Dedicated to Tessa, Petra and Tia
(My incredible wife and daughters)

Copyright © Alan McThredder 2020

Alan McThredder has asserted his right under the Copyright, Designs and [Patents Act to be identified]...

Everything in [this book is about] people in this book – it i[s mostly other] people's road stories.

Like most young adventurers who throw their lives to the winds I had no camera and kept no notes at the time. I wrote this book whilst recovering from a broken neck after a recent motorcycle accident, and all I can say is, it's as close to the truth as I can remember.

I apologise if anyone I name is not happy to be in it. As I don't have any way of asking your permission there's little I can do about that. But I think you would be proud anyway.

Warning:

Many old films played today have a warning that the language and attitudes shown may not seem appropriate to modern sensibilities. I feel the same sentiment applies to this story. There are episodes and language which many may find at odds to modern thinking. The choice was to 'modernise' the story or to retain its originality. Short of leaving out the repetitive word 'man' that our youthful language contained in almost every sentence I decided to leave it authentically late 60s to early 70s. I hope my reader will accept that I too have changed – but my memories should remain as faithful as I can make them. I beg my reader's pardon and hope I have made the correct choice.

Chapter 1. Why Yellow?

Phil, my older brother, and I are feeling extremely pleased with ourselves. It's only taken a couple of hours to paint our 1959 Ford Thames minibus with two coats of bright yellow fast drying emulsion.

The bus now stands gallantly on the roadway outside our parent's small terraced house in Thornton Heath. It looks clean, fresh, and ready for the journey overland to India. Both the paint and brushes have been unknowingly donated by our father, who's at work. Its original colours of green and cream were nice enough when new, but it seemed nobody had ever washed or polished this poor neglected vehicle in its tough fourteen year life.

It'd been a working bus, used to ferry working men to and fro from building sites. When we first saw it, every panel was dented and scratched, dirty and dull. We're doing our best, but our bodywork skills are almost non-existent, and its exhausted most of my mechanical knowledge to change the engine oil and filter, clean the spark plugs and air filter, play with the hand-brake adjustments and finally, put air in the tyres.

Phil asks for my thoughts on her condition, and I have absolutely no hesitation. Standing in Silverleigh Road, in my dirty dungarees and wiping my oily hands, on an already oily rag, I feel like a proper engineer. With an element of a 1920s racing Bentley mechanic, I say, 'I reckon she'll make it,' and follow that with a slow confident nod - as if I have the faintest clue as to what actually lies ahead of us.

We'd been disappointed to discover some areas of the bodywork were more filler than metal. A couple of large holes had suddenly appeared from the mere pressure of our paint brushes. Two fist-sized chunks falling from the wheel arches inside, revealed wads of fibreglass, supported by balls of screwed up newspaper. If these amateur repairs were stable at some point the creeping rust had undermined them now. Anyway, where we discover rust we cheerfully cover it over with bright yellow paint, and think no more about it. According to the logbook we are the seventh owners of this illustrious vehicle, that we've paid fifty pounds for. For that money we don't expect perfection, but we have convinced ourselves, out of pure necessity, that beneath its drab exterior beats the heart of a lion.

It rains all that night. Early in the morning Gill, our younger sister, grinning from ear to ear, wakes us with, 'You might want to have a look at your artwork.'

Surrounding the Yellow Bus is a strong bright yellow rectangle in the road. Much of the water soluble emulsion has been washed off by the rain. We stand on the fast-drying pavement and look at each other.

'Should have used an oil-based gloss paint.' Phil speaks mournfully.

'I don't think Dad had any in the shed.'

Mustering good grace we acknowledge that fate has dealt us this hand, therefor there must be a good reason for it. Anyway, we agree, the Yellow Bus is still predominantly yellow - it just has some streaking down it.

After Mum's full cooked breakfast, we admire it and feel it looks well-travelled without even having departed from Thornton Heath. We leave it as it is - and besides, we've exhausted Dad's paint by now. After we'd left on our travels, further rainy days gradually faded that rectangle in the road, but Mum told us that she often looked at it and wondered where we were.

Chapter 2. Sarah – Our first passenger!

Stretched for funds, we desperately need paying passengers, so we'd advertised in the local paper; a simple single line advert, 'Travel Overland to India for £50' and included our parent's phone number. We're staying in our parent's house. Neither of us have anywhere else to live at this time, let alone a phone. When we placed the ad we didn't include a departure date; there is still a lot of preparations to make. We assume the kind of person answering an ad like this'll be fairly easy going. We can work out all the fine detail later.

We've already confirmed Sarah Miller's place. Sarah's Phil's new girlfriend. I knew her father had been a Professor of History in some university or other in London, and that her mother had died when she was little. I guess Phil must have mentioned that. Her love of geology being the only other thing I knew about her.

One evening she came around to go out with Phil to the pictures. As he got himself ready, Sarah and I chatted. She quickly impressed me as an intelligent and attractive girl. Slim, with soft but pleasing features, she wore a long white cotton dress with a leaf design in brown and gold on the hem. She reminded me of those girls in the romantic pre-Raphaelite oil paintings by Edward Burn-Jones or Rossetti. Her long brown hair fell almost to her waist and she used no makeup – she didn't need any - her complexion is flawless. She's about seventeen.

'Looking forward to the trip?' I ask.

She smiles, and it's like a sun coming out to brighten up the day. 'Very much. I'm pretty sure my brother Dick is coming as well.'

'That's good. When will he know for sure?'

'Oh, first he's got to quit his job as a baker, but I know he's keen.'

A few minutes of us making small-talk later, Phil came back and whisked her off - and that was it.

In that brief exchange I'd made up my mind she'd be a good asset to the trip; sensible and easy to talk to. I can see why my brother is drawn to her.

Chapter 3. Struggles with schooling

To say the British school system had failed Phil and I may be inaccurate. No doubt, in the view of our teachers, we patently failed the schools we attended, or in Phil's case, played truant from. At one point Phil managed to get his very own personal truancy officer, who arrived every morning to collect him and supervise his attendance. Phil's school record was poor. He was 'unmotivated' they said. Needless to say, he left at the first opportunity, without any qualifications, and started immediately on a succession of meaningless occupations.

In some magical way, I managed to limbo under Phil's lack of achievement with a different brand of failure of my own making. Having fallen at the first hurdle, with a weak performance in my 11+ exam, I was carted off to a violent secondary school in Balham, South London. The teachers were there for the same reason as I was – having been judged by society as totally useless – at least that was my diagnosis at the time. Just a few years later, at the age of fifteen, I managed to get expelled for destroying school property. My epaulettes were cut off and my sword broken (all in my romantic mental imaginary of course) and I was set free on the world, like Phil, sans qualifications.

In my defence, I would explain the school property I destroyed was a set of disused concrete pre-fabricated coal bunkers, whose sole remaining purpose was as an aid in torturing young boys. The bullies would push one, or sometimes two, terrified smaller kids into one of the black sooty concrete boxes, drop in lighted newspapers, then put the lid back on and sit on it until loud and pleading cries were heard. Eventually they would let these poor victims out, with their blackened tear streaked faces, and laugh at them; and then, frequently, relieve them of their dinner money.

One day, by chance, I found my bicycle spanner fitted the nuts and bolts that held these structures together. I started undoing them. By the second day enough of the fasteners had been removed to start breaking the slabs; something I had to do to prevent them being reconstructed again. It was for this crime I was punished. The Principal of the school refused point blank to let me defend myself, and shouted loudly at me for quite a while. Then he pronounced sentence – expulsion. I didn't feel surprised or hurt – I don't recall feeling anything at all. It was certainly not something I ever felt the need to apologise for.

Phil started his working life at sixteen in a paint and wallpaper depot, where he learned valuable life skills, like how to roll his own cigarettes, waste time in the toilet reading the daily newspaper, put bets on the horses, etc. He had already accumulated a considerable work history before I joined him on the job market.

I landed my first job with John's Auto's as a car cleaner: a small business run by a couple of large genial crooks, both named John. They were more good friends than business partners. Deep down, they were both decent people, who treated me well.

One day, I turned up with a cold that had my nose running and my sinuses blocked. One of the Johns asked me to make sure there was fuel in a car, a Hillman Minx I recall, as a customer was coming to do a road test. In the workshop there was paraffin in one, unmarked, can and petrol in the other, but I couldn't tell which was which just by smell. Deeply inhaling the fumes from one can and then the other made no difference. I tried again from one then the other, then the first again over and over, but it didn't help. Well, it's a 50/50 chance I thought, so I trusted to luck.

The smart looking customer, who had the air of a brigadier, was given the keys and, without any supervision, (people where more trusting in those days) went for a test drive. A couple of hundred yards down the road the car laid down a smokescreen worthy of a World War Two frigate evading a German battleship. It obliterated the whole of Brigstock Road, bringing the traffic in both directions to a complete halt. We watched in horror as the back of the Hillman Minx disappeared into the smoke.

They say all advertising is good advertising, but that was a message lost on the two Johns at that time. The three of us stood coughing and choking under a large sign outside the showroom that proudly proclaimed 'John's Auto's - The Best Cars in the South.' Not surprisingly it wasn't a successful transaction for them, but with good grace they forgave me and even made a joke about it.

In the showroom, barely a week later whilst lying across the front seat of a large green Austin A60 Cambridge, strenuously scrubbing the fake leather upholstery, I had a clever time-saving idea. If I start the engine now, I thought, it will be warm enough for the engine degreaser to work as soon as the upholstery is finished. Stretching across the bench seat, it was difficult to get my fingers to the ignition keys to turn them. Of course the idea would have been a worthy one, had I thought to check the car was in neutral before starting the engine. But I didn't - and it wasn't.

Amazingly, the engine caught, with the car in first gear, and it drove itself across the showroom with both my legs waving helplessly out of the passenger side and the rest of me, totally panicking, inside. There wasn't time to try to press the brake or the clutch, as it all happened so quickly. It was down to luck again as to what was going to stop my progress. But this time an element of good luck came into play, and the whole front window smashed and came crashing down on the car. Where's the good luck in that you're asking?

Well, the good luck part was that the engine died at that point, for which I was extremely thankful. Otherwise the rush hour traffic on Brigstock Road would have been dealing with an Exocet Missile coming broadsides across it. The two Johns came running from their office and stood over me. As I was trying to find words, apologetic enough, to convey how sorry I felt, I noticed, nervously, that they were both fighting to control their emotions. Within a few more seconds their stern expressions gave way and they both started crying with laughter. Neither of them could speak as they gasped for air. One of them, who weighed over twenty-two stone, went bright red in the face and had to sit down and I feared for his health. They both agreed they had never seen anything so funny. Later they explained how it would have been worse to have crashed into another car inside the showroom. The insurance wouldn't have paid out. What a wonderful couple of guys they were.

But in spite of what I have just confessed, they judged I had a brain worthy of training in mechanics. They taught me to change the oil (often putting in a heavy grade to silence any engine or gearbox noises) and check all the other fluids, check valve clearances (tighten everything down so there was no nasty sounds when the engine was started from cold) and a dozen other useful tasks to aid the selling of second hand vehicles to unsuspecting punters. It was this knowledge that years later would stand us in good stead with the Yellow Bus.

God Bless those guys!

Chapter 4. Meeting Tim

Apart from a lick of paint the only other additions we make to the bus is a roof rack and some cushions. In terms of other preparations, I don't think we so much as replace the windscreen wiper blades, or even carry spare bulbs for the journey: Our youthful optimism is complete - as it is naïve.

Our roles in this adventure come naturally to us and we acknowledge each other's skills. At nineteen years old, I'm the mechanic and driver. Phil, three years older, is treasurer, navigator and organiser. Unravelling the bureaucratic spaghetti of necessary rules and regulations: understanding the required insurance, visas, and inoculations: and all the other paraphernalia we need in the many countries we're destined for (as cheaply as possible of course) are all Phil's responsibility.

We're going to accept the risk of driving the eighty miles to the Dover Ferry, our gateway to Europe, without a valid MOT certificate to prove the vehicle's roadworthiness, or the obligatory road tax; the Yellow Bus has been bought with neither. We hardly think it worth trying to get an MOT and road tax for just a few days anyway, and in our minds, we are never coming back.

In keeping with the hippy spirit of the social revolution of the time, we are proclaiming ourselves citizens of the world, beyond the reach of petty parochial laws - so the risk seems negligible. The complete excitement of adventure is upon us by this time. Neither of us mention failure. We are going to Delhi in India, in the Yellow Bus – no plan B.

The route we plot's a fairly straight-forward one. We're not interested in European sightseeing on the way. The idea is to get across the channel to Belgium, then head for: Germany – Austria – Yugoslavia – Greece - Turkey – Iran – Afghanistan -

Pakistan – India. Six thousand miles in all, as near as we can estimate.

The Yellow Bus has eight seats - really just two plywood strips running the length of each side, plus the two seats up front for Phil and me. Having been used on building sites, it isn't designed for comfort, so we need to find passengers unaccustomed to luxury.

The next day the phone rang. A strong Scottish accent asks if we are the ones going to India for fifty pounds.

'That's us,' I acknowledge.

'Och, count us in then.'

'Okay, you say 'us.' How many of you are there?'

'Just the two of us. I'm Dave. My girlfriend's name's Odette.'

'Okay Dave. I suggest we meet up and have a chat, you know, before you commit yourselves.'

I give him our address and we make a date to meet the following day.

An hour or so later the front door bell rings. At the door stands a nervous looking guy in denims with hair down to his shoulders. He's wearing a T-shirt showing a large picture of a marijuana leaf, and underneath the words 'Legalise It' printed in big letters. A friend of mine, Kevin, had been busted for a little bit of weed only a few weeks before, wearing a similar T-shirt. I wasn't inclined to be too sympathetic. I remember saying, 'Kevin, why don't you advertise with a flashing neon sign on your back saying, 'I am carrying drugs.'

These memories are interrupted by my visitor's voice. 'Hi - I'm Tim.' He offers his hand and withdraws it before I can respond.

'Uh huh!' is my only possible response to that information.

'Didn't Phil tell you I was coming around?'

'About the trip to India?'

'Yes'

'No, he didn't. Never mind – come on in, Tim.'

We go into the kitchen. I make coffee and invite him to sit at the table. Tim seems alert in a nervous kind of way - a bit like a meerkat expecting a bird of prey to swoop on him at any second. Somehow he introduces a sense of static electricity into the air, an atmosphere of impending disaster. I listen, as he hypnotically stirs his coffee about a dozen times, although he hasn't taken sugar. It is like forcing myself out of a trance to ask, 'So what do you do for a living, Tim?

He picks at his frayed jeans where his knee shows through. 'Oh, yes. I'm a train driver on London Underground.' He waves his hand as if it is of no consequence. 'But I'm getting very bored with it.' I wait for him to continue.

The frustration in his voice is obvious as he plaintively explains, 'I need adventure in my life before… well, before being swallowed up by the inevitable girlfriend, wife, mortgage, children, debt, retirement and death.'

'Wow! Neatly summed up, if you don't mind me saying.'

He sips his coffee.

'Is that the bus you are going in - the one outside?' He strikes me as nervous about the idea.

'That's the Yellow Bus. Yes. That's the time machine that's taking us to India.' I joke. 'What do you think?'

He smiles weakly, but doesn't reply to my question.

'We haven't finalised a date yet. We'll probably leave sometime at the end of next week – depends on how everyone's fixed. How do you know my brother anyway?'

'Oh. Yes, Phil. He was in Martin's, the music place in the High St, buying some strings for his Yamaha. I got into a conversation with him about acoustic guitars.'

'You play then?'

His face visibly brightens. 'Only the standards, Beatles, Dylan, that kind of thing.'

'Sounds good to me. You're welcome to come with us Tim. We'll definitely be needing a travelling minstrel to keep us happy.'

He seems relieved, as if he'd passed an interview – perhaps he had in a way.

Standing up, he pulls a leather wallet out of his trouser pocket. 'I want to pay you now, before I change my mind.'

We chat a little about passports and other requirements before he leaves.

I have my concerns about Tim. He appears nervy and unsure – on the other hand, I have his fifty pounds in my hands and, ho, hum, we need that desperately.

Chapter 5. Who needs brakes?

The following day finds us working on the bus, trying to get it ready. I'd adjusted the brakes both front and back and want to give them a trial run. Finding everything very rusty I'd had to rely on Mole Grips to turn the adjusters, and they just chewed up the heads of the bolts.

Phil jumps into the passenger seat and I start her up. At the end of Silverleigh Road I bang the brakes on hard. The bus nearly mounts the pavement as the steering wheel is wrenched out of my hands. I fight to avoid hitting a parked car.

'Shit,' I cry, 'I've done something wrong.'

'That's for sure,' Phil agrees calmly.

I turn it around and try the brakes again outside our house, with the same result. On jumping out I'm in a foul temper.

'This piece of crap won't get us to Dover let alone India.' I scream, as I give the back doors a solid kick. As I do this I become horribly aware of a couple standing on the pavement outside the house, watching us. I look over at them and swallow hard.

'Dave and Odette?'

They nod.

Dave's a tall, lanky guy well over 6 feet tall with a huge mop of long ginger hair and a matching beard. He's wearing denim jeans and jacket, and a white cowboy hat. Odette is about four feet eleven inches and looks even smaller standing next to her boyfriend. She's slim and pretty with an olive skin that isn't the result of a tanning bed or the British summers. Her hair is jet-black and straight and she wears it in a fringe, like an Orinoco Indian.

Without a word they walk around the bus a couple of times to see whether they approve of it. I look at Phil, make an imaginary pistol with my fingers and pretend to shoot myself. On the second circuit Dave and Odette stop and stand with us. There's a long pause and then it's Dave who speaks first, in a gentle voice, and with a wide grin on his face.

'So, do you think we we'll be needing to use the brakes much then?'

As they walk off together we know immediately, we're going to like these two.

Even today, Thornton Heath would acknowledge that it's not the entertainment centre of the known universe. It's depressingly suburban.

Dad made the decision to settle the family down in this, the dullest part of the world, and we suffered badly from the aching boredom that it cast over us. (He had looked at another house near Clapham Common but rejected it when someone explained how it backed on to a home for unmarried mothers; at the time he had three teenage sons, so we were disappointed but understood his dilemma.)

As we anxiously count down the hours to our departure, I know I'd rather die in any foreign desert than stay in England; this grey country of my birth.

I suppose, what I am trying to explain here is that neither Phil nor I had a career on hold; we were not taking a 'gap year' as is popular with graduates today. Between us, from leaving school to the beginning of this journey, we had probably held about 10 to 20 low paid jobs. Phil had one job which rehired him 5 times but he left every month or so. They didn't seem to mind. I had a job sanding hypodermic needles that lasted 15 minutes before I took off my apron and walked out. I managed five minutes with my eyes shut and felt a job that undemanding might drive me insane. Strangely enough, I was supposed to be taking over from a man who had done it for over thirty years. He showed me what to do in a few minutes and when I took over he said, 'Cor! You picked that up quickly.' I didn't know how I should feel about that – I still don't.

But here we are launching ourselves into the world without adequate resources or knowledge, without safety nets or backup. Once again we were trusting to Lady Luck, big time – and we already know what she can be like!

Chapter 6. Sponsorship & Theo

Over the years we had read about expeditions to Africa, India, The Great Barrier Reef, etc. Mostly from glossy magazines, stolen from doctor's or barber's waiting areas. They always showed exotic pictures of bright young adventurers, in convoys of shiny Land Rovers, resplendent with colourful stickers from this company or that. And all you need to do, in return for cash support? Simply display a company name on the side of your vehicle. What could be easier? That's exactly the look we wanted for the Yellow Bus - rugged and professional.

With this in mind, Phil and I penned some excellent (or so we thought) sponsorship requests and sent them to a dozen well-known companies. We explained, we are serious students hoping to make a study of the ancient architecture of India: That we want to record images of various ethnic races for our university library: That we are attempting to bring back an almost extinct red hooped cobra to London Zoo: That we are trying to photograph a Yeti - or any one of a dozen other fantastic fabrications.

We fell marginally short of suggesting we're Scott of the Antarctic and Doctor Livingstone, travelling on a new adventure together.

Anyway, we sat back and waited for the cheques to flood in, as they fought for advertising space on our bus. We received just two replies. One was from Duckhams, the oil people. Their parcel arrived containing a couple of gallons of engine oil, which was warmly received, with a letter wishing us good luck. The other was from Coopers, the chemicals company, also wishing us the best of luck. They sent us a dozen cans of fly spray. Undaunted, we dutifully stuck their stickers on the sides of Yellow Bus.

They could have been more generous, I thought. But at least we won't have any trouble with flies.

So now our crew comprises of Sarah and her brother Dick, Tim, Dave and Odette. We only need one more person to commit to us and we'll have our full complement. Then we can decide on a start date.

Our final character turns up a couple of days later in the shape of a well-built Greek guy with an open face and an easy manner. Theo had obtained our address from Gill, he told us. Having just received a degree in architecture from the London Metropolitan University, he wants to take a year off before starting work.

'I need to cut myself off from studying, friends, family and money worries,' he says with a grin that displays his perfect teeth. 'I feel exhausted with everything and want to spend my time staring at the countryside and doing absolutely nothing. I feel I have earned it.'

Phil and I both like him and agree he's in.

Amazingly, the phone hardly stops ringing over the next few days with so many people eager to travel with us.

'Next trip, we'll get a forty seater coach,' I suggest.

Chapter 7. Dick the Miller

Phil and I keep in touch with our passengers using Mum and Dad's phone. We agree our departure date will be the twenty-second of September, and on the allotted date, at nine am, we all meet up on the pavement outside our parent's house. The sun shines bright and clear, and we're all in high spirits. Dad, as usual, is at work. Mum prepares sandwiches, hot drinks and biscuits. She bustles around feeding people and seems every bit as excited as we are.

I'm doing some last minute checks under the bonnet when Sarah calls me over to introduce her brother, a miller by trade as well as by name. Dick Miller works for a small health food bakery, where he grinds the grain and bakes the bread. A slightly built character with a thick black bushy beard that covers his face; to the extent that few people would recognise him if he ever shaved. He's dressed from head to toe in army surplus clothing, and looks like a miniature soldier.

'Hi Dick, I'm Alan,' I say, and offer my hand.

Busy fiddling with the contents of his camouflaged military style rucksack, he hardly looks up. 'I know,' he responds in a monotone.

I wait a moment but he's too tied up with whatever he's doing to introduce himself civilly, so I decide to move off to help Phil, who's now trying to get the back doors of the Yellow Bus to close properly.

Realising Dick's attitude has irritated me, I feel a bit petty-minded and tell myself to get over it. This is a special day – a day to be happy. Later, we learn Dick was not especially meaning to insult me; he is insulting to most people he meets. Dick is an eccentric type who'll take some getting used to.

Phil and I securely lash a couple of empty twenty-five gallon jerry-cans to the roof rack, just above the cab; followed by two spare wheels and our sponsorship gifts of oil and fly-spray.

Fuel is cheaper in Belgium and we'll fill the cans there. As an investment we also tie a couple of small second hand bench grinding machines on the roof, having been told they will fetch a good price in Turkey. It's then the Yellow Bus starts to look like a real overland vehicle and we break off what we're doing just to look at her, and grin at each other.

'We're really doing it,' I say proudly.

'We sure are,' is Phil's reply.

Chapter 8. We stoop to conquer

Dick, Sarah and Tim sit down the left side of the bus behind Phil. Dave, Odette and Theo are behind me on the right. I ask if everyone is comfortable.

'Snug as a bug,' replies Dave happily.

On the floor between us lie all the possessions we think we'll need. Large cushions, guitars, books, music tapes and a 56 Kg bag of muesli. My last job before the trip was as a packer in Harmony Foods health store in London. We decided to buy a huge bag of muesli so we wouldn't go hungry. It had fruit in it, which I deemed a good idea. Having read books about the British Navy I didn't want any cases of scurvy on board.

The only hiccup of the adventure was Dick wanting to keep his rucksack inside next to him, and there wasn't enough room.

'What do you want that thing in here for man?' asks Dave. 'Put it on the roof with everyone else's bags, for goodness sake.'

In keeping with the rest of Dick's image, it looks like it comes from an army surplus store, but it isn't a particularly big rucksack. Nevertheless, with eight people in a small bus, we need all the living space we can get.

Dick looks at Dave in a challenging way, trying to stare him down. He grips the bag defensively. 'There are things I need in this. Things I want near me.' He speaks with the tone of a cross adult, telling a child off for a small misdemeanour.

I listen with growing interest, as I wonder if it's just me that's having difficulty with Dick's personality. Also, I doubt that this tall guy from Oban, on the west coast of Scotland, is the type to back down. There's a pause and Dave nods, as if digesting the information. Then he speaks slowly.

'You're right, Jimmy…'

'Dick, not Jimmy,' Dick corrects him irritably.

'Well, you're right then Dick, of course you are.' As he speaks, Dave puts his hand on my shoulder.

'Alan, Dick is right. I think I want my rucksack down off the roof. And could you get Odette's as well?'

Theo reads the situation and joins in. 'Alan, I would like to be near my stuff as well.'

Going along with it, I start to get out of the bus and ask, 'Anyone else want their stuff while I'm up on the roof?'

'Yes, me too, please,' chimes in Tim, just to increase the sense of mischief.

Before I could move any further Dick Miller relents truculently.

'Alright, alright, I can see what you're all doing. Put the bloody thing on the roof if you have to.'

Dave, to his credit, says nothing. We all watch as Dick roughly opens the rucksack and pulls out the items he can't bear to be without; out comes a book 'Siddhartha' by Herman Hess, followed by a stone chillum and a tobacco tin.

I stash his bag on the roof.

The most that can be perceived from our neighbours, as a reaction to this group of brightly dressed Hippies, milling around and chatting feverishly, is a curtain twitching here or there. Nobody comes out to wish us luck or even to enquire what's going on.

To our great joy the engine starts first time and with everyone as excited as jack-rabbits we are off. Mum stands and waves until we disappear from view. It's late in the day, for we had taken hours to get ready, and Mum insisted on feeding us as if we were never going to see food again. We're in no hurry as we want to sleep on the ferry, if possible. Phil ceremoniously unfurls the map and lays it on the warming engine hatch between us and starts to give me directions to Dover.

Dave rolls a joint and passes it around. After a few miles the chattering dies down and a curious silence falls. Some time passes without anybody speaking. I guess we're contemplating the different reasons each of us had for being here. What has driven every one of us to join such an unlikely adventure in an ancient streaky yellow bus, that's more rust than metal? Those are my thoughts as we roll towards the setting sun on a journey scheduled to last at least a couple of months, and hopefully, very much longer.

The optimistic and enthusiastic Sarah takes charge of our music and starts to feed the cassette player. On goes 'Born to be Wild' by Steppenwolf which instantly raises our mood and encourages us to sing with each chorus. We have a fair number of music tapes to choose from. Dave and Odette supplied some 'Incredible String Band', and a tape from a group called 'Family' which I hadn't heard before. Tim has some Beatles tapes like 'Rubber Soul,' and 'The White Album' but also good road music from 'The Rolling Stones' and 'Creedence Clearwater Revival'. Theo is into country sounds, and likes 'James Taylor',' America' and 'Love'. Altogether we have about a hundred tapes. Both Phil and Tim have their guitars, so whatever happens, we're not going to go without music.

As we roll down the A2 towards the coast we're all singing at the top of our voices, 'Born - To - Be – Wi – i – i –ld.' Tim shouts, 'I think we sound brilliant.' Hell, we all do.

Over the next few miles we try out different cruising speeds to see which suits us best, now we're fully loaded. Every vehicle has a speed where it feels just right - all you need is be sensitive to it. Seventy miles per hour feels too fast for the ancient high-mileage 1703cc petrol engine. It would probably do it all day, but we also need to think about noise and fuel consumption.

Lowering it to around fifty-five miles per hour proves to be smooth and stress free. We have six thousand miles ahead of us, and even with my limited maths ability I can see a few miles saved on every gallon will accumulate to a substantial amount.

The only incident on our way to the coast, a small map reading misunderstanding between Phil and me, ends up with us travelling in the wrong direction for a while. Although easily rectified, it encourages a lot of good-natured abuse from Dave, who pronounces in his strong Scots accent, 'If we canna find our way to Dover, how are we going to find our way to India at all? May we not come oot in the Gobi Desert or Timbuktu, for instance?' Then he adds with a grin, 'Not that 'am at all bothered yer'll understand,' as he turns another page of the detective novel on his lap.

Despite that, we reach Dover in good time and park up in the long queue for the car ferry. Phil runs through the cold, drizzling rain into the dingy office to get our tickets. Sarah slips The Beatle's 'All You Need Is Love' into the cassette player and we sing along to it.

When Phil returns with the tickets we settle down for a long wait. I check the odometer and do a quick calculation.

'Hey Phil. We've covered sixty miles today and with the forty we did before to check her out, we can celebrate Yellow Bus's first hundred miles.'

Phil puts his feet up on the dash, folds his John Lennon spectacles into his top shirt pocket and gets himself comfortable for the wait. 'That's a centenary celebration okay,' he agrees, 'but one hundred doesn't sound much compared to six thousand. Let's celebrate it in a week or two shall we?' His following laugh shows me not to take his pessimism too seriously.

Chapter 9. A momentary lapse of intelligence

The ferry crossing passes uneventfully. We each select one or more of the many comfy seats. The English Channel appears smooth for a September night as the white cliffs of Dover gradually disappear from view. Even with the throb of the great engines, most of us manage a bit of sleep. Theo and Tim stretch out and fall asleep instantly. Dave and Odette investigate the boat first. Sarah and Phil chat non-stop, and seem to be getting closer to each other.

We reach Belgium and with imagined dignity, and the sound of The Beach Boys singing 'Good Vibrations', we drive off the ferry into the grey, misty morning of Ostend and take to the right side of the road for the first time.

As the Yellow Bus rolls along the featureless rustic landscape in the direction of Brussels we listen, trying to familiarise ourselves with the myriad mechanical noises of the bus. I thought, 'so, this is how it sounds when all is well. We should be happy as long as all the clicks and clacks and whirring noises of the engine, gearbox and suspension carry on unaltered.'

It was the first time I'd driven on the right side of the road, so had to concentrate intently. Within an hour or so, we realise Belgium has some very peculiar laws regarding rights-of-way compared to Britain. After a number of near misses, particularly at roundabouts, our calm and happy atmosphere is often interrupted by horns and violent gestures from frustrated Renault drivers.

'What's bothering him?' I would ask, in all ignorance of some law I'd broken and Phil, equally puzzled, would shrug his shoulders.

Zebra crossings in Brussels are 'open season' on pedestrians and we try to guess why they bother to paint them at all. Young teachers, bravely stand in the middle of the road, waving furiously and shouting, a little hysterically, as they shepherd their uniformed schoolchildren across like ducklings. Mothers with prams trying to cross are slowly pushed out of the way by the front wings of the cars by gesticulating drivers. It appears very dangerous to us.

As we watch Belgian couples and families wander around outside, I think about our own tiny Yellow Bus community. I wonder how we'll all be changed by living closely together over the coming weeks. Each of us had travelled a bit but none of us could be called 'real travellers', so just the everyday architecture and ways of the Belgian people prove foreign enough to keep us glued to the windows.

The day heats up nicely and we stop at a small rural garage out in the countryside. A short chubby man, with bow legs, a drooping moustache and a blue beret, ambles over to us, as we pull off the road. A few chickens strut noisily about, while a sleepy ginger tabby cat lying on the dry and dusty ground with its front legs crossed, lazily eyes them up.

I suggest we get out and stretch ourselves. Dave and Tim, helpful as ever, climb onto the roof to lower the jerry-cans, while the man with the drooping moustache, expressionless, without removing his cigarette from his lips, winds up the handle on a vintage petrol pump to fill them. Tim speedily walks a considerable distance away and keeps looking back nervously at our smoking host. We top up the Yellow Bus to its maximum, and I pay the fat smoking man what seems to be a huge wad of foreign paper money.

Odette and Sarah come out of the Café alongside the garage. They've bought some croissants, butter and jam. We climb aboard and wait for Tim who walks very slowly back trying, unsuccessfully, to look interested in the wild flowers beneath the hedge ways.

We've been driving for five or ten minutes along a wide but deserted tree lined road. A young man in a Citroen 2CV, with a stripy red and white hood that makes it look like a mobile deck chair, overtakes us. His hand is hard down on the horn, which in these cars is hardly ear-splitting, but he's also weaving around and going from side to side and waving furiously.

'What the hell', exclaims Phil.

'A crazy man,' Theo pronounces, his Greek accent thicker than normal.

'Perhaps a lunatic who hates the English for wartime damage done to his family chateau by Lancaster Bombers,' I suggest nonsensically.

'I knew we shouldn't have put a GB sticker on the back. Is he trying to kill us?' Asks Phil with some concern in his voice.

Sarah, cuts through this ludicrous chain of misunderstanding by stating calmly, 'Alan, I think we're on the wrong side of the road.'

Now it all made sense. Thankfully I had not resorted to my very limited number of French swear words on the driver of a car seemingly made from recycled baked bean cans.

My stupidity is again, making itself painfully known to me. This man is risking life and limb to let us know we are on the road to disaster. I pull over to the right side of the road, whilst at the same time trying out new and better international gestures to proclaim how thankful I am - also trying to convey that I would now forever love him, and his nation, like a brother.

Acknowledging us enthusiastically, he drives on. Barely two minutes after this incident, a convoy of six huge lorries, laden with granite, comes thundering around a bend towards us. As they pass safely to the left of us, one after another, their vortexes sucking at our windows like the beating of a drum, the collective sigh is audible but nobody says a word for a few moments, until Phil mutters quietly 'Well, that could have been worse.'

Chapter 10. Phil becomes a bread doctor

This isn't the first time Phil and I had journeyed abroad together. Two years before, we'd set out to hitchhike around Europe and purchased a couple of sleeping bags and tents from 'Millets Camping Supplies'. A few days prior to our departure, I visited the family doctor to get the necessary injections, for we were advised not to drink the water in far off places, like France.

Dr Doust, our family doctor, well past retirement age, his hair pure white, his hands shaking and his eyesight poor, was loved by all his patients. He never wasted a second, always asking after family members by name, as he worked. Then it would be, 'So where are you planning on visiting?' and 'What plans have you got for the future?' He seemed perennially interested in everybody and everything, and becomes quite excited by our travel itinerary.

'Oh yes, you must have a typhoid injection most definitely,' he chuckles as he wrestles with a sterilised package containing a small syringe.

'Oops,' he exclaims, as the packaging parts and the needle goes flying into the wicker waste-paper basket.

'No harm done,' he smiles, as he retrieves it, and punches the needle swiftly into my arm to give me the injection.

But on trying to remove the needle we realise the tip of it had been bent, and as he pulls to free it, all that happens is a section of skin on my arm forms a pyramid, but nothing gives way. I am like a hooked fish. Eventually, after half a dozen attempts it comes free and the blood squirts down my arm.

'No harm done,' announces Dr Doust cheerfully again. 'A little plaster will sort that out.' Then, as I'm about to leave, he says, 'And remember now, no alcohol for at least a week – promise?' I promised.

Needless to say the advice from Doctor Doust went unheeded as we two exuberant vagabonds celebrate later that week on the cross-channel ferry with a bottle of Vodka, with which we frequently toast the white cliffs of Dover as they fade behind us. The following morning, when we dock in France, it's raining cats and dogs. At a loss for what to do we run towards a large nearby supermarket for shelter. From the safety of its porch we discuss our two choices; to stay in discomfort where we are, or to find a piece of land, pitch our virgin tents, and weather the storm out.

That's no contest for a couple of budding adventurers brought up reading 'War Picture Library' and 'The Eagle' boy's comics, so we run across the supermarket car park to find a piece of suitable grass to make camp.

Smarter and more experienced travellers may have rehearsed pitching their new tents in their back garden, probably choosing a sunny afternoon and, perhaps, without drinking a bottle of spirits. We are soaked and drunk, and for some reason, my arm is starting to ache like hell.

The shoppers in the supermarket have a comfortable vantage point as they watch our Laurel and Hardy comedy sketch through the windows. We fall over our packs, we fall over our guy-ropes, we fall over each other, the wind howls and the rain lashes down – but eventually, we have both tents erected.

Rushing eagerly into each tent, our joy is short lived as we quickly realise why they'd been such a bargain. The tents are waterproof only until you touch them. With any contact, water pours in like a tap's been turned on. It's impossible not to touch the sides as the tents are so small. From the swearing coming from Phil's tent I know he's made the same discovery. There's only one thing for it. Phil leaves his own tent to flood and brings his waterproof ground sheet to put over half of my tent, then he comes in and we sit, cramped together, in the one side that no longer leaks. There's little room to lie down so we sleep as we sit. We sit like that for two days and take turns to sleep. The rain doesn't relent for a second.

Gradually my arm swells up and aches badly, and I remember, too late, my promise to Dr Doust about not drinking. Dully, I realise, this is a reaction to the injection. Phil braves the rain and buys some French bread from the supermarket, which he soaks in boiling water on our camping stove and applies it, very hot, to my arm.

'Bread poultice,' he says confidently, as a witch doctor might.

Over the following day I become feverish and weak. At one point Phil heats a can of Heinz Beans and Sausages. On handing them to me, my arm, without the strength to keep the plate level, lets the metal camping plate tip its contents onto the muddy, twig-strewn ground. I cry then. Phil is wonderful and constantly renews the bread poultice. I'd never heard of bread poultices before, or since, but the pain is getting really bad. I'm happy to try anything.

And then the rain stops.

'Listen.' Phil says.

'What?'

'Nothing.'

'Has it stopped?'

'I think so.'

Phil gets to his knees to open the tent flap, and realises he has both knees in an inch of mud.

'Ugh'

I try my arm. It hurts a lot less - so I become quite a believer in the magic power of bread poultices.

There is precious little dignity in us getting out the tent. Our legs have seized up from being bent so long. We are pitched on a slope that runs down to a pond.

We smell too; so it appeals to my perceptions of what a rugged adventurer would do in this situation when Phil suggests, 'We can wash in the pond.'

Collecting our soap and towels together we start to walk down the incline, when we realise we can't stop ourselves. Our numbed legs have stopped responding. We really can't stop ourselves! We are like those little toys you place on steep slopes that run down by themselves. Both of us have to fall over on our sides or risk staggering like crazed zombies into the water - more entertainment for the supermarket shoppers.

Oh yes, we were experienced travellers all right.

Chapter 11. Hitching with a goat

To allow those of us carrying illegal substances to hide them, we stop a couple of miles short of the German border. Satisfied we've done what we could, we pull up at the border behind another over-lander, a forty-two seater coach with 'Sundowners' written on the side of it.

While we're waiting for papers to be checked, the driver and I get talking. He's an Australian, unsurprisingly called Bruce, and he looks every bit the travelling-man, wearing a brown safari suit. He has creased tanned skin, a full beard and china beads in his long hair that rattle together when he moves - the way some West African tribes wear them.

We both lean against the customs building.

'Ah man.' He says wearily. 'Never travel with a South African.' He pulls out a tin with rolling tobacco in it, takes out a paper and a wee bit of tobacco, and offers it to me. I don't smoke frequently, but like the tradition of sharing, so accept.

'Politics?' I venture.

He lights his rollup and exhales strongly. I follow suit. It's a bonding thing.

'You bet. Every border now takes forever. They check everything. It's almost like they want to make life difficult for South African travellers and anyone who helps them. As if I give a damn about apartheid, and their crazy politics.'

I nod in agreement. Politics is the last thing I want to get involved with. Friends of mine had gone from being bright hedonists to dull worried people, after getting involved with politics. 'Not my cup of tea.' I say simply.

He laughs at my Britishness. 'Not mine either, but I picked up this South African guy at a hotel. He wanted a lift. He had some cash - so what can you do?'

Phil comes out of the border building, waving a piece of paper and smiling, so I know we are through okay without being searched. I commiserate with Bruce and we wish each other luck on our journeys.

Under a sun, both warm and friendly, and a lightly populated blue sky, we cross the border into Germany.

We agree we can still get a few more miles in before resting up for the night. When we do stop its early evening and I pull into an open field.

'I'll get some firewood,' Theo immediately volunteers. Piling his thick black hair into a top knot and fixing it with an elastic band, he strides off towards the trees.

'I'll come with you,' says Tim, jumping up.

Sarah and Odette organise the tea-making. Phil and I share thoughts on our progress and decide we're happy. He leaves me to investigate underneath the engine for oil leaks or anything else out of the ordinary.

Tim plays a little guitar music and sings a melodic Simon and Garfunkel song. Phil accompanies him on his guitar, and the rest of us drink tea. We eat the croissants and chat until the sun sets and the night turns chilly. Then we all turn in for a wonderfully undisturbed night of sleep.

We rouse ourselves surprisingly early the next morning. The sun is just starting to prise an opening in the darkness and cut across the sky in golden streaks. *It's the earliest I have been up for years*, I think guiltily. *It's so beautiful.*

With lively enthusiasm we strike the little tents and chat excitedly, except Dick, who is always a little jittery and concerned about everything, even when stoned. Already, we are losing all sense of urgency and an easy relaxed vibe is developing in the group, as we help each other as if we're old friends; this at the end of our second day!

If anyone has a watch it's never checked unless we have a ferry to meet, and nobody talks about time. After lashing down the packs and getting ourselves sorted out, we set off down a long deserted road that seems to stretch towards the horizon. I'm starting to have more confidence in our bus and believe she will roll along until the second coming. The regular noises are still there and nothing has worn out yet.

Occasionally, we stop to pick up hitch hikers, usually young people just going to the next town or village. Mostly they're students who speak English well; who have some favourite tales to tell to keep us entertained. In Germany there's an established hierarchy for giving lifts. It runs: First: young military men, as most families have someone who's been conscripted, Second: single girls, Third: two or more girls, Fourth: – a couple, Fifth: - a man alone, Sixth: – more than one man or three or more of any gender. Whilst driving through Frankfurt we are flagged down by a category we had never seen before - two men and a goat.

We get out to chat with them. Both men (and the goat) have scraggy beards and long unkempt hair. One is wearing an old stained Afghan great-coat, the other, a kind of duffel coat with a number of badges badly sewn on it, protesting against nuclear power and some other causes: my lack of language prevents me from discerning what they represent. They are French hippies living in Germany who have decided to head to Asia. They both speak excellent English.

The goat is fully grown and looks at me with satanic eyes, which are unnerving. I wouldn't like to turn my back to it when it's off the thick rope they lead it with.

'But why the goat?' I ask.

They look at me, as if the answer is obvious to any half-wit. 'For milk of course.'

'When did you start out?'

"It's been 3 days now,'

'Where did you start from?'

'From a village near Dieburg.'

'But that is only about 25 miles away,' exclaims Phil, 'I saw it signposted earlier.'

The taller of the two, the one wearing the Afghan coat, makes a classic French gesture of resignation. 'Mon Dieu! We have walked because no-one will give us a lift with our goat.'

We roll and share a couple of cigarettes, but even the smell of good grass can't disguise the rank odour of the goat. We wish them luck with their journey, and carry on without them. To give a goat a lift was stretching the hippy code to breaking limit. We often wondered how far they got.

Shortly after, we pass by Stuttgart. Dick fills and lights his chillum for the first time. The clouds of smoke start to waft up.

'Smells good,' I remark.

After a couple of strained gulping sounds to keep the smoke in, Dick just says the word, 'Nepalese.'

After what feels an age, he exhales a huge cloud of smoke. The bus is so full of it that I have to wave my hand furiously in an attempt to see through the windscreen. Everyone waits patiently for Dick to pass the chillum around, but he makes no move to do so. Instead he cups his hands for another mighty lungful.

The bus becomes so full of smoke it looks like we are suffering an engine fire. Phil and I simultaneously open our windows to release the great billows. At that precise moment I find myself looking down on a police car that's overtaking us. The uniformed driver looks up at me, no doubt seeing a startled hippy appearing like he was self-combusting. He smiles and slowly shakes his head from side to side before speeding up and disappearing into the distance.

'You meet such nice people when you travel,' remarks Phil.

Chapter 12. The efficient German policemen

The impressive thing about the German autobahns is their lack of speed restrictions, so it feels to us travelling at fifty-five miles per hour is slower than an electric milk cart. Big Mercedes Benz and BMWs come past at amazing speeds, as if we're stationary. Looking down at the fuel gauge it's showing nearly empty. Cripes! I hadn't noticed. The distraction comes from a game we've been playing since Cologne where you have to name a musician, band or music track from every letter of the alphabet.

Dave suggested the game and started it off. 'A is for Al Green.'

Odette's turn. 'Arnold Lane – Pink Floyd.'

Phil says, 'All Right Now – Free.'

Sarah. 'Astral Weeks – Van Morrison.'

Tim. 'Anyone Who Had a Heart – Sandy Shaw.'

'Not Sandy Shaw.' Odette interrupts. 'That was written for Dionne Warwick. But you could have said Cilla Black or Petula Clark as well. They had hits with it too.'

Everyone looks at her in appreciation.

'Sorry Tim', she says demurely.

'No, no. That's fine', Tim grins.

Theo says loudly. 'Asikis'

'Who?' we all chant in unison.

Theo grins widely. 'Grigoris Asikis. He's very big in Greece. He composes lots of songs for the outi, lyre, and bouzouki. My parents have many of his records.'

'You bugger,' laughs Phil, 'you could make anything up and we wouldn't know it.'

Theo looks innocent and shrugs his shoulders. 'But it's true. Why should I make it up? There are many wonderful Greek musicians whose names start with Q and Z, all the difficult letters you guys are going to be struggling with later on. For instance we have the famous female singer and composer 'Qualotto', who has an album called 'Zanzanni.' I think I shall win this game.'

He can't carry it through though, and his handsome face splits into another grin that gives him away. It's then agreed, only American and British names are allowed.

Then it's my turn. 'A Day in the Life – Beatles'

Now Dick vigorously shakes his head and says truculently. 'If you have one that starts with 'A' then you can't just have 'A' as the first word. It's like having 'T' then you could have any band that starts with 'The' like '*The* Monkeys' or '*The* Rolling Stones.' It's too easy that way.' He's right, of course, but I argue the case just to annoy him.

And so it goes on. We all have our own idea of the rules. Everyone is passionate about music, and everyone challenges almost everything. Odette resolves most problems about which bands produced which albums, or who wrote which songs. We learn she'd been a receptionist for 'The Who' when they had a secret recording studio. It was behind the fake front of a scaffolding company in Battersea, London. She's incredibly knowledgeable about the music scene and has no trouble in refereeing our disputes. Having been quiet so far she now opens up, showing where her real expertise and passion lies.

It's just past Mannheim on the A5 (we are only on the letter 'L') when we pull into a large motorway service station for fuel. Whilst filling up and admiring the view of the nearby hills a large BMW police car pulls up. Two very large officers get out and head straight for us. They are both tall and wear immaculate olive green uniforms. *'That's one thing the Germans do really well – uniforms,'* I think.

'Who is the driver please?' Asks the taller one. His uniform bulges as if filled by an air-compressor. It appears to have been specially made for him, as he has the build of Johnny Weissmüller, the blond actor who played Tarzan in Hollywood movies for many years.

'I am,' I volunteer.

Neither of them speak again for a while, but they stand together looking at the horizon as if we're no longer of interest. They let us fill up and Phil go into the garage to pay. Then they direct me to park the Yellow Bus in one of the parking bays near their BMW.

What follows is one of the most thorough MOT (Ministry of Transport) tests we have ever witnessed. They don pristine overalls, open the trunk of their car and pull out an array of different tools, including one that makes my heart sink. This is a little hammer that's blunt on one side but spiked like an ice pick on the other. I have seen it being used before and know only the toughest metal survives its spiteful attack. Our passengers melt away into the nearby shops and cafes, as they have no idea whether a full bus search, or perhaps even a body search, might follow.

I admit, they're a pretty efficient team, these two policemen. Hardly speaking or acknowledging each other, except to comment on some mechanical fault, or laugh as another piece of chassis collapses under the ice pick they wield noisily. One of them writes things on a clip board and appears terribly amused by it all. They put the handbrake on, then both lift the back by the bumper and push the bus forwards without too much difficulty. I want to explain that we never normally encounter body-builders on our travels and anyway, I always put it in gear on hills, but Phil holds my arm. He knows that kind of pragmatism isn't what they're after just now. Eventually they finish and put everything away.

'Well, is there anything wrong officers?' Phil smiles cheerfully.

'Ha, ha! Everything is wrong,' Tarzan laughs. 'This vehicle is a danger on the roads. The tyres are uneven and worn. The horn is kaput. The steering has too much …how you say….play? The engine and gearbox drips oil and ……….' and so he went on with a litany of faults, and as he talks our hearts sinks lower and lower. The prospect of having the Yellow Bus confiscated looms large.

'Where do you come from?'

'England.'

'Ja, I know this much already. Where in England?'

'Thornton Heath.'

'I haven't heard of such a place. Where are you going?'

'To Delhi, India'

'India eh?'

Now they chat amongst themselves in German for a while. It's hopeless trying to guess the content, as nothing gives us any clues. One thing's for sure - they can scupper all our hopes on a whim – they have that power. I can see Tim and Theo over by a tourist shop pretending to try on sunglasses but keeping a firm eye on the proceedings. Then the darker haired one of the two slowly walks over to us. He grins widely and speaks in a low confidential tone.

'Personally, I would not take my wife to the shops in your bus. I don't think I could be sure we would arrive safely. My mother-in-law however, I would encourage her to drive it.' He laughs so sardonically I'm not sure if he's really joking.

There's a long pause.

'However, we are impressed by your er…. adventure, so my colleague and I are going to find other work to do this morning. If you are out of this area by this afternoon we'll forget that we have met with you.'

With that he turns and they both get into their car and drive away with a cheery wave. I let out my breath, which I now realise I have been holding for a while. And at that moment I forgive the German people for the many fruitless and weary hours we've spent thumbing lifts in the past and decide there are saints to be found among them, after all.

The passengers now all start to reappear from their hiding places, like a clan of chimps after the cheetah has moved on, nervous and eager for the news. They're amazed when Phil and I explain what happened.

'How dare they laugh at the Yellow Bus,' says Phil theatrically, as we get under way. 'She's a fine machine.'

It begins to rain a light shower and as I flick the windscreen wiper button the passenger side windscreen wiper comes free and clatters onto the road. And we all fall about laughing.

Chapter 13. Why aren't people having fun?

We enter Austria at Salzburg having driven the billiard-smooth A8 road from Munich. Hearing that the sniffer dogs at the border are the best in the world is concerning: that they were trained in England does little to activate our sense of patriotism. Surprisingly, they wave us through after a very perfunctory inquiry about our destination.

One of the border guards even shouts. 'Have fun, Hippies', in English. We all think that's decent of him, although we rarely called ourselves Hippies, preferring the term 'Freaks.' Media and big business were busy commercialising the word 'Hippy' to sell beads, wigs and plastic flower-covered hand-bags. It was embarrassing to identify ourselves with the fashionable 'Celebrity Hippies' that filled King's Road and Carnaby Street of London.

Dave and Dick breathe a sigh of relief as we head out onto the open road and celebrate by smoking some dope. Sarah puts on 'Light My Fire' by The Doors.

Theo, who has hand-washed his white T-shirt, asks if he can attach it to the aerial of the Yellow Bus to dry, so he threads it through the arm holes and it fluttered above us for miles like a battle flag. We last see it an hour or so later through the rear window when it sails away over to the other side of the motorway to be scooped up by the traffic. Theo isn't too happy, but he learns to tie them on better after that.

Entering Yugoslavia near Maribor we're immediately struck by how badly maintained the roads are. Much of it is cobbled and uneven, with water-filled potholes which throw us around a bit. I slow down the cruising speed to about thirty-five. The Yellow Bus proceeds painfully, passing mile after mile of boring turnip and potato fields. Many of the small towns we pass look deserted, like old prospecting towns where the gold has run out. Yugoslavia is the first communist country most of us have been to, and this part at least, is no advertisement for the success of its politics.

'Well, if this is Communism, you can count me out,' I announce. 'I've never seen...'

Sarah interrupts me - and her normally soft voice has an edge to it. 'You'd feel the same about capitalism if you drove around some of our northern cities.'

'Maybe you're right,' I concur, both through a desire to keep the peace, and my complete lack of knowledge on the subject. 'But capitalism doesn't make any pretence at sharing for the common good.' Sarah doesn't respond to my immature attempt at pride saving.

I suppose, I just felt disappointed. A political hippy at that time was called a 'Yippie' and I wasn't one of those. All I knew about that movement was that its leader, Jerry Rueben had written a book called 'Steal This Book'. And people did. W. H. Smith, the bookseller, found so many copies being stolen they locked them up and you had to ask for it at the counter. I hadn't read it. My innocent concept of communism was as uninformed as you could get. Perhaps, I thought everyone would be having street parties all day celebrating their freedom from the bosses.

In comparison to the countries we have travelled through, this country is very poor. There are run down farms with dirty, broken windows and doors falling off their hinges. Obviously, people still live in them as drying washing flaps on the lines, or half-starved dogs run out and bark at us. The people, when you do see them, look depressed and shabbily dressed. Some of the towns we pass through are almost deserted, with twenty closed shops to every open one. It's in desperate need of cheering up.

'These people need the healing power of Rock and Roll,' Suggests Phil.

'They bloody well need something,' I agree.

We contemplate heading south to the coast of the Adriatic, then running down to Dubrovnik. We could then head east just above Albania, but none of us want to stay in Yugoslavia any longer than necessary. Instead, we take the direct route inland and head for Beograd.

Typically, in every poor Christian country, people erect huge elaborate churches and cathedrals, and Beograd is no exception. It strikes me as strangely perverse how so much wealth can be gathered from the poor and channeled towards gold leaf for church ceilings or jewel encrusted crucifixes and robes. *Why can't it be used to improve the infrastructure and their standard of living?* That thought might be considered naïve, but I've never heard an answer to it.

As we trundle along, slowly eating the miles, I consider my attitude to religion. I am a member of the Buddhist Centre in Ecclestone Square in London. I never deliberately pray, but I like to meditate, even when driving if the roads are clear. It seems to me that praying is all about asking for the fortitude and courage to accept pain and poverty, to continue in much the same life-style without breaking down. But, I think, 'What if it's not the courage to accept life that you need, so much as the courage to rebel? That would explain why royalty and politicians are so keen on fostering religion. Tell the people to pray to God for forbearance and not to blame them for taking everything for themselves. Then you have the perfect solution to those who raise their voices. Simply accuse them of being driven by envy and claim they have no spirituality.

These thoughts are interrupted when the engine of the Yellow Bus complains bitterly about the quality of Yugoslavian petrol by running hot and lacking power. A garage attendant who speaks English tells us they dilute the petrol in his country, but with what he isn't sure. 'Why?' we ask. He put his right hand out and rubs his thumb over his index finger – the universal sign for greed.

Chapter 14. An unexpected trip

The Greek border guards look tanned, relaxed and happy, as we enter Greece at the Evzoni Border Station on the E75. We feel the sun shine on us like we're being barbecued and instantly forget the greyness of Yugoslavia.

We pull in the first garage we come to for some decent fuel. Phil looks over the map, with a very happy Theo, now back in his home country.

'Kavala,' Theo says. 'That's where we should head. Trust me, it's one of the most beautiful places in Greece.' We all gather around the map.

Everyone agrees it's in the right direction. It takes us a little closer to India, so why not?

'But we need to go to Salonica first, because it's easier to drive that way.'

Phil looks at the map intently and then at Theo. 'I can't see Salonica.'

'You call it Thessalonika. Look, it's there.' Theo puts his finger where the Mediterranean had washed a large semi-circle into the land, like a huge natural harbour. 'It's about 50 miles. If we have breakfast now, we can be there in an hour, and then head east to Kavala.'

We find a lay-by and cook up the eggs and beans we've bought from a small cluttered supermarket. The girls now discard their jumpers and change into cotton dresses and sandals. The guys are in T-shirts, but not yet brave enough for shorts. I notice

that Tim was still wearing his marihuana T-shirt, but I haven't the heart to have a go at him. I just hope he's bought some others in his pack.

Breakfast over, we pack up and head south to Salonica. We avoid the busy centre as much as we can, get lost for half an hour but don't really care, then find ourselves on the right road to Kavala.

Theo is right about Kavala. As we drive towards it the Mediterranean looks like a warm blue bath with diamonds shining just below its surface. The beaches are wide and clean. We find a place to park and turn the engine off. There comes the sound of hot metal complaining, with a series of clicks and pings that sound almost symphonic. *'Maybe this was the first time the Yellow Bus has experienced real sun,'* I think. After putting a couple of rocks under the rear wheels to compensate for the weak hand-brake, we all strip down to underwear and run to the sea.

Perhaps deferment of gratification is a big hit with some people, certainly not us. When we find ourselves swimming in the clear blue sea and lazing on the fabulous sandy beaches of Greece, we give ourselves over to sweet hedonism. Some years previously I'd asked a wealthy self-made business man how to make money. His advice was simple. 'Stay hungry.'

I understood what he'd meant, even then, but his advice was wasted on me. I didn't like being hungry, even in a metaphorical way. It's true that Phil and I had mapped out an itinerary for the entire journey, which should have seen us getting to Delhi with a small profit. We figured this would allow us to stay in India for a while, but as soon as we hit Greece all our capitalistic persuasions evaporated like morning mist, and our tight timetable was discarded. We are already starting to hear the calls of those mythical Greek sirens. Boy, they work fast!

Over the next few days we gorge ourselves on Greek yoghurt and juicy peaches until the juice runs down our chests and we have to dive into the sea to wash it off. We light bonfires every night on the beach and induce young Greek kids to join us with our music and party life. Then we sleep on the beach. We are happy. We are suddenly living a life that some people dream of living after they retire, but probably never will. The local people come and chat with us and have no worries about us being there. They bring food to cook on the camp-fire, dance and play music and make us feel like part of their family.

Only days into the journey, a shift is taking place in the group. Rather than being a disparate group of travellers we are becoming a little community, looking out for each other. Phil is spending more time with Sarah now. Their easy way together is noticeable. For my part, I feel Odette is seeking me out to talk to and spend time with. Dave doesn't seem to mind, so there's no friction.

Theo's ridiculously happy to be back in the land of his birth. Although he'd been clean shaven less than a week ago he soon sports a thick black beard. I've never seen anyone grow a beard so quickly. He seems a different man, full of enthusiasm and energy.

Sitting on the beach one day, staring at the horizon and trying to see the curve of the Earth, I enquire. 'Why would anyone leave this wonderful place to go live in England?'

'He thinks for a while. 'Perhaps I needed to leave home to really appreciate it,' he laughs. 'Then it had to be done. Now I love being back here.'

One morning, lying on the ground of a pine scented forest, I wake from a warm snooze to find a piece of paper in my mouth. I run my tongue over it but can't understand what it's doing there. Then I see huge smiles on the faces of Theo, Tim and Dave, and I know, before they tell me, I'm scheduled for an LSD trip.

'Oh you bastards,' is the only thing I can think of to say. To which they all nod in agreement.

After a few moments of mentally checking whether there's anything important I need to do today - sew my shirt? - find some wood for tonight's fire? - I quickly decide there isn't, so relax into it. Theo is tripping too, and he and I go for a walk while the others head for the beach.

As we sit on the hillside, we can see the island of Thasos far away in the motionless blue Mediterranean. Far below us, in the bright sunshine, a number of bronzed men are working inside the white ribs of a fishing boat they're constructing. The sound of wood being chopped echoes up to us, and as the acid starts to take effect, I can visualise each sound as it floats by. It's like watching anemones swim up from the ground and head into the clouds.

Theo tells me his family comes from a fishing village and explains how each fishing boat is still built by hand, in the traditional way, with the ribs being hewn with sharp tools called an adze.

'In the hands of an expert an adze can chop a big chunk of wood like your hand or a sliver as thin as a finger nail. When I was ten years old my uncle showed me how to use it properly.' He points at the boat being constructed below us. 'I have worked on boats just like that one.'

As I listen to him talking about being a young boy growing up in a fishing village, and watching those men working below us, I couldn't have been happier if Socrates had taken an afternoon off to confide in me his latest thinking.

Theo also explains how he'd managed to get to London to study architecture. His parents saved every penny they could. His father had worked all hours, fishing, building new fishing boats, repairing damaged ones; his mother had taken in cleaning; his uncles had contributed what they could. It was a joint family effort, and now he represented all their hopes and ambitions.

'Don't you want to go home and celebrate with them?' I ask. 'I mean you've done it, haven't you - got your degree?'

'I want to, Alan, I really do, but first I need to make some money in London working for a successful architect. Then I will go back in a good car, wearing an expensive suit, and be able to help them financially.'

Seeing I'm about to say something, Theo put his hand up to stop me.

'I have to do that, not just for me, but for them. They need to see the results of all the sacrifices they made. They need the neighbours to see what they've achieved. It isn't what I have achieved, but them. You know many rich kids rack up degrees in this and that, without being particularly bright. It isn't the studying that's the hardest part. It's the struggle for money and time and motivation that are difficult. If your parents buy you a flat around the corner from the University, and you don't need to work evenings in a bar, well … it's not so difficult.'

'Okay,' but it was you who did the work. It was you who studied…'

Theo broke through my train of thought. He knew exactly where I was going with it.

'Parents can't make their children succeed, they can only help them blossom. They're like gardeners. It's not enough just to plant the seeds. They need to pull up weeds and claw out the rocks from the ground that would choke them; digging the earth and making it fertile for them. They do much of the really hard work, but it's the successful child that gets the praise.'

There's no bitterness in Theo's voice. It's all so accepting, as if he'd had the easy bit to do, whilst everyone else took the burden. He hooks his hands around the back of his head as he lies on the grass. He studies the sky for a while, then he looks at me and smiles broadly.

'Don't get me wrong; my degree wasn't easy for me. It's the hardest thing I have ever done and I do feel proud of myself. A lot of people dropped out and some failed near the end of it, some of them from well-off families. I suppose I'm glad it's over, but for now, *this* is all I want.'

After a couple of hours of chatting, I decide to go for a walk in the forest, and we agree to meet up later.

The walk is fascinating. I head inland, with my subtle mind slowly dwelling on the little Greek mythology I know. I soon become Jason searching for the Golden Fleece, then I'm Prometheus challenging the Gods. The wispy white clouds above resolve themselves into the outlines of Zeus and his wife Hera playing around with humanity, as if in a game. I am in an adventure and I'm their chosen golden child. The sky is my home, and the whole world my playground.

I feel I'm travelling back in time with every step. As I walk through the heavily perfumed trees, listening to the joyful sound of the cicadas, I am lost in my own world. There's no sign that any humans have been here before me. No houses or paths, no trace of humanity. It could be any era since the world began.

Gradually, the sound of the cicadas seem louder and more constant, although they cannot be seen. It gives me the uneasy feeling the sound is coming from the earth itself, and it's demanding something of me, but I can't understand the language. The smell of pine, strong in the hot sunshine, is becoming almost suffocating. Every breath sears my lungs with hot heavily scented air. Slowly my sense of delicious freedom ebbs away from me and I experience a deep worry, like a great black cloud rising inside. Thinking hard about what this feeling is I try to put a name to it. It's utter and complete loneliness.

The logical part of my mind, the 'guardian at the gate,' so to speak, is aware of what's happening and reminds me, *it's just the trip*; that I should breathe deeply and stay calm.

There's a palpable change in the air, and a growing hostility in the world around me. This is no mild inclination or passing desire. My need to seek other humans is becoming greater and more demanding; if only to prove that other human beings inhabit this place. I scour the area for as much as a discarded piece of litter. (Somehow, I've found myself in the only part of Greece not littered by empty chocolate milk bottles). It's easy to think that I've entered some kind of portal and am now alone on Earth. This realisation hits me almost like a physical assault - without doubt, I am the only human being in the entire Universe.

There is still part of me that clings to a more rational explanation, but I walk faster and faster, trying not to get into a panic, trying to remember the direction back. This is not a good feeling. Anyone will do. Anyone at all.

God knows what would have happened if I had come across some strangers then. I imagine there would have been unwelcome full-on embraces of relief, followed by some screaming, and then an attack by angry husband or friends. And I still would have welcomed it.

Finally, accompanied by the greatest feeling of delight, I burst into a clearing on the hillside to see my own travelling companions, as tiny figures, swimming in the sea below. Somehow, I've arrived back to near where the Yellow Bus is parked, just a lot higher up. I sit and cry with gratitude.

My pride in fancying myself a bit of a 'lone wolf' took a blow, from which it never recovered: I like people - and need them too. Smiling and crying and knowing I will be too embarrassed to tell anyone what happened, I scramble down the hillside to join them.

After a couple of happy hours splashing and laughing with them, I decide to do some clothes washing in the bay. There's a tourist type of clean water shower available to rinse off the salt water, so that's fine. I retrieve my rucksack from the bus and pull out a few items in need of a wash. In my rucksack is a pair of dirty socks that I'd not worn since the sun started to shine and I'd changed into sandals. Still under the effects of the acid trip I begin to work out these dirty socks in the clear Mediterranean Sea. As I do so, the water becomes stained, dark and dirty.

Mesmerised, I watch this mysterious pollution spreading out in all directions. Soon, the whole of the little cove I'm sitting in is turning black. Further washing just makes the stain travel beyond the cove and start out to the open sea. Oh, my God! My socks are going to pollute the whole of the Mediterranean - from North Africa to Spain - Italy to Israel. The responsibility is a heavy one and I sense I will serve some kind of unimaginably long custodial sentence for it. But I'm laughing now. Everything seems so funny for some reason. It takes some effort and a moment of sober thinking to realise that with my vigorous washing I have been stirring up the very fine black silt that lies beneath the shallow water.

My socks are not the culprits at all.

Chapter 15. I meet a Greek god

Our planned three day stay in Greece turns into five weeks. We find less and less reason to leave the beaches and warm sea for the drudge of the road. We're sleeping either in the bus or on the beach, eating supermarket food, surviving on a tiny budget, and having a fantastic time.

One morning on coming out of our local supermarket I see a crazy guy. Standing in the road, and shouting what must be Greek swear words, dressed only in the briefest of swimming trunks and a pair of sandals, he is trying to start his motorcycle, and not doing too well. He looks like a candidate for a Mr Olympia competition. His superb physique dwarfs the little CZ two stroke bike. Every time he slams down on the kick-start the fragile bike looks like it's about to break in half. But there's nothing even close to life in the engine.

It's fascinating to see the different muscle groups alternately delineating and subsiding in his body and legs. I find myself looking at him in admiration to the extent that I had to inwardly remind myself that appreciating the human form is no challenge to one's own sexual identity.

'Need a hand?' I ask. Knowing that if he didn't speak English it would spell the end of the conversation.

He looks over at me and shrugs. 'Do what you can. I'm going to throw it in the sea if I can't make it start.' It comes across as a simple statement of truth, rather than a baseless emotional rhetoric.

Hanging from the saddle next to the rear wheel is an open leather pack with a few tools in it. I sit on the kerb and do some basic checks for the obvious, fuel tap open, spark plug lead on, that kind of thing. As I work I can't help but stare at one of his legs. There is an amazing pattern of puckered scars around his calf muscle. He notices me looking and proudly presents it so I could see the whole thing.

'Octopus,' he says simply. And he holds his hands far apart to give me an idea of its size. 'Oh', I say, not having a clue that an octopus could do that.

'I'm Alan.'

'Mikos.'

As I work he talks. He tells me he was a professional goalkeeper for the Athens football club. He lives in Kavala. He likes women. He loves swimming and is in the sea more than he is out of it since the age of three. He likes women. He has travelled a lot with the Athens football club – and that he likes women. The expression, 'I like women' comes pretty well on cue after any attractive Greek girl walks by.

I dry the spark plug while he's talking. On replacing it the bike starts first time.

Amidst the blue swirl of the rattling engine, he beams at me and shakes my hand.

'Alan, you are a genius. I thank you. Do you have a pen and paper?'

He writes down an address.

'This is my father's restaurant. It's on the beach to the left over there.' He indicates a block of a dozen or so restaurants a few hundred yards away. I invite you to come and have a drink with me at eight o'clock tonight, so I can say thank you.' He then bestrode the little bike, which sinks beneath his weight, and with lots of noise and smoke, makes his way down the road.

That night I go for the drink and meet his father, who's just an older version of Mikos, with the same generous expression, broad smile, laid-back attitude to life and large athletic build. It doesn't surprise me at all when he confesses, like his son, that he also likes women. I can only imagine that women like them both right back.

We eat freshly caught fish and drink various wines. They show me how Greek men dance and encourage me to join in. When I am really drunk Mikos invites me to go swimming with him the following day. Normally, I would refuse as I am an air sign – or that's what I would say as a joke. Instead, I enthusiastically accept.

As I don't have any swimming trunks I use a cut down pair of khaki trousers. He laughs when we meet at the beach the following morning, but is polite enough to say nothing. He has turned up equipped with a spear-gun and a large knife strapped to his leg. Feeling my hangover can only be improved by the water, I go swimming with him; rather, he swims as I paddle about or just sit in in the cool water. He is the closest thing I have ever seen in real life to a Greek god.

My pale and shapeless body feels rather pathetic in comparison. I make a mental note to myself to get fitter.

Years later, as I watched the film 'Zorba the Greek' I recognised us both. He was Anthony Quinn, full of life and the decent forces of nature, welcoming every obstacle as a challenge. I was the Alan Bates character, full of British working class 'forelock touching subservience,' scared of the needs and desires within me. Our upbringing was as different as butter and margarine; his natural and healthy, mine in comparison, felt like an artificial and cheap substitute.

Chapter 16. Not waving but drowning

A few days later, walking along the beach on my way to get some shopping, I run into Mikos again.

'Hi Mikos.' I wave.

'Hi Alan, good to see you. How are you today?'

Sitting on the sand next to him I light a cigarette I'd cadged from Tim. We chat about this and that for a while, when I notice he has snorkel equipment.

Trying to sound like I wasn't cadging a favour I mention, 'I've never tried snorkelling before. What's it like?'

'Give it a try,' he says, motioning to the equipment.

'Can I really?' But I'm already moving eagerly towards it; just trying to appear as polite as possible.

In truth I can't swim at all; never had been able to, even in the safety of Balham Swimming Baths when I was a child. But I'd once borrowed a mate's flippers there, and believed they tipped the balance between being able to swim and drowning.

Excitedly, I pick everything up and walk towards the sea. I'd watched people carrying flippers with them to the water's edge first, so that's what I do. When it comes to putting on the lead weighted belt it feels unbelievably heavy, and I'm not sure about it. But I can't go back, and certainly can't just leave it on the beach. With satisfaction, I notice it has a quick release mechanism, should the need come to discard it.

Slightly nervous, but trying to appear confident, I walk as far as I can into the sea before experimenting by flipping along the surface. It isn't easy trying to breathe without gasping down the plastic tube, but soon I'm captivated by the sight of thousands of brightly coloured fish in this water. Miraculously, it's as clear as air. There are metallic blues, greens and yellows flashing everywhere like mirrors. And they all dart under me, unconcerned by the great white whale above them. I'm transported with delight. Memories of 'The Undersea World of Jaques Cousteau' on TV comes back to me; although I feel unlikely to discover a ship wreck when I can see the legs of people around me who are standing up and talking to each other.

Flipping harder propels me further out. There are all manner of incredible shells makes me wonder why they have such exquisite patterns on them, although I could never see a scallop shell without thinking of my Auntie Jean, who used them as ashtrays.

I see sharp-spined anemones and try prodding them gently to make them move. *Ow! Their needles are as sharp as – oh yes, needles.* The water is warmer in some places than others, as if hot geysers are coming out of the rippled sandy bed.

Venturing a little further out, I tentatively try my hand at diving the eight feet or so to the sandy floor, and that feels fine. Then, as my confidence grows, I try going further and further from the beach.

Suddenly, the ground falls away like a cliff edge and I'm panicking. In a desperate attempt to turn away from this chasm I breathe in some water and flip my feet as hard as possible until I'm safely over the sandy bed again. Fighting the chocking feeling, I berate myself for being such a coward. *'I'm swimming – it doesn't matter what's underneath me, idiot – I'm swimming on the surface.'* My self-mockery helps me to gain a sense of proportion, so timidly, I swim back over the ledge again.

It's a sheer drop, disappearing as far as the eye can see into an impenetrable depth. '*Good chance to try out the weighted belt,*' I think - and before common sense can collect its wits to stop me, I dive vertically down. Compared to a professional diver, it probably isn't very far, but it's much further than I'd ever experienced. Down I go.

Pretty soon, common sense does wake up, and slaps me strongly in the face. I try to take control by pushing the stop button on my runaway elevator. However the descent doesn't seem to slacken. It's amazing how the temperature of the water drops as I descend, almost as if an icy hand is pulling at me. It's a disconcerting feeling to be flipping madly to go up but watching the undersea cliff-edge telling me I'm going still descending.

Now the beams of light from above can't penetrate, and things are getting blacker all around me.

Kicking my feet to go up is not as productive as I'd hoped. As far as I can tell I am still heading for the basement. My fingers grip the quick release mechanism of the weighted belt, but before pulling it, a thought comes into my head. *How much do they cost?* My budget is on a shoe string. Can I afford to replace this fine piece of diving equipment? *If there's any chance to get back with it, I must.*

Praying to be spared from cramp, flipping like a man possessed, after what feels like an age, I start to come up. My legs are hurting and the muscles in my thighs and calves are beginning to knot.

Now it's just air I need to worry about, and hope I can hold on long enough. The light of the sky is visible above me but it seems forever before I break through to the surface and gasp in a huge breath of wonderful air, and frothy sea water. I choke and cough. My legs are starting to complain badly as I head away from the chasm towards the security of the beach, where I can thankfully stand again with my head above the waves. Still coughing and choking, I look up at where Nikos is sitting. He merrily waves and gives me a thumbs up. I smile and wave back. Trembling from the exertion, I take off the flippers and start back.

Walking casually up the beach towards Nikos, I'm wearing what I consider to be, a rakish James Bond type of expression.

'So, how was it?' asks Nikos enthusiastically, 'Good, yes?'

Calmly surveying the beach for a few seconds I pretend I haven't heard him whilst I try to calm my breathing and lower my heart rate"– I am trying very hard to be 'cool, or maybe, I just can't trust myself to talk yet. "Yes, It was good – very good.'

Nikos lights a cigarette and blows out a long stream of smoke followed by a perfect smoke ring.

'I was worried for you for a moment,' he says. 'You had all the weights on the belt. I usually only have two or three when I dive, and I am a strong swimmer. I'm glad you are okay.' I look for any sign of mischief in that statement, but he remains expressionless.

Chapter 17. The mad bee man

We love everything about Greece; Ouzo and the cheap wine made from pine resin called Retsina (how forgiving is the young palette!) but especially the food. We've taken to dripping honey into yoghurt, and eating this with firm peach slices. We name this 'Ambrosia' after some notion of it being the true food of the ancient gods.

It's with this in mind that Tim and I go to the little supermarket to pick up some groceries. As we stand outside, deciding what we need, a wizened old man approaches us. His skin looks like ancient parchment stretched over bony skeletal protrusions. He wears a dirty pair of brown corduroy trousers done up with a piece of string, and a tattered shirt with a sun-faded pattern. He moves incessantly from side to side as if he has St Vitus Dance. He opens a toothless mouth.

'Meli? Meli? Meli?' he repeats in a squeaky voice over and over.

'That's honey isn't it?'

Tim nods.

I do a pantomime of opening a jar, spreading something with a knife over an invisible piece of toast, then with a big appreciative smile on my face, start to chew.

This little excitable gentleman dances more vigorously than before, 'Nai, Nai, Meli.'

Using the established international way of asking where this honey is to be found, I look all around me and shrug my shoulders as if to say, 'I can't see any honey from here.' Perhaps we half expect him to point inside the shop, and confirm our suspicions about his sanity, but instead, he waves for us to follow him up a narrow path.

It's a torturous rocky little path up a hill. After a mile or so our confidence in our guide is wearing thin. We begin to suspect that we're being used in a game by the village idiot. But just as we enter the forest, he rushes into a clearing and proudly points to four or five large bee hives. These are stout wooden affairs, painted white and obviously professionally set up.

The din from the bees is pronounced and we both hang back a little; what Tim and I don't know about bees is encyclopaedic. I have some vague recollection of watching bee keepers, with fully enclosing white uniforms and masks, pumping smoke into hives to make the bees drowsy before messing with them. But hell, what do we know? This old man had probably kept bees all his life and could wear them as a living beard if he chose; so when he beckons us to come closer to watch him, we do.

He lifts the heavy wooden lid to one of them. Smiling at us, he throws the lid aside. For a brief moment we see a great black viscous ball, which appears to be squeezing itself upwards in slow motion. Fascinated, we stand like statues. This ball begins to separate and fan outwards to reveal itself as a condensed cloud of very angry bees. The last sight we have of the old fraud, is of him screaming and running and clutching his face, as he disappears into the forest, enveloped in a garment of stinging bees. Tim and I also run, but in the opposite direction – to the sea. It's every man for himself.

Pulling my white T-shirt from my waistband, I run and slap myself around the face with it, as hard and as fast as I can. My body will have to take care of itself, for my only concern is to protect my eyes and mouth. There are too many bees around me to let up for a second. Kicking off my loose fitting sandals, for they were slowing me down, I run as fast as possible in the direction of the beach, and the life-saving water.

How many bees stay the whole journey without laughing victoriously and turning back, I don't know, and I wasn't prepared to count. I am still being stung, as I dash into the water and fling myself under the surface to safety.

Holding my breath isn't easy after all that exertion, but I do my best, and when I come up for air - there isn't a bee to be seen.

Now it's time to request a structural report. After feeling myself all over, the report isn't good. Just about every piece of exposed flesh has been stung; as I'm only wearing shorts, that's most of me. Thankfully, my face has escaped, all bar a couple of stings on my cheeks, although they got me in the neck a number of times. I think about whether the old man has survived, but feel angry with him, and know I won't go looking. *'How about Tim,'* I wonder, as I make my way, like a wounded soldier, back to the Yellow Bus.

In all we count over one hundred bee stings, or I should say, Odette does, as she goes over me with a pair of tweezers, picking out the little barbs. Tim arrives shortly after, having fared about the same, although his tactics have been very different. He'd run into an open apartment block and slammed the door behind him. Then he'd set about the bees that managed to follow him, with both his sandals in his hands, until the walls ran red, or whatever colour bee blood is when squashed.

Odette went over Tim's damaged body the way she had mine.

We are smeared all over with a bottle of calamine lotion, until we resemble a couple of Zulu youths being made ready for a tribal initiation ceremony. In way of consolation Theo cheerfully tells us, every sting we have represents the death of a bee. He says they can't sting twice like wasps can, but die shortly afterwards.

'So that makes you both champion bee killers,' he laughs.

'Just shut up and pass the Ouzo,' is my reply.

Chapter 18. Coming into Turkey

It's on a cloudless sunny morning, that Yellow Bus cheerfully presents itself to the gun-carrying guards at Ipsala, the border post between Greece and Turkey. We park it where indicated, and all walk into a spacious air-conditioned room and stand, appreciating the cool air and shade.

A Turkish policeman requests our passports and peruses them carefully, before validating each one with an ink stamp. Unlike the practical square entry-stamp of Greece, which just has the name of the crossing and the date of entry, the Turkish stamp is a work of art. It has words from the Qur'an in a flourished font. It makes Turkey feel very different to us. This is the gateway to Asia.

'Why are you coming to Turkey?' the dark moustachioed guard asks sternly.

Phil always deals with border problems, so we wait for him to reply. 'We are tired of the awful people and the bad food and wine of Greece.' We all stare at him in disbelief.

Dave laughs. Tim looks at Theo and shrugs his shoulders as if to say 'What the …?' Theo raises his eyebrows and shakes his head disbelievingly as a reply.

Suddenly the border guard throws his head back and laughs out loud. 'I like that. Ha, Ha. That's the best reply I have ever had.' He claps Phil on the shoulder and, still laughing, he says. 'Okay, you can go.'

We file out without a word. As we climb into the Yellow Bus the border guard is still laughing, and waving at us.

'Okay. What was that all about?' Dave asks, when we are a half mile or so down the road.

'Have you guys not picked up on the friendly – well mostly friendly – competition that goes on between the Greeks and the Turks?'

Theo grunts in confirmation but from the silence Phil assumes nobody else has.

'Look, the Greeks have Ouzo, the Turks have Raki. They're almost identical; but they'll say each other's tastes of bat's piss. The Turks and the Greeks both have moussaka. You ask any Greek who invented it. "The Greeks invented it," they say. The Turks are just the same and will tell you moussaka is an Arab word. It's hilarious. The similarities between the two people, at least in this area, are obvious, but they will mock each other at the drop of a hat. That's why I said that to the guard back there.'

'But what if he didn't have any sense of humour?' asks Dick drily. Nobody speaks. This is a question without an answer

We could have convinced ourselves to turn back at any time - up to now. Everything changed when we entered Turkey. For us this is the beginning of our real metamorphosis from tourist to adventurer, going beyond the familiar and recognisable, and entering a fundamentally different culture: A place where we have to learn how to conduct ourselves, and not just assume everyone will think we're a good bunch of people. Values are different, dress and body language is different. You can give offence without realising it or take offence where none is meant. Because of the difference in mannerisms and gestures you can misread situations; befriend the local drug dealer or contract killer believing them to be pillars of society: To Odette - it was home. Maybe, at that time, only Dave realised Odette was half Turkish, and had been born in Bursa, about one hundred miles south of Istanbul.

The journey of one hundred and fifty miles from the border to Istanbul begins uneventfully. Because of the splendid mountainous vistas, we take a couple of stops at open cafes to sit on carpets, usually with the owner's family, sometimes playing with their children or admiring their babies, and look at the mountains whilst drinking a bitter yoghurt drink. This is not to everyone's liking. The nicest description would be that it is a 'challenging taste' that most of us found interesting enough (or polite enough) to finish. Wanting to get a true taste of the culture, or possibly as a personal challenge, we would order it again at the next stop.

Tim decorously described it as, 'Tasting like an alcoholic's vomit mixed with goat urine.' After his first taste, he ordered a Fanta orange instead.

Soon our road becomes more demanding, and the going gets slower and more dangerous. We often find ourselves tucked behind a line of large trucks, without the power to overtake them, as they belch out thick black diesel smoke. Choking and coughing, we're often forced to drop back so we can breathe decent air.

Dick, who normally keeps to himself, reading Herman Hess novels and smoking his chillum, decides my driving can be improved. He moves forward, so as to almost stand over me, and stares out of the windscreen. 'You're taking the bends too fast, man. You need to use the gears more. Look out! You only just missed that rock!'

Trying to concentrate on driving on these tight, rough roads is taking all my concentration. I can't spare any for Dick. After a few minutes of this, I pull the bus over and leave it in first gear so it can't roll. Those on the right side have the view of a sheer drop into a chasm.

Climbing out the driver's seat, I rudely push past Dick and sit down next to Sarah.

'She's all yours Dick.'

'Oh shit! No,' Dave exclaims.

Dick stutters. 'I don't want to…. I mean I didn't want to…'

Sarah interrupts. 'I think what Dick is trying to say is he can't drive. He doesn't have a driving licence.' She then adds laughingly, like a nursery school teacher to a naughty child. 'Come and sit back down sweetie – and do shut up.'

Reaching the peak of the climb and we can see the vast plains stretching out below us. There's a heat haze rising from the ground of this great expanse, like a rippling mist that makes it difficult to focus on any detail.

I climb back into the driver's seat with a quick warning look at Dick. 'Thankfully, it's all downhill from here,' Phil says, and follows it with a laugh. He can see that the downhill part looks like a rugged roller coaster ride that's going to get a lot tougher.

And he's right to think so. The downhill stretch is more dangerous than going up. The brakes need so much pressure on the twisty down-stretches, my leg aches. Frantically looking out all the time for escape routes should our brakes fail I use the weak handbrake almost continuously, for the minute extra assistance it gives. A few times we stop to let the brakes cool down before pushing on. The water we throw on the wheels boils with an angry hiss and I check and recheck the hot brake fluid, terrified that all this extra load is going to burst a brake seal: This would leave us helpless at best - dead at worst.

Eventually we come down to the plains and the level road again. Stopping the bus by the first grassy field, we all get out and lie down with relief, and let the accumulated stress pour out of us. Because of our poor progress, we decide to camp overnight before entering Istanbul. Crossing the mountains has left us too exhausted to bother with making a fire or singing. We camp by a stream and listen to it gurgle until we fall asleep, under a canopy of twinkling stars.

Chapter 19. Istanbul and finger modelling

The following morning, as we drive into the capital city of Istanbul, we decide to call it by its old name of Constantinople. This sounds more exotic to us.

The first thing we notice when we arrive is the number of huge American cars. We can identify Cadillacs, Buicks, and Studebakers and just about everything else produced from America's Motor City in the 40s and 50's. Here, big is beautiful when it comes to vehicles, and the bigger the wings and more outrageous the design, the more desirable. The oddest thing is they are mostly taxis, plying their trade in some of the narrowest streets in the world. Using the horn must be the first driving skill they learn; if you don't lean on the horn you don't make progress.

When two of these leviathans meet head on in a narrow passageway it usually means a lot of gesticulating and shouting at each other. Initially this makes us apprehensive, as if knives are about to be drawn. It takes a while to realise there's no aggression attached to these exchanges, and they're as normal as bartering – more pantomime than serious.

Everywhere we drive or walk there is the handsome face of Kemal Ataturk on posters. This stern character stares out at us in every taxi, in shops and schools and even bus stations. When we enquire who this man is from a couple of English-speaking Turks, they explain how he had revolutionised Turkey single handed. Ataturk had changed the written language, the monetary system, the way people dressed, and created a secular society. The more they told us the more impressed we were that one man could be so influential; and so admired too. I dare say he had created enemies, but all the time we were in Turkey we found no one who would hear a word against him.

We pull into a coach parking place outside of the Blue Mosque at eleven am. The sun is already scorching the pavements and it's getting hotter by the minute. Our long sojourn in Greece had given us the beginnings of a tan, so we all feel a little more capable of staying out in the sun, but it's still undeniably dangerous to spend too much time in it.

'Okay – it's agreed then, we take today off for sightseeing and doing the tourist thing,' Phil announces. 'Make sure you don't leave anything valuable on the bus because no-one's going to be with it all day. We'll meet back here at six o'clock.'

Being the only driver is tiring, and I'm feeling the responsibility heavily after yesterday's mountain adventure, I want to be by myself for a while. After locking the bus as best I can, which really involves wrapping a bungee cord around the rear door handles, I walk along Kennedy Street, the road bordering the peninsula. To my right is the deep blue Sea of Marmara and the famous square-built 'Maiden's Tower' on the jagged rocks, a short distance off.

I turn into the breath-taking church called Hagia Sophia in English and Ayasofya by the Turks, which some westerners refer to incorrectly as St Sophia; it was never dedicated to a St Sophia. Its builder, Emperor Justinian the Great, is supposed to have cried, 'Solomon, I have surpassed you,' when he saw the completed structure.

Looking up at it I can understand his pleasure. Its main dome is huge with a diameter of over one hundred feet, an amazing feat of engineering. Trying to think where I'd seen the shape before, it comes to me - I realise it's like a soldier's helmet from the days of Genghis Khan. I pick up a brochure in English and read: "The original church was completed an AD 537" (too early for Genghis to have influenced it). "It remained the largest cathedral in the world for over a thousand years. In 1453, after Constantinople fell to the Muslims under Sultan Mehemet 11, it was converted into a mosque and a number of minarets were added." (To me the minarets, one on each corner, gives me a sense that the whole thing has landed from another planet, and that the minarets are its control rockets.) I carry on to read: "Kemal Ataturk had it turned into a museum in 1934."

The sense of peace and space inside is impressive. I wander in hushed silence, like an awe-struck child, amongst its towering columns. The sensibilities of both Christian and Muslim visitors are accommodated in a difficult balance. Islam forbids the creation of images, so huge plaques hang from the ceilings with Qur'anic words etched in gold. Early Byzantine images have been painstakingly restored, revealing its original Christian ancestry. As an atheist I'm not affected by the messages these icons present, but, as an ordinary human being I am thrilled by the superb artistry and the craftsmanship of our ancestors.

After the coolness of the Ayasofya, the heat outside hits me like a body blow, as I meander further down Kennedy Street and along to the Topkapi Museum.

Looking at the museum makes me think of the Peter Ustinov film, 'Topkapi'. He played a jewel thief trying to rob the museum. The scenery had been staggering in this movie and I remember wanting to visit it one day. It is a fabulous historic building. Topkapi Palace had been the administrative centre of the Ottoman Empire for nearly 400 years.

Peter Ustinov, if I remember the film correctly, climbed in through the roof; it must have been because he saw the ticket prices!

I nearly walk away because of the cost, but then feel it would be a pity since I don't know if the chance to visit will ever come again. There are a number of different areas to the museum: the kitchens, the harem, the porcelain collection etc. and each needs a different ticket. Because of the film I'd seen I buy a ticket for the section housing the jewellery.

The real treat for me is the 'Spoonmaker's Diamond,' which sits in the corner of the room in a softly lit cabinet. This large single stone, as big as a duck's egg, is extremely beautiful and fabulously valuable. As I admire it a camera flash startles me. A well dressed Turkish girl explains in excellent English. 'We're doing some photographs for a new brochure,' she says. 'Do you mind if we use your picture in it?'

'Not at all.' I smile, although why or how they're going to use a picture of a long haired, bearded, English hippy is beyond me.

Vainly, I try to remember my exact expression at the time of the flash going off. I think I had the look of a hungry fox staring into a chicken coop. Perhaps, I had been salivating? *Too late now*,' I think, and make my way to the next room.

After a while even treasure gets boring, so I leave Topkapi and go in search of the Grand Bazaar I've read about. Flagging down a dolmus I am surprised to find Phil and Sarah in it. The 'dolmus' is unique to Turkey. Any small bus or converted van does the job, as long as you can squeeze six or more people inside. They run along regular routes, but can be flagged down in any place, and you only pay for your part of the shared journey, so are very cheap and efficient.

'Hi guys,' I greet them.

'Hey, get in Al. Where have you been, brother?'

I tell them about my little tourist trip. They have visited Galata Bridge for a meal in a restaurant, but after seeing the prices, ended up buying some fresh fish just cooked and served from one of the many fishing boats tied alongside. On the wide wooden handrail each vendor has napkins, salt and vinegar, so you can help yourself.

'The whole bridge is a succession of restaurants, so the choice is amazing,' Sarah says with joy. 'But your brother refuses to eat any sea food except cod. I need to educate him.'

Phil laughs. 'Ugh! All that slimy stuff – humans shouldn't eat any of it. Some of it's like eating salty snot.

Sarah smiles. 'Where are you heading, Alan?'

'The Grand Bazaar.'

'Us too,' she nods. 'I want to get a present for my father.

'Any idea what you want to buy him?'

She shakes her head. 'No, But I'll know it when I see it.'

Phil paid the driver the few lira for the ride and we walk into the long bustling hall of the bazaar. There's surprisingly little hassle inside. You'd have to have a fragile nature to get offended by the shouts of persuasion and friendly banter, as owners try to encourage you into their shops. Carpets, porcelain, brass and copper goods are stacked everywhere. Intriguing bits of antiques peep out from beneath layers of goods that appear to have been built up over the generations, like strata of rock on a cliff face. It would have been impossible to do an inventory in some of the shops, as generations of owners have added more goods, until only the very brave would try to buy something at the bottom of the pile – the antediluvian offerings.

We are fascinated by the intricate carvings of the meerschaum tobacco pipes. One shop owner tells us meerschaum is a fine clay-like mineral that can be found floating in the Black Sea. The French call it *écume de mer* which translates as 'sea foam'. Patriotically, he tells us the best meerschaum in the world is mined in Eastern Turkey.

At one point we lose sight of each other in the fuss and flutter of the crowd. After a few minutes I spot Sarah admiring an antique silver ring in a jeweller's shop. The owner is a broad man wearing a fez, which is a traditional piece of Turkish headwear, now almost obsolete. He grins and nods when I come in.

'Salaam-Alaikum,' he says. The traditional greeting that means, "Peace be upon you".

'Wa-Alaikum-Salaam.' I reply with the tradition response – "And unto you peace."

Sarah hands me the ring she's been holding, and I remark on how heavy it feels before handing it back.

'What does the engraving mean?' she asks the proprietor.

He sticks a jeweller's magnifying lens in his eye and squints at the Arabic writing.

'Good luck and many babies,' he laughs.

'And what about the smaller inscription underneath?'

'He takes the jeweller's eyepiece again and looks at it again.

'That is the date,' he announces. 'It says 1357.'

'That can't be right surely,' Sarah says incredulously.

'The big man shrugs his shoulders as if to say, 'it's not so unusual.'

Sarah asks me to slip the ring on to get a better idea of whether she likes it. It's a tight fit on my ring finger, but I manage it, and ostentatiously act out my role as finger model.

'You like it?' asks the owner.

Sarah appears undecided and starts to look at some other things. The owner keeps a close eye on me as I try to remove it, but it's too tight. It's stuck fast. Licking and twisting the ring is getting me nowhere. I look at the man, who once again shrugs his big shoulders, but this time, as he does so, he reaches under his counter and brings out a large curved knife, which he lays gently down on the glass display case.

Sarah is now moving closer to the front entrance, still looking at various items as they catch her eye, but seemingly intent on leaving. Waving my hand in the air, I call nervously, 'Sarah, are you going to buy this ring or not?' She doesn't respond. 'Sarah, please!'

She turns, nonchalantly flicks her long brown hair with her hand, and smiles sweetly. I suddenly realise she's totally aware of what's going on, and is just making me sweat for a while. It works. I sweat. She purchases the ring but it's over an hour later, after I soak my hand in cold water and then olive-oil, that we manage to get the damned thing off. 'I hope your father has thinner fingers than me,' I moan. To celebrate we buy some sweet pistachio halva from a street vendor for sharing around later.

At six o'clock Phil, Sarah and I are sitting in a tea shop where we can keep an eye on the Yellow Bus. We notice Theo's jaunty walk before recognising his face. We call out and beckon him over. He seems even brighter than normal.

'You're looking very pleased with yourself. What have you been up to, Theo?' Sarah asks.

'Ha, ha, man, I've just had the first Turkish bath of my life. It's something I always wanted to do.'

Sarah studies him closely. 'You sure you're not pregnant? You have a strange glow; I would almost say you were looking radiant – No, you are definitely pregnant.' Theo laughs.

'They beat me with branches – I'm not kidding. I had to take off all my clothes and they gave me a towel to wrap around myself. Then I went into a steam room so hot it was difficult to breathe. I may have passed out for a while because I was really woozy, when a big fat guy came in and took me into another room He made me lie down on a block of wood and then he beat me up.'

'What?' We exclaim together.

He chuckles, 'Well, nigh on beat me up. He bent all my limbs in ways they shouldn't bend and then when he did bend them the right way he went further than I thought they could go. Then when I was crying for mercy he started pummelling me with his fists. He must know I'm Greek, I think. When I couldn't take it anymore he bought out a tree branch and beat me with that.'

He sees our looks of disbelief.

'Alright, they were just twigs, but they still hurt like hell. Then, when I thought he was going to beat me to death he picked me up bodily and dumped me into an icy pool. It was freezing. He stood over me and refused to let me out until I'd dunked myself completely under a couple of times. I thought I was going to die. When I finally climbed out I thought I had left my penis in the pool. I couldn't find it until it warmed up again.'

We all laugh and Theo continues, 'He threw me a dry towel and walked away, as if he had changed his mind about killing me. No doubt he was going for someone else. Maybe another Greek guy had walked in. When I got dressed and walked out of the place, I felt like I'd been reborn. I've never felt so clean and... I'm not sure of the right word for it... flexible, yes flexible.' We could all see the difference for ourselves.

We notice that Dave, Odette, Dick and Tim are standing around the bus, so we get up and prepare to leave.

We can't stay long in Istanbul. Cities are expensive. We soon find ourselves on the ferry, crossing the Bosporus, looking back at one of the most wonderfully famous skylines in the world, hoping to see its beauty and meet with its friendly people again someday but we still have a few miles to go.

Chapter 20. Do even mosquitos like mosquitos?

Over the coming days we get to see Odette in her element. Being bought up in South London she'd never learned the Turkish language fluently, just the basics her father had taught her. But now suspicion drops away from people's eyes when Odette shows up and speaks a few words of their language.

There are small mannerisms she has now that create a subtle shift in the way she speaks and moves. Body language plays a subtle role in communication, and it can't be taught, only unconsciously copied. Every nation has slight shades of movements when speaking that signal the difference between a linguist and a native. It's in the nature of all people to mimic those around them. It gives out the message, 'I am the just same as you and no threat.' It's wonderful to see those changes in her, that are usually imperceptible, taking place in front of our eyes; it's like seeing a plant growing using slow frame photography.

It makes her slot in somehow, in a way that's difficult to explain. Just as Theo had become more 'Greek' in his homeland, so Odette becomes more 'Turkish' in hers.

It's always welcome, although no longer a surprise, when the Yellow Bus starts on the first turn of the key. We drive off the small ferry boat, with the fierce, blood red sun setting behind us, and enter the district of Üsküdar. Briefly, we stop to look back at the skyline of Istanbul. The sun seems to be alighting on top of the dome of the Blue Mosque, precisely between its minarets, as if intent on resting there for the night.

Western Turkey marks an even greater cultural shift for us than Eastern Turkey. Now, the Yellow Bus has made it to Asia! We feel so proud of her.

Once again we can't tarry as we need to find a field to camp in. With the sun so bright in my rear-view mirror, I have to turn it awry to see where I'm driving. Üsküdar looks almost as fascinating as Istanbul, but our budget precludes overnight stays in cities so, with Phil navigating, we head east.

The sun goes out like a light being switched off. Within seconds we go from broad daylight to pitch-blackness, in an unknown countryside.

'These headlights aren't designed for Turkish nights,' I mutter to Phil, as I try to make out the road ahead. He leans forward and peers out the windscreen as if to help me; or maybe it's just to brace himself in case we crash.

'Al, I don't believe they were designed for anywhere dark at all.' He says.

Realising we can't choose an ideal place to camp if we can't even see the road, we pull up near a copse of trees. 'It will have to do guys,' I call out. 'I can't see much anymore.'

Dave yawns loudly. He speaks for everyone when he says, 'I'm knackered. Let's get into our bags and sod using the tents tonight.' The general consensus is, It's a warm night, so why not?

We sit in the Yellow Bus for an hour, telling each other stories of our adventures in Istanbul, drinking Raki and smoking a few joints, before calling it a night.

Phil takes off his glasses and rubs his eyes wearily. 'I'm staying on the bus tonight.'

'Me too.' Staring out the windows, I agree. 'I don't fancy trying to walk around out there. 'I don't think a bat could navigate this.'

Theo laughs, and drinks from the Raki bottle. 'Face it boys – You're just afraid of the wild boars – or maybe it's the poisonous snakes.'

Dick's head snaps up. 'What snakes? Odette, is he serious? There's no way I'm going to sleep out there if there are snakes – particularly if I can't see them.'

Theo's mischievous spirit rises as he hears the panic in Dick's voice. 'It doesn't make any difference if you *can* see them Dick. They can outrun a man. Just a quick flash to your throat and...,'he makes a lightning fast move to Dick's throat, '...it's all over.'

Dick jumps. He's very stoned, as always, and this is affecting his gullibility. He looks around at Odette, the only one of us with any experience of Turkey. 'He's joking right?'

Odette's voice is calm and consoling 'He's joking Dick. There's no wild boar or snakes here. He's pulling your leg.'

Dick, continues to roll up his sleeping bag on the floor of the bus. He doesn't seem too convinced. As he climbs out the back doors he stares threateningly at Theo. 'If anything happens tonight I'm going to blame you. Okay?' The others follow, all looking like naughty children trying not to explode with laughter.

Ah! Immediate and tranquil sleep. Blessed sleep - with dreams of exotic architecture and the echoing plaintive call to prayers from the mu'azzins... What? Already it's sun-up. And with the morning light comes a loud and incessant thumping on the windows. Phil and I wake with a start. It's Sarah. 'We have got to get out of this place. I mean – now!'

The others, carrying their belongings, are running fast across the field towards us.

'What's going on?' I try desperately to rouse myself from my wonderfully deep sleep. 'Sarah just says one word, 'Mosquitos.'

We hear Theo shouting. 'Where's Tim? Has anyone seen where Tim went?' Nobody has. In the darkness of the previous night it'd been impossible. Theo dumps his stuff in the bus and runs back to find him. Everyone else scrambles inside, tightly closing the doors and windows.

'We are all bitten to hell,' says Dave. He pulls off his shirt to see the bites all over him. 'Tenacious little buggers. I heard them buzzing around me but thought little of it. My God, they got me well and proper.'

Sarah and Odette check each other's arms, necks, and backs. They have both suffered badly.

Just then Phil shouts. 'Here comes Theo. He's got Tim. Christ...'

Theo, holding Tim's sleeping bag over his arm, is leading him like a World War Two veteran helping a gassed soldier back to safety. Tim looks like he's blind, and has his left hand on Theo's shoulder. Pulling on my sandals, I shout 'This doesn't look good,' and run to help them.

It's difficult to recognise Tim. His face looks like a stretched balloon. His features are hidden in folds of swollen bumps. His eyes have closed until the tops and bottoms have joined, and even the slits between them have vanished. He moans, and seems unable to move his mouth to talk. Quickly we lie him inside the bus and sit around impotently, astonished that mosquitos could wreak that amount of havoc on anyone.

'We must get him to a hospital fast,' announces Sarah. Within two minutes we are on the road, desperately searching for anyone who can help us.

Apparently, we'd stopped at a swamp; a perfect breeding ground for mosquitos. Tim had slept closest to it, almost at its edge. And we agree, he must have the most desirable blood group for these insects. Everyone had swellings coming up, but nobody has anything close to Tim's condition.

The wonderful foreignness of Turkey, that we've been revelling in, now plays against us. We don't have a clue where we are. Phil's road maps are on too big a scale to show smaller roads and hospitals. The whole of Turkey fits into just two pages.

We drive east along annoyingly deserted roads looking for someone, but apart from a few early rising farmers working in fields off in the distance, see nobody at all until we come to a small town.

The Yellow Bus

After parking in a road near a few shops, Odette leaps out. She hurries up to an old woman to ask her if there's a hospital nearby. But Odette's basic language skills are useless here. There are two dozen languages spoken in Turkey, and this woman's was not even close to the one Odette has a smattering of. After a few fruitless minutes we see her beckon the old woman towards the Yellow Bus.

We lift Tim up so she can see his bloated face. Studying him with care she mutters a few words to herself. Urging us to stay where we are, with one of those international hand-gestures, she goes into a nearby shop and re-emerges with a smartly dressed middle-aged man wearing a light blue suit and patterned red waistcoat – a surprising attire in these surroundings.

He introduces himself. 'My name is Mustafa and I can speak a little English. My mother tells me you have an ill person. Can I help?' He looks at Tim's face and appears deep in thought for a moment before going back into his shop. On his return he has a number of ointments and tablets.

There are no obvious signs or advertisements, but we realise then that it's a pharmacy. He's a trained medical man – what luck! In reasonably good English he explains what each of the medicines do and how we should apply them.

'But you must get him to a clinic for injections – we have malaria here. I will draw you a map.' Promising we would, we thank him. After paying him for the ointments and pills we take turns in shaking his hand until he must have felt like royalty.

We divert for an hour and drive to Bolu. Here we've no problem finding the main hospital where the receptionist speaks good English; so Tim receives his much-needed injections without further incident.

Afterwards, with Tim lying on the cushions full length on the floor and still moaning gently, we set off towards Ankara, the capital city. We've no intention of sight-seeing there – it's a city, and we need to keep our goal, India, in mind. It's the agreed plan that all cities are to be avoided. Unfortunately, they're the places where all the good roads lead.

The people here are very different from the ones on the European side of this huge country. The women's clothing is more Muslim and modest, covering most of their bodies, although still revealing their faces. The men wear long cloaks of coarse woollen fabric with a hood, called a burnous, and openly carry large curved daggers on their belts. We are told that those wearing white cloaks are the richer and more important people.

All of the men have moustaches and most have beards as well. They look severe and are not taken to smiling unnecessarily.

The women and the children are infinitely curious about us and stare, sometimes intensely, in a manner considered most inappropriate to westerners. It feels disconcerting sometimes. Whenever we stop at a tea shop we are immediately surrounded by women.

The men tend to stay at a distance warily keeping an eye on everything. My hair is below my shoulders, which the women find amusing and, a couple of times when we're made to feel welcome with a group, take delight in braiding, and adding beads to it. Male and female, we all get the same attention, but I notice their menfolk look more and more uncomfortable about it. Ineffectually, we try to get the women to desist in case of a jealous flair-up, but they giggle wildly and won't be diverted. Meanwhile they continue to serve us sweet tea, all the while chatting and laughing in an unknown language; a language which sounds like a country brook flowing over pebbles; to my ears, the most beautiful musical language I've ever heard.

For some reason this lessens any sense of danger I imagine ourselves to be in.

When they ask us to stay and eat with them, we decide that we'd taken their hospitality to the limit as far as their men-folk were concerned, and politely decline.

Chapter 21. Crashing in the mountains

'If you want to know where hills are – ask a cyclist.' This is Phil replying philosophically after I criticise him for navigating us up yet another stretch of mountain roads.

Not getting the gist of this obscure comment, I remind him, 'You know we need to keep to level roads as much as possible, Phil. The Yellow Bus is an old lady – she doesn't do stairs very well.'

'Every slight gradient for a modern car is a bloody mountain to us. Our maps don't show hills.' He pauses. 'Anyway, she seems to be doing fine.'

Our daily progress slows noticeably. Across Europe we have travelled at a steady fifty-five miles per hour. Now we find the Yellow Bus feels happiest at about fifty miles per hour on the level. This is the speed when all the mechanical noises sound like they should. I assume the constant hills are taking their toll – but there's still a long way to go, so we try not to be impatient and drive any faster. In mountainous country we are reduced to an average of about twenty miles per hour. Looking at our progress on Phil's map we make a decision to drive longer each day, which means me, being the only driver, driving into the night.

By any geographer's definition of a desert, there are no areas designated as deserts in Turkey. But some long and wide expanses in its centre look very much like it. The roads east of Ankara are stupefying monotonous, and at night they become dangerous.

When driving at night, Turkish driving protocol demands I turn off our lights and count to five every time a vehicle approaches. At the same time the vehicle coming towards us turns theirs on to full beam - and they also count to five. At the count of five we simply reverse things. I switch everything on and they turn everything off.

So for a horrifying five seconds, which feels like eternity, especially if the oncoming driver counts slowly, we can see nothing at all except the blinding lights of the oncoming vehicle.

I lose all sense of where the road is, where the ditches are, or even how near we are to hitting the oncoming vehicle, because their lights are rarely on the extremities of the vehicle. It could be pulling a trailer that increases its width by some feet. Our lights are like candles; standard issue on a 1959 British built Ford Thames minibus. We have no extra spotlights like the powerful ones sported on many Turkish vehicles. I doubt if we could cause much of a problem to anyone. On the contrary, we are often as blind as new-born mice.

Dick, having learned his lesson about back-seat driving, keeps quiet. In fact, we all keep quiet. If will-power alone can steer a bus there are seven more drivers driving it, although I'm the only one with the controls. I can sense everyone's fear and try to drive as safely as possible.

We decide to keep going until we hit a small town. We're out of the desert and climbing up a mountain, but the same crazy driving rules apply here too. It just means the stakes are even higher. Driving a truck in Turkey is still a macho-man's job. You can always tell a group of truck drivers because they have arms like Popeye; power steering is not commonplace. Hearing from other travellers, about the large death toll among them, it doesn't surprise us much. We have taken to spotting large lorries, even petrol tankers, wrecked at the bottom of the canyons.

The constant noise of the Yellow Bus screaming in second gear is getting to me as we climb higher and higher into the southern part of the Turkish mountains.

"Jesus that was close!" becomes a regular cry.

Large trucks sweep around hair-pin bends, threatening to send us over the side of a vertical drop. Driving on one side of a chasm, we can see the occasional distant lights of trucks winding down the slopes opposite. Night must be the chosen time to drive these big vehicles, as there's no other traffic on our road. Plenty of stars twinkle in the sky, but there is no sign of lights from any dwellings, and little moonlight to help light our way.

Trying to dispel our worries, we sing along to the gravelly voice of Roger Chapman of Family.

> *'Hunted me out, sapped me of strength and of will*
> *Showered affections, baited me, loved me until*
> *My defences and cautions were gone, babe*
> *And you did it just for the thrill'*

As we swing around a tight bend, our headlights reveal a landslide in front of us. Huge boulders thrown on top of each other block most of the road. My heart jumps. As I react to avoid the rock fall, we run into the dazzling glare of a truck's headlights. I'm blinded completely.

Desperately, I hit the brakes and steer with the information I had before I lost sight of the road; unfortunately it's not enough to save us. Two wheels go over the edge and we slowly tip over. Tim lets out a high-pitched scream that I hardly believe possible from a man.

Suddenly life goes into slow-motion. The noise inside the bus is awful. People are thrown on top of each other; there's the crashing sound of guitars being smashed by flying bodies; food and crockery, plates and cutlery hit people and rattle and bounce off the metal interior. Loud swear words go unfinished as the need for self-protection takes precedence. It's a few long seconds of shouting and screaming, all of which seems to happen in slow motion.

With a solid thump, we roll over onto the driver's side then over again, down momentarily on the roof, then on the other side - where we finally come to a halt.

I check myself out and believe I'm unhurt, having had the advantage of gripping the steering wheel tightly throughout. The others have been ferociously thrown around, with nothing at all to hold on to. I quickly turn the engine off and we sit in complete, blackened, silence.

'Is anyone hurt?' I ask tentatively, afraid of the answer I'm going to get. Nobody speaks, so I ask them individually.

'Odette?' 'I'm okay, I think.

'Sarah?' 'A bit shaken up but no bones broken.'

'Phil?' 'Nothing's broken – that I can feel anyway.'

One by one, everyone reports themselves as shocked but unhurt.

Only then I realise that I'm soaked in the engine oil that's leaking on me through the engine cover. It's burning hot - I try to pull my cotton shirt off.

'Have we stopped… I mean…are we safe?' asks Tim in a trembling voice. 'I … I'm sorry I screamed. I was dozing. The last thing I saw before going to sleep was a sheer drop. I thought we were going down to the bottom.'

'Me too,' agrees Dave. As the driver, I thought it wise not to admit to it - it's what I feared too.

'Look,' says Phil. 'We might not be safe. I can't get out my side. We're going to need someone to climb out and check our position. Can I suggest nobody moves an inch until we know where we are?'

Although my side of the bus is now pointing at the sky, my door is twisted and jammed. The headlights have remained on, but are just pointing into total blackness and give us no reassurance about our predicament. Are we teetering on the very edge of a sheer drop? We have no idea.

Odette, who ended up closest to the rear doors says. 'I'll go. 'Anybody got a torch?'

Nobody has, or at least, we can't find one. 'Has someone got a lighter or something?' Tim passes her his Zippo. She pries one of the rear doors open as gingerly as a safe-cracker dialling a bank lock, waiting for the click.

'Be bloody careful then,' instructs Dick unnecessarily, but whether in concern for her safety, or from fear of her sending us down the chasm, I'm not sure.

The rest of us sit in total silence. Thankfully the scorching oil I am covered in is cooling fast as the chilly mountain air howls in through my window. The only light comes from our headlights pointing uselessly at the sky. Nobody speaks until we see the Zippo flame outside and the little flickering patch of light moving around.

'There she is,' says Theo.

The light comes around the bus from the road side towards the vertical drop on our right.

Then the little light comes flickering towards the bus and the rear door opens. 'You wouldn't believe it.' Odette grins.'

'What?' Comes the immediate chorus.

'It's alright. You can all get out. We're quite a distance from the drop.'

As we very gently climb out one by one, Phil calmly says. 'Suggest you put out that lighter, Odette. We're probably leaking petrol.'

She flicks it closed.

We sit on the grass a safe distance from the bus. Sadly we study its dark outline, lying on its side. I have turned off the lights. The bus now looks like a huge defeated animal; its life extinguished. The amazing star-filled sky continues to twinkle above us, totally oblivious to our disaster. Theo pulls a blanket from the bus and wraps it around me when he sees me shivering. Dave rolls a joint and passes it around. Having got clear of any petrol fumes, Odette uses Tim's Zippo to check us for any signs of bleeding. It is quickly ascertained, apart from Tim's pride, we're all safe and sound.

There's a lot of laughter, gallows humour, as we release our pent up nerves together, like a support group.

'Sorry for smashing your guitar Phil. It certainly saved my face from hitting the floor though.' Sarah laughs.

Odette immediately went over with her lighter to investigate Sarah's face. Sympathising, she laughs, 'I made an effort to fall on top of Dave, but missed.'

'How are you Al.' Phil asks.

'Well, I'm okay Phil, but I think I'm a bit oily. Best not to bring that Zippo too close, Odette. Immolation would be a tough punishment for my bad driving.'

'It's a beautiful night though,' observes Dave, as if it's the most natural thing to say in the circumstances. 'Anyway, Al, there's no way you could have done anything else. Who the hell parks a truck with its headlights full on like that?'

Looking up the gradient to the road we see the truck is still parked, with its blinding lights on, seemingly waiting for its next victim.

Theo interrupts us in an urgent tone. 'Quiet! Be quiet for a moment. Listen!'

It's then we became aware of the faint sound of music from a radio.

Chapter 22. "I'll deal with it tomorrow"

The Yellow Bus lies on its side, a couple of dozen yards from a sheer vertical drop. As we sit on the chilly mountainside listening to the mysterious Turkish music filtering through the night, our entire adventure feels doomed. Knowing it's too dangerous to try find the source of the music without torches to light our way, we gather the sleeping bags from the belly of the dead beast, we had recently, respectfully, called the 'Yellow Bus'.

There is little to say, and precious little we can do in the dark and cold. Everyone climbs in their bags and tries to sleep. By common unspoken consent we decide to behave like Scarlett O'Hara in "Gone With The Wind" and just 'deal with it all tomorrow'.

All except me, that is. The hot engine oil that cascaded over me when we upturned also saturated my sleeping bag. This had been spread over the engine cowling to reduce the noise from our screaming motor as we ascended the mountains. I just tuck myself into the debris in the back of the bus, wrap whatever unknown pieces of cloth I can feel around my shivering torso, and go to sleep.

In my dreams we go over that cliff edge, and fall hundreds of feet, over and over. I wake each time sweating and wondering if I'm dead.

The Yellow Bus

Sunlight coming in through the windows is not welcome to me. It's early and I have probably managed two or three hours of sleep. Of Walt Disney's seven dwarves I could only have auditioned for the role of Grumpy; maybe mixed with a bit of Dopey. I don't want to face reality, but have little choice. Apart from the wind whistling outside, all is silent. The music of last night has stopped.

The inside of the bus reveals the chaos. I try not to focus on it at that moment; not until we are all together. What I do see makes a lump in my stomach. Of course, I had taken my rucksack down from the roof to get at my sleeping bag and hadn't bothered to put it back. Being stashed temporarily behind the engine cowling, it's now richly stained with dirty engine oil.

Squinting out the hole where a window used to be, I can see my fellow adventurers sleeping in a row of blue and green bags very close together, as if for safety. I wrap an Indian blanket over my oily torso, grab my sandals, and walk over to the colourful little maggots on the grass.

'Anyone awake?' I ask quietly.

'Fuck off.' Dick raises his bushy head, and for the first time I see that he's going bald on top. I realised then I'd never seen him without his military camouflaged Tilley-style hat. He turns over and tries to go back to sleep.

'I'm awake,' Phil answers, 'Tell me it's just a dream Al'.

He sits up and gasps against the chilled air of the mountains. Rubbing his arms vigorously to generate some warmth, he contemplates the Yellow Bus where she lies on her side.

'I wish I could.' I reply. 'Let's inspect the damage and see where we are.'

Both Theo and Dave respond by climbing out of their bags and braving the mountain chill. The four of us visually inspect the crash site.

Our first thought is, how close to the void were we? We stand at the edge of the ravine and look down the sheer drop of a few hundred feet, the updraft of freezing wind make us shiver as it whips and tangles our long hair into knots. Then we look back at the bus which seems so close.

'Another full turn and we would be at the bottom of that,' says Dave; and as if to illustrate the point, picks up a large rock and throws it over the side. We don't hear it land.

Then we turn our attention back to the bus itself. Some of the windows have popped out and are laying on the grass. I look at them and think, *'That explains why I felt so cold last night.'* Dave climbs inside the bus and pokes his head out one of the window holes; he looks like a tank commander. Grinning, he cracks, 'On to Moscow.'

One body panel lies a few yards from the rest of the bus where it has been ripped off; it's the lower section that runs from the driver's door to the back. The driver's door itself is punched in at the middle, maybe by some rock, which makes the top stick out about a foot. There's no rear bumper anymore. We guess it's disappeared down into the ravine.

'Ha, ha.'

I look up. 'What's so funny Phil?'

'Every bit of filler has fallen out.'

He's right. Some of the bodywork now resembles gruyere cheese. The years of fibre glass repairs had not been able to take the punishment.

'Shit it's cold. I'm going to make a brew.' Shivering, Dave sorts through the mess of bits and pieces in the bus and locates the tea making equipment, which we return with, to wake our friends.

'What's the verdict guys?' Sarah and Odette ask.

'Dead as a dodo.' I shrug.

'Oh, that's a shame.' Odette looks over at the wreckage. 'I was beginning to think it was going to get us there.'

'What do you mean 'beginning'?' My curiosity is aroused.

'Oh come on! I don't think any of us really thought we would make it – did we?' She looks around for support. None comes. Everyone is too busy rolling up their bags or stamping and slapping themselves to get some blood flowing; puffs of breath are visible like a group of heavy smokers. 'Oh, maybe it was just me then. Anyway, let's have some tea.'

Chapter 23. Blame the Raki

After warming ourselves with a hot drink and a few mouthfuls of muesli, which is now scattered all over the inside of the Yellow Bus, we take in the amazing craggy mountains and valleys all around us. It's wild country. For a moment I feel a strange pleasure at being there – even in the present circumstances. What's an adventure without danger, after all?

Dave does a funny Charlie Chaplin walk up to me and says, 'Now this is a fine mess you've got us into,' and flicks an invisible tie.

We all laugh. Gallows humour again – so valuable. I say, 'You're mixing up your comedians Dave. That was Laurel and Hardy's catchphrase.' Then I feel embarrassed at mentioning it.

Dick, sits up, holding a metal cup with tea in it, still in his sleeping bag, but now with his hat on, and asks in an imperious tone, 'Would you care to explain how we are going to get us out of this mess, Alan?'

What an insufferable little shit he is,' I think. But it's important not to create divisions between us, particularly now, when we need everyone to work together. So, I just say, 'That's what I'm thinking about, Dick,' and leave it at that.

Seeing a potential argument about to brew, Sarah interrupts. 'Anyone got an idea where that music was coming from last night?' We all look towards the truck on the hillside above us.

'C'mon Al.' says Phil, wrapping his sleeping bag around his shoulders.

Phil and I climb up to the truck, the big Mercedes, whose lights had blinded us the previous night. Those lights have now been turned off and it's empty. We check to see if it had a radio but it hasn't, so we deduce the music wasn't coming from there. Then we see a stone cottage a hundred yards further down the road in a clearing. It had been hidden from sight from where we slept.

It's an old place but obviously still functioning as there are lights in the window. Two small vans in front of it bear the sign-written insignias of the council. We knock on the stout wooden door, which opens almost immediately to reveal a group of six rough-looking men playing cards around a long table. The air is thick with tobacco smoke which forms a lazy cloud under the bare light-bulb over the rough table. The seventh man, the one who opened the door beckons us in and goes back to his place. They stare at my oil-stained Levi's and my long oil-clotted hair with some amusement.

If we had known the cottage was there we would have taken Odette with us for a bit of translating, but all we could do is say,'Merhaba,' the Turkish for 'Hello.'

A giant of a man with a full black beard, every bit as outstanding as Dick's, rises from his chair and directs the man who opened the door, to give us tea. More tea. Tea to celebrate and tea to commiserate, I think to myself.

Then he asks, in excellent English, 'What brings you two here?'

Phil replies. 'We crashed last night. There are eight of us.' The giant translates this into Turkish for the others, and then nods at him to go on.

'We came around the bend and saw a rock-fall. Some idiot has left a truck there with its lights full on and we were blinded.'

Again, the giant speaks in Turkish, but this time they all start to laugh uproariously. When the laughter has died down, he nods for Phil to continue. We must have both looked puzzled at the mirth we were causing because he said, 'yes, go on, go on.'

'We are trying to get to India from London. But we crashed and - our bus is dead...' Phil ran out of things to say.

The giant signals to another man, a rough looking man with a healed slash wound across his cheek and lips, and they each grab a thick coat from the pegs on the wall. The giant and the other man follow us back to the crash scene. When they see the Yellow Bus, the giant says, 'We had loud music on last night, and drank a bottle or two. We didn't hear a thing,' as if he was already producing a defence.

They walk all over the crash site and speak seriously to each other. After much discussion and nodding, the giant says, 'Get everyone together and come back to the house.'

By now the bags have been unlashed from the roof-rack and people are inspecting their goods to see what has survived intact. For the most part everything is okay, as it's mostly clothing.

'My bloody pipe,' says Dick angrily, displaying half of his chillum in each hand before tossing it into the bushes.'

'Good,' laughs Dave, 'Now we won't have to wonder if you're ever going to pass the bloody thing around.'

Chapter 24. Theo wants a Viking funeral

The card players in the cottage vacate their seats at the table and the giant motions us all to sit down. They disappear into another room and leave the giant and his scarred friend with us. Perhaps they think listening to our English is going to be a strain.

More cups of tea and bread, and a number of small complimentary plastic packs of butter and raspberry jam, are presented, which we all welcome.

'What can be done?' Phil asks the giant.

'Nothing, until this afternoon.'

And then Phil asks the question we all want answered. 'Who parked the truck on a blind bend with all its lights on full-beam?'

The giant unashamedly grins and nods. 'Yes, we did that.'

''But why?'

'Because there was a rock-fall and we needed to warn the people.'

He pauses, and we all wait, fascinated as to what possible excuse he could have.

'Yesterday afternoon we came here to move the rocks. Ibrahim here,' he nods towards his friend, who grins, as far as his scar would allow, which turns it into a kind of snarl, 'had a bottle. Mehmet had a pack of cards. Then Hüseyin pulled out another bottle from his truck and then…. Well, you know… it got dark; too dark to put up our warning signs. Hüseyin went out and parked his truck to warn people and we decided to have a little party.' He shrugs his shoulders as if to say *'it's is the most natural thing in the world to leave a rock-fall covering a road if having a party is an option.'*

'Hold on,' says Tim in perplexed tone, which his swollen lips have turned into a kind of lisp. 'Sho you *had* been shent up thish mountain to put warning shigns about the landshlide, and to clear it away, but you got drunk inshtead? And becaush you got drunk you parked a bloody big…'

'Hold on Tim,' I interrupt. I understand Tim's anger. The injections had reduced the swelling in his face from his previous mosquito bites, but now he looks like an angry Charles Laughton in The Hunchback of Notre-Dame. The giant is still grinning and showing absolutely no sign of recognising his own poor and dangerous decision. But I'm not going to let Tim create bad feelings. We are up in the mountains without a vehicle. This giant is possibly the only one who speaks English. We need him.

'So, what can be done? I ask.'

The giant pulls at his beard, leans forward, hunches his shoulders, and says, 'Nothing can be done until this afternoon. We have work to do.'

'Work you should have done yeshterday,' interjects Tim, somewhat comically.

I wave him down, 'Okay Tim. But what will happen this afternoon?'

The giant simply says, 'This afternoon we will help you.'

Looking around the table at our party we look a bit beaten up. Odette, dressed in a lacy white top and a wide black gypsy dress, has fallen asleep with her head resting in the corner of two walls. Theo, with his boundless energy sapped, appears dejected for the first time. Dave, still in denim top and jeans, is just looking down into his cup of tea. Dick is totally disinterested. Tim looks like he should be in a hospital ward. Sarah is fighting to stay awake. It's just down to Phil and me – after all, it's our responsibility to get us to India.

'Okay.' I say. 'Let's rest up for a while. Pretend we're on a mountain camping trip for the day. Anyone got a better plan?'

'What about food?' Sarah asks. 'We don't have much.'

The giant stands up. 'Don't worry little angel. I will get something for you this afternoon. One of my men will drive down to the village. And you can stay the day in here. It will be warmer. We have a fire in the other room.'

Then I ask the question that's been on my mind since we first saw this place, 'Do you have a shower I can use?' If I wasn't so pissed off with him I could almost hug the man when he points to a door on the other side of the room and says, 'There's a bathroom and shower through there. You can stay here while we go to clear the rock-fall.' With that he ambles through the door and we hear him shouting to his men.

In the cold brick built shower, with a solid block of white soap in one hand and something that looks like an old tea cloth in the other, I scrub myself over and over, until all the old engine oil is out of my hair and beard, and my skin stops feeling slimy. The water is only tepid but that's enough for me to start singing with joy. The feeling is fantastic – to be clean again! I shiver as I try drying myself on the tiny hand towel and, still damp, pull my oily pants and jeans back on with difficulty. But I feel like a million dollars. Happiness is so relative!

The cottage is empty by the time I'm finished. As I leave it, I notice that both of their vans have gone. Walking towards the road I see the giant and his group of men using some kind of crane on the back of the Mercedes truck. They're moving the huge boulders into a clear area, one at a time; finally doing the job they were supposed to have done the night before. I can't identify the mixed emotions I feel when I see the new road signs, on both sides of the avalanche, warning approaching motorists.

Everyone is back at the site of the crash. The sun's starting to warm the day and the chill in the air, whilst noticeable, is much more bearable. Odette and Sarah have collected all our remaining food together. The muesli has been retrieved into the large paper sack and we also have halva, nuts, rice and some apples and some bananas that escaped relatively intact. A large red watermelon, we had recently bought from a roadside seller, is crushed, but mostly still edible.

The others are pulling everything else out of the bus and laying them on the grass. The two guitars are ruined and lie together in a tender union of musical destruction. Personal belongings like books and small bags, beads and bangles are laid on the cushions so as not to get trodden on. The three side windows, all unbroken, have been collected up and stacked. Our unused Chinese socket set, hydraulic jack and a few other tools are in another pile.

Theo is seemingly getting his energy back, and he shouts enthusiastically, 'Why don't we give the Yellow Bus a Viking funeral?'

Crouching down and pushing some of his belongings back into his rucksack, Dave says, 'And how do you plan on doing that my crazy Greek man?'

'Over the side.' Theo points towards the edge of the cliff.

That gets Phil riled. 'Holy shit, we can't do that. We don't know what's down there. Maybe there's some village, or something else we can't see.'

'They'll think it's just another crazy Turkish driver with too much Raki in him.' Theo laughs, then pauses and thinks for a while. 'Okay, how about we set light to her?'

What? Now that thought upsets me. 'Hold on guys. Before we talk about Viking funerals, let's see what these Turkish guys have in mind. We only have to wait a few hours. Anyway...,' I slowly turn around with my arms outstretched, taking in the huge desolate mountain ranges like a demented Julie Andrews in The Sound of Music, 'what the fuck else can we do?'

My oil-spattered rucksack lies on the grass and I kneel down to see what can be saved. Everything at the top is soaked with engine oil. I have a roll of toilet paper that is now dark grey. I throw it in with the guitars as I figure a fire will be on the agenda at some point. Underneath that is my favourite blue shirt with an African gazelle design on it – that has to go onto the fire as well. My trainers and socks are only slightly marked so I immediately swap my sandals for them to warm my feet. The few other bits and bobs are relatively okay. My book "The Bold Saboteurs" by Chandler Brossard is just damp at the edges – I keep that. The rucksack itself and my sleeping bag are unceremoniously dumped with the rest of the pile.

Then it occurs to me; I feel strangely and quietly numb. I suppose I've been waiting for a convenient time to allow myself the luxury of feelings, but there's too much to do just now.

Chapter 25. Phil sets himself on fire

By midday the dense mist, that fills the valley ahead of us, dissipates under the power of the sun. Jackets and hats are discarded as the day warms, and the chill mountain wind that has been freezing now drops almost completely. The majestic mountains around us look like they've been painted by an artist without any skill for detail. Great daubs of colour and triangular gashes of shadow make the view seem like a rugged paint-by-numbers art-work on a vast scale. There are few trees to be seen on the mountains just jagged granite slabs supporting various clumps of bushes. In the distance we can see pure white snow glinting on the peaks.

Up the grass slope from us, the man we now know to be the boss and his co-workers, are busy moving the largest of the boulders that spew across the road. The crane on the truck clinks its grappling chains, as the powerful Mercedes motor roars with the effort of lifting and swinging them to a safe area. Black smoke billows out of the vertical exhaust pipe, which, the now gentle breeze, turns into a ghostly wavering, battle-flag.

Not a single vehicle comes our way in the three hours they work on the rock-fall. I now feel unsettled at just how dependent we are on the good will of these rough-looking Turkish men. On the grassy slope, a dozen yards apart from the sad wreckage of the Yellow Bus, my brother Phil calls us together and tells us to gather around. He has wrapped a white sheet around him. With his long hair and beard, he looks the very image of Jesus. 'We need to have a proper ceremony,' he shouts.

Tim, Theo, Dave, Odette, Sarah, Dick and I, all drop what we are doing to listen to Phil's sermon. He stands in front of the pile of our wrecked things; a wooden bowl full of petrol next to his feet.

Here are the busted guitars, my oil-soaked rucksack, sleeping bag, and a few of my clothes, too oil-stained to be saved; also a couple of books and one or two of the thin blankets that I had wrapped around my slimy body the previous night.

We form a circle. Phil raises his hands like a preacher at a pulpit. In a theatrical stentorian voice he begins. 'Dearest brethren.' We all smile. 'We are gathered here to pay tribute to the two finest guitars ever made, and a load of stuff my idiot brother here destroyed by his inability to drive.' He looks over to me and smiles. *'He's my brother – he can say that kind of thing without upsetting me.'*

The sermon is a short one; at this point he picks up the wooden bowl and vigorously splashes a generous quantity of it over the pile. 'Ashes to ashes. Dust to dust.'

'Amen,' we all chorus.

He steps forward and strikes a match and - WOOF! Having been over-generous in splashing the petrol it ignites in a great ball of fire, and throws Phil backwards. As he slips, he accidently drops the bowl with the remaining fuel and the contents flow towards the fire and catch immediately. We all run. I look back to see Phil on the ground desperately rolling away from the fire. Some dribbles of petrol have gone onto the grass and he is rolling in them and setting his shroud alight.

'You silly bastard!' I shout as Sarah and I run towards him. He throws the sheet off and we rapidly check his back and hair for damage. Underneath he is unharmed – eyebrows and beard a bit singed, that's all.

'You too, are a fucking idiot brother.' I tell him. He laughs and I look him in the eyes - and am glad to know that this crazy guy, my brother, was in my life.

Hearing laughter, we look up to see the Turkish workers had stopped to watch our pantomime, and are laughing their heads off.

The fire burns fiercely for a short time, but there is little in it to keep it alight for long. Theo pokes the books with a stick to encourage them to burn. Not liking to see books burn I don't ask whose they are, or even bother to read the titles.

Then we hear the sound of motors approaching. One of the workers pulls a green flag from the back of the Mercedes truck, and walks towards the oncoming vehicles, ready to wave them to stop, but this new found sense of responsibility isn't required. It's the two council vans that had been parked outside the cottage earlier. They pull up behind the truck and open their back doors. A number of men and women clamber out. The women are wearing gaily decorated skirts with black and red blouses – more gypsy style than the severe Muslim fashion we are used to. Many are carrying bags. One of the drivers points towards the bus and everyone makes a bee-line down the slope towards it.

We see the boss and Hüseyin, the man who parked his truck in the cavalier way that led to us crashing, join the group coming towards us. There's lot of laughing and good natured shouting in Turkish.

We've no idea what's going on.

The boss comes over to where our group are standing, while Hüseyin shouts instructions to the new party.

'I told you we'd help you, didn't I,' says the boss proudly. 'Now watch this.' He points to the new arrivals.

We all sit down on the grass where we'd been standing - and stare.

There are about a dozen people – half of them women. First of all, they muster their combined strength, and gripping the roof line, lift up one side of the Yellow Bus. By feeding their hands further and further down they push the Yellow Bus up to a point that it thumps down on all four wheels.

There's a gasp, then a round of applause, not just from us, but the workers on the roadside above us as well.

The bags are opened and pop-rivet guns are produced. The long body panel, shed in the crash, is held in place by a few of the men. Some holes are drilled. Two women apply their shoulders to the panel and expertly operate the guns to fix it in place; then they strengthen another couple of panels that appear to be about to fall off. They stand back to admire their handiwork.

We all look in appreciation at our saviour. He grins. 'Just watch,' he says.

In teams, our new visitors grab the three windows that have popped out, from where we had stacked them. They have them inserted in their appropriate holes in the bus within two to three minutes. Two are outside holding the glass up. One person is inside, using a knife to slide the rubber holding strips back to grip it.

'It's like watching a team competition on TV,' says Sarah. She's voicing the astonishment we probably all feel.

The boss, sits next to her on the grass and dwarfs her with his bulk. He claps with childlike enthusiasm. 'I told you, didn't I?'

He then points down the valley, and we all follow his finger. There's a dark storm approaching in the distance. It's still bright and clear where we are, but we can see rain clouds casting great shadows a few miles away. The boss shouts to his friend, 'Hüseyin!' and points to the storm clouds. Hüseyin acknowledges him and issues commands in Turkish to the crew working on our bus. They stop, look at the storm coming, nod and get back to work again.

Little can be done to get the driver's door shut, as it has been bent out by forty degrees, but it's pushed hard until there's only a six inch gap at the top; then lashed permanently closed with a piece of rope.

A women in her thirties is directed over to me by Hüseyin. She had a full, symmetrical face, like a Mongol. It takes me a few seconds to stop looking at her with admiration, and to realise she wants the keys to the ignition. Taking them with a smile she returns, climbs into the front passenger seat and slides over to the driver's side.

A man comes down from the Mercedes truck feeding a long hawser behind him. He lashes it to the front bumper and calls up to a colleague. There's a whirring sound of a winch, and the long cable moves like a snake in the grass before lifting itself clear of the ground. The group working on the bus get behind it, and push the front around with the help of the winch, until the Yellow Bus faces uphill. Then, with the winch, and the group aiding it, it ascends the hill bit by bit.

We all stand and cheer its progress: British and Turkish together grin at each other, like proud parents of a new born child.

With a lot of clever winch work, and brute strength, the Yellow Bus is dragged and positioned on the roadway, facing the direction we need to go.

Theo, Tim, Odette, Dave, Dick, Sarah, Phil and I grab any belongings we have and clamber up to it. I climb up on its roof, unlash one of the undamaged gallon cans of oil that we had received from the Duckhams Oil Company, and pass it down to Phil. Now we are surrounded by grinning Turkish people, who are chattering and slapping us on our backs, as if we had won a race of some kind. We, in turn, thank anyone and everyone with handshakes.

After filling the engine with oil and checking the level is right. I turn the ignition on and try the starter. The Turks all cheer and urge it on. The engine turns but won't catch. I try it again. This time it coughs a couple of times and sputters. More shouting and cheering. On the third time it bursts into life.

After a lot of embraces and handshakes, we are all aboard just in time for the storm to break above us. The Turkish people, all heroes to the last, flee from the pelting rain to the cottage. Some of them stop long enough for a last quick wave to us.

Regarding the Turkish workmen I am in two minds, whether to be angry for the irresponsibility of their crazy acts, or to love them for the enthusiastic and generous help.

I put the Yellow Bus in gear, check if we have enough petrol, try the brakes a few times to build my self-confidence, and start along the mountainous road that we should have travelled many hours ago. The rain comes gushing through the gap at the top of the driver's door and within seconds my right arm and chest are soaked. I have to tilt my head away slightly to avoid raindrops splashing into my eyes – but we were on our way!

Chapter 26. Horses in the trees

Two days after the crash I start to feel ill. We've made good progress across Turkey. The wonderful repairs done by the Turkish people have remained reliable.

'I've got to stop. I feel awful.' I groan.

'What again?' asks Phil, rolling a cigarette.

'No choice.' I moan, and push him out of the passenger seat, so I could dive behind some bushes to pee, project vomit - or worse.

'Drink this,' says Odette, when I climb back on board. She hands me some real cow's milk bought from a street vendor.

'Thanks Odette.'

'Maybe we should rest up for a day, so Al can get better?' suggests Theo.

My stomach feels like it's inhabited by angry creatures. They're all fighting to eat me from the inside. It's getting difficult to concentrate on driving with so much pain.

'I've only eaten watermelon for the last two days,' I said. 'Can watermelon be poisonous if it grows in dirty water? I mean, does fruit naturally filter dirty water, and grow the same, as if it's in clean water?'

A quick buzzing conversation within our group reveals nobody has any idea of the answer. We sit in blessed ignorance. (This is twenty years before Google has been invented.)

Phil takes charge and tells me to stop and rest until I recover, and I'm only too happy to agree. We're in the process of looking for a suitable camping place when the engine gives up the ghost. It's overheating and chugging along on two or three cylinders, seemingly as sick as I am. I try revving the engine but there's little response. Then it's firing only on two cylinders, and it becomes difficult to make any progress. Yellow Bus feels like a bucking bronco ride at the fun-fair, and I have to slip the clutch to keep her going.

It's pure luck that we manage to find a decent field to drive into, just as it gives a last gasp and rattles to a stop. We all disembark and stand around talking. I spot some welcome shade from a tree nearby, stagger over to it, and lie down. Within seconds I'm fast asleep.

The next two day are lost to me, as I lie in my tent in a high fever, passing in and out of consciousness, being fed soup and tea, and having my forehead constantly bathed by Sarah or Odette. I wake up long enough to thank them and then fall back to sleep.

Then I'm having a surreal dream with six or seven white horses in a deserted landscape. They're caught high up in oak trees; and I am the only one who can help free them. There's one in each tree. I have no idea how they'd got there. They're panicking; their eyes bulge and stare wildly. Hooves crack against branches as they thresh around, desperate not to fall. But I know they'll fall if I can't do anything. I have no rope. There is nothing around me that can use to help. They are big, fully grown beasts;

too big for me to do anything.to help Helplessly, I look on.

Then I'm in a modern city. The sky glows crimson, swirling in a turmoil of stormy patches. Thousands of flecks of black within the incandescent heavens spin and dance within each blood red cancer-like patch like an unholy flock of starlings; they're dark coals on a fire; unburnt fuel awaiting their time. Then they rapidly flare in bursts of sharp lightening spears, adding to the liquid movement of the billowing masses.

Great areas in the sky coalesce and turn to vast troubled clouds which insidiously streak down like ink through water. But that rain is hotter and more fluid than volcanic lava. This liquid streams from the clouds like a furnace sluice has been opened, and pours its bursting load over skyscrapers, roads and people with a heat so intense that concrete explodes instantaneously and the huge buildings crumble, their steel girders, like flaming skeletons twist agonisingly in tortured slow motion before falling to the ground.

The people and the cars are incinerated in a fraction of a second. Where they coalescence is not so extreme and millions of sparks the size of small houses shoot out and punch deep craters into the Earth itself. These rockets of fissionable rock wipe away everything, like a cloudburst wipes the chalk off a blackboard. Nothing can survive in those places. It's worse for those on the outskirts of each occurrence because they can only witness the death and destruction of their neighbours. It might be happening only a few hundred yards from them. They can see everything but not know which way to run. Where will these clouds of swirling plasma deposit themselves next? I am screaming and writhing in the heat.

The fever lasts two full days, and then goes as fast as it came. I wake alone, unable to speak because of my parched throat.

The tent is flapping in the hot wind and I think it's someone knocking to come in. Confused, I look around to remind myself where I am. Then I find a cup of water next to me and gulp it down. It's daylight. I have no watch to know what time it is. Crawling out of my tent I realise its early morning. There's Theo and Dave starting a fire to brew morning tea with.

'Och, so, you're alive then?' remarks Dave as he catches sight of me.

My voice is shaky. 'Yeah. At least I think so. I had some pretty weird dreams.'

Theo laughs. 'You didn't dream you crashed the Yellow Bus in the Turkish mountains, by any chance?'

'No,' I say, 'I wouldn't dream anything that ridiculous. How's tea coming on?'

It was then I remember the problems we were having with the Yellow Bus. 'I've got to have a look at our engine today. I remember it's not doing too well.'

'Your too late Al. Theo and Tim have fixed it,' says Dave. 'Tell him Theo.'

Theo throws some more kindling on the flames and explains. 'Apparently, Tim's a bit of a mechanical wizard. He took a look and diagnosed a blown head gasket.'

'Oh! Christ,' I moan.

'No. Christ had nothing to do with it. Tim and I hitch-hiked about 80 kilometres to the nearest town and bought a new head gasket, and some other bits and bobs he said were needed. Apparently they use these Fords for dolmuses all around here, so parts are not difficult to come by.'

Dave places a saucepan of water on the fire and throws some tea-leaves into it.

Theo continues. 'We got a brilliant lift in the back of a tractor. It was slow but the guy stopped at café's and insisted on buying us Coca-Colas. He thought we were Americans and kept talking about New-York. I think he has relatives there. Anyway, we got back and Tim spent a few hours working on the motor and – well, it runs again.'

Just then Dick comes out from his tent, looks at me suspiciously, and says sourly, 'I thought you were going to die.'

I don't know what to say. Dick has a way of phrasing things that perplexes people. He sits down cross-legged on the grass, waiting for the tea to boil.

Odette comes out to join us. 'You made it then,' she says with a smile.

She sits next to me with her legs bent behind her, but her feet pointing outwards. I find that enchanting. 'Thanks to you.' I look into her beautiful face....'*But, she is with Dave,*' I remind myself.

She's about to say something, but stops when Phil and Sarah crawl out of Phil's tent and come over to join us. It surprises me to realise they have slept in the same tent. Up until now Sarah has always shared a tent with Dick, her brother. Phil deliberately avoids my knowing smile. 'Any tea ready,' he asks enthusiastically. If auras can be seen, I feel I am seeing one now. They sit together and their body language speaks a love story without words. Every gesture, expression and sound they make became part of a private language between them. My brother is definitely in love.

'Tim was trained as a mechanic by the London Underground, Al,' Theo says, breaking my reverie.

'What? Oh!' I collect my thoughts. 'I thought you said you were a train driver, Tim.' We all look at him. He's embarrassed by the attention. 'You're a dark horse.' I add.

He stammers. 'I, I, didn't really like it. So I asked to be reassigned to driving. Mechanics is too dirty. I could never get my hands clean.' He laughs then shakes his head as if remembering difficult days. 'No, it wasn't for me, but I did learn a lot.' He looks over to the Yellow Bus, ten throws me the ignition keys. 'I think it'll be okay now. Give it a try'

Dave jumps up and takes the keys from me. 'You need to rest some more, my man. I'll give it a go.' He climbs into the Yellow Bus and starts the engine which responds immediately - and it sounds so smooth! He revs it a couple of times. It responds well.

Tim is grinning with delight. 'Oh just a word of warning; we had nothing to make sure of a perfectly clean surface, so I used shellac on the head gasket. You know what that is don't you?'

I did know. Shellac is a resin secreted by the female lac bug from India and Thailand. It creates a formidable coating or glue when used as a liquid. I knew that motor mechanics sometimes used it, but it was never meant for engineering purposes. It's a fix that's never mentioned in workshop manuals.

I laugh. 'Well, that's never going to come off again.'

Dave returns. 'Well done guys,' He shouts. 'What a fantastic job.'

Everyone gives Tim a round of applause, not forgetting the assistance of the effervescent Theo. They have done a good job. Now the Yellow Bus is better, and ready to go even before I am.

Another half day of resting follows before I'm feeling capable of continuing. When we set off the Yellow Bus purrs along the road more smoothly than ever before. The motor sounds so different. The symphony of mechanical click and clacks, whirs and taps, we're all used to, has changed; becoming somehow more refined. It was the difference between "Electronic Funk" and "Beethoven's Pastoral", in musical terms.

Well done London Underground for giving Tim such good training!

Although, it must be said, Tim had been lucky using our cheap Chinese socket set without incident. The next day we have to change a tyre when we pick up yet another puncture. I stand on the end of the bar of the socket in order to undo the wheel nuts. The customary sharp crack of the nut coming loose is loud, but I am surprised to find the noise comes from the socket itself, having split simultaneously down each of its six sides; fortunately we also have an old-fashioned wheel brace. As I change the wheel and swap it for a spare on the roof, Phil checks the map and declares aloud to everyone, 'We should make Iran before nightfall.'

Chapter 27. Entering Iran

We park in a lay-by outside a town called Van, about fifty miles before the Iranian border. Dave and Dick roll up the last of our dope.

Other travellers have warned us about Iran. "They don't have a tolerant attitude to us Hippies, man," we were told by a remorseful Dutch guy, who had done prison time in Tehran. A small crumb of hash lost in a crevice or under a cushion, a pipe with a little oil residue, anything at all, he told us, would spell disaster.

But, sitting in the bus and getting stoned didn't really help allay our sense of paranoia.

'Guys, are we all really sure nobody has anything in their pockets, or in their bags?' asks Phil.

Sarah and Odette inspect their shoulder bags again. Dave, Theo and Dick check their pockets, tobacco tins and anything else they have with them. Afterwards, we pull everything out of the bus and clean it thoroughly.

'I'm going to get all the bags off the roof and we can check those as well.' I announce, waiting for Phil to move so I could get out the passenger side.

'That's not necessary, Al' says Phil. Then he thinks about it for a few seconds. 'Oh, okay. Maybe you're right.'

I climb up on the roof, unlash the rucksacks and hand them down to Phil to distribute. Everyone empties their bags onto the tarmacked lay-by and goes through their possessions one by one. When satisfied, we tie the bags back in place and drive on.

At the border hostility shows in the eyes of the thin moustachioed border guard as he directs our battered and bent Yellow Bus to a parking spot. Waving his machine gun threateningly, he indicates he wants us to get out. The fact that we don't speak any of his language doesn't seem to deter this twitchy gun toting individual from shouting at us continuously. He marches us to the customs-shed to show our paperwork. Seemingly, out of thin air, a team of four men dressed in overalls, pulling a trolley with tools, start to search the Yellow Bus - and what a search it is.

They remove the seats. They throw every piece of luggage down, without care, from the roof and investigate each bit thoroughly. Meanwhile, we're taken, one at a time, into a small room and body searched. It didn't involve undressing, but every part of our bodies is manhandled. They call a mean-faced matron of a woman over to search the girls.

An electric drill is produced and a number of small holes are drilled in both the bodywork and the chassis of our bus. A couple of big Alsatians are brought out, straining at their leads, and encouraged to smell the areas that had been attacked.

We watch from a distance through a large window, appreciating the air-conditioning, even at this time of the evening. I hear Dave murmur to Phil. 'I hope we've done a good clean-up job Phil.' It was then I realise I haven't breathed for a while, and my heart has gone on hold, waiting for one of these guys to shout a whoop of victory; a small roach-clip held aloft.

The search continues for an eternity. Some of us try to get some sleep on the hard wooden benches – I can't. Somehow I feel I am instrumental in them not finding anything; as if my will-power is influencing events. Phil feels the same.

The fuel tank is tapped with little hammers to listen for odd noises that might suggest a hidden compartment. To us every tap sounds suspicious, even knowing we have nothing to hide. As dark falls powerful lights are brought out to give them more visibility. Everything we own is reduced to its smallest component and checked. We are kept there until the early hours of the morning. After six hours of this microscopic examination the team of men suddenly walk away.

A guard casually calls over to us from his office in one corner of the yard. 'Go. You can go.' Then he waves us away dismissively as if we're unwanted itinerants. We stare at our belonging strewn across the area. It looks like a bomb wreck. Halfway through the laborious task of fitting everything back together, a young smartly dressed officer comes over to us. Pointing to Phil and me, he waves us to follow him and sits on a low wall outside We three sit and look up at the twinkling stars that are starting to fill the night sky.

'Beautiful aren't they,' he says.

Cautiously, we both agree with nods and grunts of, 'Ah-ha.'

This immaculately dressed officer then offers Phil and me a cigarette each from a pack of Marlborough's. As he lights them for us, he says in a confidential way, 'You have done a very good job. My men are completely baffled. So, where did you hide the drugs then?' He looked astonished as Phil and I burst out laughing. 'Obviously subtlety is not his strong point,' Phil says as the officer walks off in a bad temper.

Eventually, we reassemble everything, without assistance from the Iranian customs people, and start on our way. It isn't much of a welcome after the friendliness we've received by every other country, but at least we're being allowed through. We drive all night in a subdued spirit. We know we need to be very alert in this place if we are to stay out of trouble.

Chapter 28. Suicidal sheep

A couple of days in and we start to relax a bit. We're making good progress with anything up to three hundred miles a day possible. Petrol's cheap, and the roads are good. The country appears vast, often without a building in any direction, and the continual mountain range in the distance is beautiful to look at.

Ahead of us a lonely sheep herder drives his flock, which is scattered messily along the side of the road. I slow, although most of the coaches and trucks we've seen here just kept going full pelt. We've passed flocks of sheep many times in Turkey and throughout our first couple of days in Iran; the reaction is always the same. The herder leads his sheep off the road and into the scrub until we pass by. That's the accepted method.

This time seems no different; the man walks into the scrub and the sheep follow. But suddenly one sheep breaks away from somewhere in the middle of the flock and runs directly at the Yellow Bus like a ram on heat challenging for mating rights. It lost.

This poor thing must have been dead before it hit the road, and it all happened before I had any chance to take avoiding action.

It's unheard of for sheep to do this, surely? I think. *They're supposed to behave like – well - sheep - aren't they?*

Parking up swiftly, a few of us jump out to inspect the damage. Sure enough, our suicidal sheep who, maybe acted as an individual for the first time in its life, is dead. I'd avoided running it completely over, for which I was thankful. As we start to manhandle it out of the road we're surprised by three men in their late twenties or early thirties dramatically sliding their motorcycles to a halt in front of us. They don't wear crash helmets. We have no idea where they came from.

They park their trails bikes across the road ahead of us in a way to prevent us from going forward. The leader dismounts. He looks like a denim covered body-builder with a Freddie Mercury style moustache. I could almost smell his self-love. He comes up to us with a swagger and starts shouting, which, our last two days had shown, is the way many people in Iran communicate - at least the men. With an exaggerated motion he pulls off his expensive looking sunglasses, folds them slowly and puts them in his top pocket. Then he pulls himself up and stands arrogantly, like a rock star on a stage, and points at the dead sheep. He grins and puts his hand out in an unmistakably aggressive gesture that demands money.

To build self-confidence I stand my ground and, without confirming whether or not they understand me, I say firmly, 'Hold on. Hold on. Who the hell are you guys anyway? I will pay him for the sheep, but not you.' Phil moves alongside to give me psychological support.

But, as we turn to look for the sheep herder, we see him running away from us as fast as his old legs can carry him, with all his sheep in hot pursuit. This is extremely confusing. These guys have shiny motorcycles and wear nice clothes and wrist watches. I can't for the life of me think what connection they would have to a shepherd; or why this old man, who had done no wrong, should be furiously running away across the scrublands.

By now everyone has climbed out the bus to see what's happening. These three tough looking guys, sporting large knives in their belts, couldn't have felt we British Hippies were much of a threat to them. On this deserted road in the wilderness they apparently figured they were the law.

They continued to demand I pay them. Just as hard, I continued to demand they return with the shepherd, and let him know we were prepared to pay him for the sheep we had killed. Things were heating up, and I could see we were not getting anywhere fast. It reminded me of the bullies at my school who had to go through the initial stages of words and slight pushes before launching into the rough stuff. *The rough stuff here will be too rough for our liking.*

The leader puts his hand on his large bowie- style knife.

'Everyone back in the bus,' I shout.

Smoothly and without too much fuss we all climb on board and slam the doors. The motorcycle guys seem perplexed on how to handle this unexpected turn of events. They shout angrily at each other, but don't appear to have a plan. I start moving the bus forward and judge there's just enough room to squeeze between their machines. There's a chance. We take it and accelerate as fast as we can. Poor old Yellow Bus is obviously no match for the three powerful motorbikes, but any chance to avoid a bowie knife in the stomach feels like one worth taking.

We go barely half a mile, with our engine screaming fit to burst, before the burley leader pulls alongside my side of the bus, between the road and the scrub, and shouts at me to stop. There's another motorbike close to the passenger side and the third one close behind us. Understanding from this that the words, the pushing and the shouting stages of the game had now passed, and that we were down to the 'rough stuff', we were determined not to stop.

'These guys are either going kill us - or themselves,' I shout in panic.

'Don't stop, whatever you do, Al.' Phil is as tense as a cat.

'If someone's going to die, make sure it's not us,' commands Dave. It's the first time I had heard the big Scot sound nervous.

The motorcycles roar, accelerate and brake, easily manoeuvring around us at will. At times they take to the scrublands at speed or change places with each other. There's a thump as one of them punches the side of the bus as he flies past. Then another and another, as they laughingly take turns.

We have no plan except to drive to the next piece of civilisation, be it a town or a village, where we can get some explanation of what's going on. The decision is taken out of our hands when the man on the motorcycle behind us accelerates to the front.

A couple of hundred yards ahead he slides to a heroic stop, and sits facing us.

The leader is still gunning his motor on our inside and I take the tactical decision to take him out - and I do just that. When there's a gulley I swerve sharply to the right and give him no road.

We watch him fly into a field at about sixty miles per hour. Whether he hit a rock or something I don't know, but we see him fly high in the air like a bird for a while, before pounding into the ground and, in a cloud of dust, rolling for a few more yards.

This gives us the room to go around the stopped bike in front, and keep going. I pray they care more for their friend than they do for our blood, and hammer the gallant Yellow Bus for every possible ounce of power.

Odette and Sarah take a rear window each and stare intently down the road. 'There's nothing behind us,' and then every few seconds ... 'Still nothing.'

'What are we going to do now?' Dick cries. 'We have to stop. Report it to someone.'

None of us know the answer. We talked about stopping in the next village or town. I'm not up for that as I envisage the town sheriff being like Rod Steiger in 'The Heat of the Night', and finding out these three hooligans are the beloved sons of the local mayor.

'They'll hang us for sure,' I said, maybe a little melodramatically, but I am also bloody scared. My heart is racing, my palms are sweaty. The thought that I may have just killed someone in this country is something I'm trying my best to suppress.

We drive on past a couple of towns without stopping before the need for fuel forces us to – by then we feel far enough away to relax again.

Chapter 29. An unexpected event

Unusually for us, we decide to drive into the seven thousand year old city of Tehran, the capital. I suppose we just want to say we've visited it. Like all cities it's overcrowded and difficult to navigate through. The traffic comes to a standstill every twenty feet or so and then everyone just has to wait.

Tired of the heat and traffic we stop at an outside cafe and sit under the umbrellas. We order long non-alcoholic drinks and look at the noisy traffic-choked streets. After some contemplation I say to Phil. 'Why is everything here so stressful? Even driving down the roads is a totally nerve racking experience.'

Phil studies the busy road for short time before saying. 'It's easy. Nobody plans ahead. If they can move their car three inches closer to where they're heading, then they do. That's all there is to it.'

It's easy to see what he means. A line of traffic is being held up by a truck trying to turn right. It blocks the vehicles behind which queues back to where the traffic is crossing further back. This prevents any movement ahead which could allow the truck to go forward. In other words, it's a total square. I expect someone to hold back, allow the truck to go and free up the whole situation. No way. The cars all shuffle forward as soon as any tiny gap appears, filling every space and blocking the lorry again and again.

'You're right. It's insane.' I say. 'You'd expect something smarter from such an ancient civilisation.

Eventually, the burley driver of the truck gets out, and by threatening gesticulations, forces the drivers who are blocking him to drive onto the pavement. Then he strides to a car further back, and using a wagging finger, instructs him to stay stationary. He shouts so loudly we hear every syllable from a hundred yards.

We sit for about twenty minutes and witness a number of incredibly stupid actions from drivers who refuse to help each other. Phil confirms his theory. 'It explains why traffic moves so slowly here.'

I challenge him. 'I bet you a pound we don't see anyone do a good deed for anyone else in the next half hour.'

'You're on,' he says.

We study the way people drive, and look for any unselfish action - but without luck. After ten minutes a black clad woman, carrying a huge bundle of washing on her head, comes into view. As she walks along the street the knot holding her laundry bundle works its way loose and the clothing falls onto the pavement. We are astonished to see people walk on the washing, without any apparent concern, as she scrambles about to save it. Not one person stops to help her. I won my pound. We decide to leave Tehran without doing any sight-seeing.

Not far from Tehran we find a small lake and decide to make a stop there. Parking the Yellow Bus under the shade of some trees I decide to investigate the area a bit. Being the driver I'm free of all other duties. After climbing a rock strewn slope to get a better look at the water, I sit under a tree to rest. Ten minutes later I hear someone coming and keep very still to find out whether it's local people. But no, it's Odette. Her hair, long and flowing, catches the sunlight: Her beautiful face framed by that Orinoco style fringe.

I don't move or say anything – just watch. She's wearing a flowing blue cotton dress with small motifs, maybe flowers, maybe just dashes of colour, I'm not sure. On top she has a white gypsy blouse with short ruffled sleeves. Stepping cautiously over the loose ground her movements look so feminine. I feel magnetised and dumb.

She looks around and I admire her slim but well-shaped outline. Then, seeing me, she smiles and comes over.

'Hi.'

'Hi.'

Odette sits down close to me, picks a long piece of grass and starts to peel the end of it.

'That was pretty scary, y'know, with the sheep and those guys. Were you scared?'

I smile at her. 'Oh hell no. Big guys with knives don't bother me. I'm an Englishman.'

She pulls an expression of disbelief and laughs.

'Honestly, I was petrified.' I say.

'Me too.'

Leaning towards me I thought she was going to lay her head on my shoulder for comfort. Instead she puts one hand around the back of my head and kisses me softly on the lips. It was a kiss to be remembered. Perhaps I'm not as surprised as I should have been. Only a total fool could ignore the way we always avoided each other; the way we made sure we were never alone together. Well, we were together now.

For a long time we kiss – if time continued to exist at that point. When our lips part I say, 'That's what lips are for then?' My humour isn't the cold water of doubt; it's more fuel to an inevitable fire. She laughs as I pull her down in an embrace - and we make love.

'What's going to happen when Dave finds out,' I ask when we are resting together; somehow confident this isn't to be a one-off experience. I like Dave a lot. I respect him and don't want any bad feeling to affect our journey. There's also the consideration of being beaten up by this tall fiery Scottish guy in a fit of jealous rage.

Odette moves up and kisses me again. She says simply, 'Dave and I are more like brother and sister. He won't mind.'

I chew on a stalk of grass and stare at the wispy clouds in the blue sky above us and think, *I really hope you are right about that.*

Chapter 30. A road full of dead people

Alarmed by the strange sight Phil shout, 'My God. What the hell is that ahead?' There's a scramble as everyone pushes and shoves behind us to see out of the windscreen.

'It's friggin' Armageddon. That's what it is.' Dave's Scottish accent sounds stronger than ever.

'It looks really ghastly,' opines Tim, nervously.

There are bodies - bits of bodies - strewn across the road a couple of hundred yards ahead. The sun glints off the wet, red, bloody chunks scattered over the entire road. Is it a butcher's truck in a terrible collision with something, or have these victims, perhaps been cut down by some act of war? Maybe the result of an explosion of some kind? It's so difficult to make out.

Ahead we can see a truck down a gulley, leaning at a crazy angle. There are a crowd of people milling around, but we're too far to see what they're doing.

Dick groans, 'Oh shit. Let's get out of here.' I start to brake to turn around, but realise Dick's suggestion is not possible. 'There hasn't been a turnoff for miles.

'We'll need fuel soon. Sorry Dick, we'll just have to go through it.'

I search for a way of driving around this gore from some recent catastrophe, at a loss to explain what has created so much carnage. There's no way. The gullies either side of the road run too deep for the Yellow Bus to cross.

'You can't just drive through this, Al.' Phil is silent for a few seconds. 'No, this isn't right. Nobody gets smashed up this much. That's not just one or two people. It would have to be…'

'Watermelons!' cries Theo. 'They're fucking watermelons.'

'Oh Christ, he's right.' My heart leaps at the realisation. The heat haze shimmering over the road has distorted the picture. As we come closer the truth becomes obvious.

Theo starts to laugh. 'For Fuck's sake. What an optical illusion that was…'

But he is interrupted by a hysterical shriek of laughter from Tim. 'Fucking watermelons. Fucking watermelons.' His voice is shaking, and I can see his face in my rear-view mirror is distorted with panic.

Sarah grabs him and pulls him down next to her. I hear a sound like a clap as she slaps him hard across the face. 'Get a grip, Tim. Everything's okay. They're just watermelons.' She pulls him towards her and buries his head in her shoulder. His body shakes as he sobs.

That isn't the first time we've seen Tim go into a panic. The first time was when we turned over in Turkey. We had forgiven that because he thought we were going over the cliff; at least, that's what he said. Phil and I exchange looks that speaks volumes about our concerns.

Nobody speaks as we slowly navigate through the wrecked fruit strewn all over the road. We can all see what the problem is. Someone has failed to secure one of the rear tailgates on the huge lorry and it's swung open. There must have been a thousand watermelons smashing down on the tarmac just before we arrived.

An Iranian man in a long white turban beckoned us on. Because of our first impressions, I realise I am trying hard to avoid running over any of the debris.

Phil says, 'C'mon Al. They're just watermelons.' We laugh, and drive on.

We're two days drive out of Tehran and stop in a small town, more a village really, to get some food. It's a rundown little place. Houses are made mostly of wood and in bad need of repairs. It reminds me of cowboy towns in the movies and I expect to see whirling dust storms and balls of tumbleweed blowing past.

'It's like something out of a spaghetti western.' Phil observes. 'I can hear that coyote-howl theme tune from Ennio Morricone.'

Sarah and Odette jump out to buy some things from a shabby little shop on the corner of an intersection. I haven't really had a chance to talk to Odette to find out how things are between her and Dave. She and I had made love yesterday afternoon by a lakeside. I know this isn't the time. That I just have to be patient. Unsuccessfully, I try to put it out of my mind.

Feeling more protective than usual, I stand outside the shop when the girls go in. A few locals walk by when it strikes me that everyone who comes past appears to be suffering from Downs Syndrome. Having had a neighbour in Thornton Heath with Downs I could recognise it immediately. A few more people came along the street, and they had Downs Syndrome as well. There was a whole family, mum and dad, with a couple of kids. The mother was holding a baby. They were all Downs sufferers.

This feels remarkable, and slightly spooky, so I go inside the store, which is a general store selling ironmongery, foodstuffs, and all the regular items. Making sure the girls are okay, I pretend to look at some of the hand-tools they sell. Four Iranian men with that strange dreamy Downs look come up and stand around me, far too close for me to feel comfortable. They speak to each other in Farsi and constantly grin and chuckle in an unsettling way. They take it in turns to look very closely into my face and then laugh loudly as if generating courage to do something. I don't know what I should do. All I can think is, '*I can't fight people with a disability.*'

I'm wearing an Indian cotton shirt with a buttoned flap, which is open. One of the Iranian men reaches forward and quickly pulls a clump of hair from my chest. He shows it to his friends and they all laugh. It hurts a hell of a lot, but I try not to react as I genuinely believe they're as mad as hatters. Another man reaches forward to do it again and I bat his hand away. The laughter is loud, and I know the people in the store can see what's going on.

I look over at the owner of the shop, he too looks like a Downs sufferer, and is laughing with them. The other people join in laughing and suddenly, everyone is looking like actors in a horror movie. The girls pay and grab their things and we rush outside, jump into the Yellow Bus and pull away, with a few of them banging on the sides of it.

As I rub my chest I think, 'What's to blame for these people's condition? Perhaps inbreeding, perhaps chemicals from a nearby factory. Although I can identify Downs I have no knowledge of its causes. What I do know is, it affected the entire village. We can see that as we drive through.

We are all mighty glad to leave them to it.

Chapter 31. Cultural differences

Mashhad is the second largest city in Iran. It's on the ancient 'Silk Road' and is huge both in size and influence. The name means 'place of martyrdom' or 'burial place of the martyr' and it's one of the holiest cities in the Shiite Muslim world. It's a strange and dangerous place to be if you are a blue eyed foreigner with no money. You feel like an intruder on a private gathering you have no right to attend.

Any appreciation of the architecture, or the gardens, which can be fabulous, is spoiled by the looks of unbridled resentment in the faces of the people, and a sense of being positively unwelcome. Many years later I learn the reason for their attitude, but at this time I am a political innocent. Right now we were simply western hippies with long hair - and we generate no respect.

The day after we arrive, I'm walking by myself near the Imam Reza shrine. This is the largest mosque in the world, and famous for being the burial site of Imam Reza, the eighth Imam of the Twelver Shiites, and a descendent of Mohammed.

In front of me are two American tourists, both girls about twenty three years of age. I wonder about the appropriateness of their clothes in such a holy place. They're both wearing short skirts and blouses and no headwear. They start taking some photographs of the people and the awe inspiring architecture.

Immediately an old man rushes forward and, with a cry, starts to hit them with his cudgel - and I mean a cudgel rather than a stick; this is something capable of staving someone's head in. Only his physical weakness prevented a murder taking place. I rush forward to intervene and receive a glancing blow to my head. People are shouting loudly, and the old man is encouraging them. He appears to be someone of authority, and I can see the crowd is very much behind him.

As the crowd gathers tighter around some people start pushing, trying to unbalance us. Looking for some inspiration I put my hands together like a Hindu. It's the most respectful figure I can make of myself. *Okay – it's the wrong religion - but it's a pretty universal attitude for any human who wants to send out a peace message.* So, I bow in a gesture of supplication and apology, and repeat, 'They are very, very sorry for any offence.' Really, I don't know what to say. I'm not sure anyone understands English anyway, but I reckon that the sound of an apology will work in any language.

And it does appear to work. The old man calms the growing aggression in the crowd with some stern words, and they fall silent. There are a few shouts from those around us, as if calling for extra punishment, but the elderly man pacifies them. I do my best to usher the crying girls to safety. I feel extremely vulnerable as I turn my back to force a passageway through the mob.

After a few hundred yards we reach a park where we feel safe enough to stop and talk. One of the girls, a pretty brunette, introduces herself as Toni and her blond friend as Jennifer. I'm now beginning to feel the effects of the blow on my head. I reach up to find blood on my fingers and a searing pain where I touched.

'Let me look at that for you,' Toni insists. Jennifer helps me to sit down on one of the benches. My head starts to swim. I feel a little sick - but more important than that - I'm angry.

'Are you girls not aware that taking photographs of people is offensive to religious Muslims? And walking around like a couple of Coca-Cola advertisement pin-up girls might get you killed here?'

'We've only just arrived here – nobody's told us anything,' Jeniffer explains. They start to cry again and apologise, and insist on taking me back to their expensive hotel and to get a medic to look at my head wound. The head wound isn't that serious, I tell them. The girls both have bruises on their shoulders and arms. After a couple of whiskey's together – thanks to an understanding manager going to his own room and retrieving some, along with a clean bandage which he expertly wrapped around my head, we say goodbye, and I make them both promise to get some advice on the local customs here.

(Many times I have pondered on this event. Some would say it was the girl's fault for not learning the rules of another culture, and perhaps they deserved it for being inadvertently insulting. In my years of travelling since I have been to many parts of the world where someone has accidently insulted a host by being ignorant of their ways. Usually a simple word in their ear, an explanation of the required behaviour, is met with an astonished and profuse apology. Nothing more need be said. Only with fanatically religious people is violence the first resort rather than the last.)

I'm pleased to get back to the area where we're parked, and to see all the others. My head bandage causes some questions and I explain the strange incident. Theo and Tim had gone out for a walk too, but hadn't travelled far, when they decided the atmosphere was not too healthy for people like us.

'They don't like us, do they?' observes Theo. We all decide it might be wise to get out of Mashhad and hole-up far outside in the countryside.

Now I am having internal troubles of my own. Every night Odette is sleeping with Dave. I'm finding it difficult to sleep at all. My inner thoughts are a whirl of conflict and I'm also finding it difficult to know what's right.

What it is I really want? Do I want Odette? Yes, of course I do. Can I take Odette away from Dave? I think I can. Odette has more or less said it's what she wants. But I like Dave a lot. He is a friendly, generous guy. Do I want to hurt him? No, of course not. Do I want to travel with a girl, any girl, with all the extra problems that brings? No. That's why I chose to travel alone in the first place. Do I love Odette…? Christ! I don't know. I haven't ever been in love before.

And so the thoughts go on and on without me finding mental peace or making any resolution.

It takes us five days to cross Iran and that's as quick as we can make it. It's a big country. I must say the best Iranians I have ever met have been in England as refugees fleeing the Ayotollah's revolution and, years later, I met with other travellers who told me that the people of Southern Iran are a different kettle of fish, and much more friendly to foreigners. It's not a culture that won my heart nor those of my companions, so we were glad to arrive at the border of one of the most wonderful countries in the world - Afghanistan.

Chapter 32. Entering the sanity of Afghanistan

Afghanistan – a wonderful but unfortunate country, with an organised ancient culture that has existed in its lands since between 3000 and 2000 BCE. Without many natural resources it's poor, but regarded politically as a 'buffer' country occupying a strategically important location.

Its tragic history was decided by its geography; being located between Russia and India in the days of the British Empire. This led to Britain invading it three times to ensure that a puppet government was installed in Kabul, to protect British interests. The goal then was to ensure movement of its own goods and military, and to prevent the Russians from interfering with the jewel in the British crown, India.

More recently history has seen both of the modern Superpowers, Russia and America do exactly the same; attack the fourth poorest country in the world in order to control a strategically placed country, using propaganda as justification.

So, the Afghani people, although never officially defeated by any foreign power, have known war brought to them by foreigners for many generations.

This story takes place in the early 1970s during one of those rare periods of peace.

***

The crossing between Iran and Afghanistan is a substantial drive across the barren desert landscape that is no-man's land. Our next destination is the Afghan city of Herat, the third largest city in Afghanistan after Kabul and Khandahar.

As we look back at the receding Iranian town of Islam Qala, Odette is brushing out Sarah's long hair that she's recently let down. Sarah, trying to see the progress, is holding a small circular mirror. 'I'm not sorry to be leaving Iran,' she says.

Odette nods in agreement. 'That's a dangerous place. I liked the countryside but everyone seemed to hate us for no reason. The last few days I never felt safe.'

'Too right,' agrees Dick morosely.

Dave rescues the mood by passing Phil a tape of The Rolling Stones 'Beggars Banquet' to put into the player. As soon as Mick Jagger belts out… *"Please allow me to introduce myself. I'm a man of wealth and taste…"* we all join in and sing "Sympathy for the Devil" at the top of our voices at the desert scenery. It's cathartic and much needed, and we grin at each other as we use Rock and Roll therapy to forget the depressing place we've just left.

Phil looks over at me and says, 'Let's hope Afghanistan's better eh, Al?'

But for us, this no-man's land between Iran and Afghanistan is totally barren and deserted. We feel a bit uneasy – just hoping the bus keeps going as we've heard stories of woe from other travellers about what happens if you leave one country with a vehicle stamped in your passport, and then turn up to the next border without it. The assumption is that you sold it on the black market – and there are no breakdown trucks operating here.

But without a glitch, we arrive at the white border post and stop at a large wooden sign next to a lowered barrier which has Arabic script on it, but nothing in English.

'May as well get out and stretch our legs,' I suggest. 'Who's got any tobacco left?'

'You're a tobacco ponce Al,' Phil murmurs.

I reflect on that for a moment. 'It's true. I am. But I smoke so little, if I bought a pouch it would all dry up before I got to the bottom of it.'

Phil chuckles. 'You could buy a pouch and pay back all the people who've supplied you with a smoke.' He throws his tobacco tin at me as he speaks.

'Thanks Phil. I will definitely give some consideration to your suggestion.'

We are interrupted by Theo. 'We have a visitor. Looks like Quick Draw McGraw to me.' Then he adds, 'No, not Quick Draw McGraw; that was the horse wasn't it. Who am I thinking of?

A shambling, tall, thin figure with a drooping moustache like Fu Manchu's, is slowly making his way towards us. We can see his lower arms and ankles are exposed because he's wearing an old, threadbare army uniform, far too small for him.

'I don't mean to be cruel but he looks more like Sad Sack,'[i] Sarah giggles. Is he wearing his son's uniform do you think?

It takes an age for him to traverse the thirty yards or so of ground between us. Then he calls out in good English. 'Who drives the vehicle? I raise my hand and he motions me to follow him back to his little office.

'Cmon Phil,' I urge jokingly. 'He saw us laughing at him. He might shoot me when we get back to his command post.'

Phil and I walk at the tortoise speed of our guide, back to his office. At the rear is another area we hadn't seen. There's a room, and we can hear people's voices coming from it. There's a conversation going on, involving a number of men by the sound.

Sad Sack ushers us into his office, which has a large mahogany desk with drawers, which remind me of map draws. He takes a seat behind the desk on a swivel chair, plays with a leather fly swatter for a moment and then, with a hand gesture, invites us to sit on the two rattan chairs opposite him. His long face appears friendly, although his skin is dry and very gaunt, without a shred of spare fat. The ligaments play in his neck like wire hawsers as he moves his head. We are fascinated, having never seen a man so desiccated. It's like an anatomy lesson.

When Phil and I are sitting he stops playing with the fly swat, swings around in his chair and looks us squarely in the eyes.

'Drugs? Hashish?' he demands, his face suddenly stern.

'No, no, absolutely not,' I stammer, wondering how he thought we got across Iran with any drugs on us.

He studies the ceiling and watches the slow pulse of the fan overhead for a few seconds. 'You want some?'

Phil and I stare at each other, unable to speak.

With a smooth motion, Sad Sack pulls open a large drawer in his desk and waves us closer. In the drawer sits a large selection of different coloured blocks of hash, which he points to in turn.

'This is from Pakistan, this is local from the south, this is from India and this is Nepalese.'

Looking at our bewildered faces, he laughs. 'I don't think you expect this perhaps?'

'No. Not at all,' I murmur.

Phil and I are unprepared. We know there are other men, probably soldiers, nearby. If we buy some, do they just arrest us, throw us in prison - and then do it to the next guys that come along? I can tell Phil and I are thinking the same thing by our total reluctance to say anything.

Sad Sack grins, displaying good white teeth. 'I know you think this is odd, particularly coming from our Iranian neighbours; they have their culture and we have ours. What can I do to assure you…? I know. Follow me.'

He leads us around the building and back to the room we'd passed. As he opens the door a cloud of smoke billows out. It takes a few seconds to focus our eyes to the darkness inside, but we soon make out a circle of about a dozen uniformed men sitting around a hookah. One of the men is sucking on its mouthpiece with verve, we can hear the water bubbling like a boiling pot. I have to admire his lung capacity. The smell in the room is definitely of good quality hash. We wait for a few seconds before the man on the pipe directs a huge cloud of smoke towards us and everyone laughs.

Sad Sack says a few words in their language. It appears he is the commanding officer of this ragamuffin group of soldiers, who are sitting around taking little notice of us.

We later learn that every Afghan soldier has to buy their own uniform, so a single uniform can be shared by a number of brothers, as and when, they are on duty – then the uniform could also be passed down from father to son. Not surprising then, the soldiers in the Afghan army are less than spic and span.

We return to his office. I suggest we get the others here and he agrees, so I walk back to where our friends are clustered around the Yellow Bus. There's a look of anxiety on everyone's faces as I approach.

'How's it going Al? Asks Tim warily. 'Are they making it difficult for us?'

Attempting to keep a straight face I reply, 'No Tim. We're just buying some hash from the border guards.'

'No - You have got to be kidding. No way!'

'That canna' be right, can it?' asks Dave, with a confused look.

'Dick thrusts his hand down his pants and pulls out a chillum. 'I'm game for that…..'

Now I'm the one who is shocked. 'Dick, did you have that all the time we came through Iran? How the hell did you manage it… I'm amazed at your stupidity…'

'…says a guy who is buying hash of off the border guards in Afghanistan?'

He has a point!

After a quick explanation, we all troop back to Sad Sack's office to listen to a demonstration of his encyclopaedic knowledge about the different types and strengths of his products.

Using American Dollars we buy what we need and shake Sad Sack's strong thin hand to thank him. I felt that he would be a very handsome man, if he were to be soaked in a bath of water for a couple of hours and allowed to fill out.

We are welcomed officially to Afghanistan by Sad Sack as he opens the barrier as we get ourselves organised to go. He stands to one side of the raised post and salutes us seriously.

'Good Luck on your adventures, English,' he shouts. We return his salute and wave as we pull away.

'What a nice man,' Tim says. Within minutes Dick is filling his chillum. Dave and Sarah are rolling joints.

Phil, chuckling at the weirdness of the experience adds, 'Oh well! There's nothing for it, if we want to make friends, we must accept their age old customs. What a welcome.'

'I think I'm going to like this country,' says Dick.

Chapter 33. Too much bounce for our springs

Stopping at the first roadside tea shop we order fresh mint tea and some qatlama, an Afghan cookie, and we gather around the map that Phil's been studying. 'There's a road from Herat to Kabul which is almost direct, however some guys I met a few days ago assured me we wouldn't make it in the Yellow Bus. The terrain is too mountainous.' Phil traces his finger along the route. The road is clearly marked and a great deal shorter than the Kandahar option.

'I calculated how much further it is to go south to Kandahar and then back up again to Kabul. It's an extra 200 miles to go the long way around.'

'Phew. That's a long way,' observes Theo. 'Why don't we give it a try along the shorter route?'

'It's tempting,' agrees Phil, 'But the guys I talked to said better equipped outfits than ours didn't make it. Remember the wrecks we saw in Turkey at the bottom of the ravines.'

That settled the argument. It's to be Herat and then Kandahar.

The road becomes difficult to drive. It isn't old or full of potholes; in fact it's an excellent surface having been laid by the Russians. The problem is simply that it's prefabricated in large concrete sections and then laid edge to edge; there's a gap left between each section to allow for expansion under the terrific heat and cold of the Afghan seasons, and our wheels thump across them.

The gaps produce the same effect as old train lines, creating a rhythm of 'clunks' from both front and back wheels. The continual double 'clunk-clunk,' is irritating enough, but even that's not our main problem. Gradually, the suspension builds up sympathetic vibrations where the thump from each gap adds to the bouncing effect. Within a mile we are bouncing up and down like kids on a bouncy castle.

Tim tries to compose a song that fits with the thump of our tyres on the concrete.

"She broke
My heart
Tore it
Apart
Just want
Her back
....."

But realising the song was as tedious as the sound he was using for inspiration, he let it drop.

'Thank you Tim, says Dave, lying on the floor and trying unsuccessfully to sleep. 'I prefer the sound of the road to that.'

To protect the suspension from destroying itself, we have to constantly change our speed and break the sympathetic vibrations. We all stop talking as the monotonous thumps of our wheels rob us of any thought - apart from the quiet determination that this torturous noise must eventually come to an end.

After an hour, it's with a mighty cheer that we hit the American built section. Suddenly all is smooth and quiet, and we roll along the perfect asphalt surface. We stop for a tea break and Phil and I check the suspension. The Yellow Bus is feeling a little lower than before. Sure enough we have broken springs on both front struts. There's little we can do about it but to drive as gently as possible, no easy task considering the terrain we still have to cross.

Phil and I agree to keep this grim news to ourselves.

Within three hours we're crossing the Hashemi Bridge over the fast flowing Harirud River, and on our way to the outskirts of Herat. On the way we see number of brick built minarets rising from the desert floor. They look like fingers. Lopsided and decidedly haphazard as if the builders had been drunk.

Because we decide we need a treat, we stop at the first budget hotel, called 'The Agra Hotel'. It's cheap, has showers and appears well kept. The manager, who reminds me once again of my favourite actor Peter Ustinov, a portly man with a lot of energy; he welcomes us enthusiastically. Like Peter Ustinov, he speaks a number of languages – English perfectly.

'Please, my friends, sign the register.' He swings the large book, on the counter, towards us. 'You are English, yes?'

We assure him we are, except for Dave who is Scottish.

He appears delighted. 'Fantastic, I have worked in Dundee for six years. Perhaps I still have a slight accent. I was the manager of the Hotel Magan near the University. Do you know it?'

Dave has to admit that he doesn't.

I interrupt. 'We haven't changed any money so we don't have Afghanis with us. Can we pay in American dollars?'

He beams. 'Of course. We are international people. That will be perfect.'

He issues us with keys and shows us around. The hotel has a central courtyard that is elegantly tiled in beautiful blue-patterned geometric shapes. Graceful Arabic arches complete a circle around it. Our rooms are simple, nicely furnished, all on the second floor, with balconies looking down on a palm tree growing in the middle for shade, and a water fountain.

There is still plenty of daylight left so we decide to roam around a bit.

'Be careful everyone,' Phil warns.

But it's a needless warning. The Afghan people are as foreign to us as the Iranian; like the Iranians they are Muslims; like the Iranians they are tough. But they are such a kinder and more decent race of people. How good it is to be with people who don't shout at every opportunity; people who hold hands as they walk together, and laugh, and often hold little birds in their hands to enjoy their singing (which don't fly away because they are being fed hash seeds, we are told).

Alone, as I often prefer, I stroll around the local market place off of Mhabas Street and am greeted only by smiles and respect. Not the overblown friendliness of the trader spotting a 'rich' tourist, but by a genuine warmth that is surprising. Turbaned men form in groups outside of tea shops and seem to discuss things quietly and with humour.

Women, frequently unadorned by any headwear, and wearing modern western style dresses, walk freely together. It's so unlike Iran. I watch a group of a dozen youths all dressed in traditional robes. They laugh and nod as each of them speak. I wait for the 'playful' pushing and shoving I would expect from people of that age in my own country, but there's none. Even at that age they appear to have a dignity about them and just be happy to talk.

It's with a feeling of growing safety I wander around looking at the different fruits and vegetables on the stalls, investigate the inside of stores that sell vinyl records, watch hairdressers at work through their windows. It all seems so modern and wonderfully peaceful after Iran.

I take a little time off my roaming to return and inspect the damage to the Yellow Bus where she is parked, outside the hotel. The broken springs now give her a slightly wacky angle. The exhaust system is blowing, which makes her sound like a much bigger bus. We are lucky that the fumes don't come in when we are moving. She is starting to burn a little oil now but nothing to worry about. I've been checking it two or three times a day. The gearbox and clutch feel sound. The back bumper had been ripped off in our accident back in the Turkish mountains, but the police don't seem too concerned about stuff like that here.

When the windscreen wiper motor failed in Iran, Phil cleverly tied a long piece of string around both wiper blades and we each held either end of it. We taught ourselves to synchronise, pulling the blades back and forwards perfectly well as we drove; it was as good as the real thing. Luckily, we didn't get too much rain, as it always soaked me through the yawning gap in the driver's door.

My major concern now is our tyres. I can't remember just how many punctures we have picked up so far. Presently, we have a punctured tyre on the roof that needs mending, but none of the others would ever pass as legal in England. One of them is showing canvas all the way around the tread area. Not getting decent tyres before we set off was definitely a mistake, however money was tight, and the road conditions tougher than we'd ever imagined.

I return to our hotel and take a shower. Shortly after, the others all come back smiling and laughing and we sit on the cane furniture in the courtyard and swap stories.

Odette has a new dress. 'I've got to try it on. I love it,' she cries, as she runs to her room.

Shortly after, she returns looking like a princess. It's a Kuchi Tribe dress, in thick cotton to protect from the desert cacti - and it's beautiful. The colours are predominantly red and blue with strong gold thread designs around the hem, the sleeves, and across the breast and shoulders. It has a myriad of different patterns that confuse the senses. Sewn into it is a hundred tiny mirrors that sparkle with reflected light. We all applaud as she does a twirl in it, sending it spreading out like a flamenco dancer. She's so delighted, it makes us all feel happy.

Lying alone in my bed that night, I think about the next thousand miles to Delhi: I'm having doubts as to whether the Yellow Bus can make it. I fall asleep to awful imagined mechanical noises that sound like engine death-rattles.

Herat is an enchanting place, the people friendly and dignified. Many Afghans who speak English use the opportunity to practice on us, and we feel welcome wherever we go.

Chapter 34. Afghan bread

It's 10 am on a beautifully clear, sunny day. None of us can name what day it is, and we don't really care to try. We're all having breakfast outside a café Theo found, around the corner from our hotel. It serves omelettes in the English way rather than in the undercooked Afghan style. We're all well rested, scrubbed up and looking good. Odette's wearing her white blouse and a thin cotton skirt with the red flower patterns, Sarah's similarly dressed in a light blue blouse with Chinese style lacework.

Tim has bought himself a light straw hat and a white ribbed Afghan T-shirt with long sleeves. The rest of us make do with our regular jeans, T-shirts and sandals, especially Dave who wears his denim jacket, jeans and cowboy boots, regardless of the weather.

Theo is describing a scene he witnessed yesterday about how Afghan bread is made. He gesticulates wildly as he talks, with enthusiasm.

'....the domes are made of brick and clay about three or four feet high. Big enough to crawl into. They make up the dough in large bowls and then, using a long wooden spatula thing, stick lumps of the dough to the ceiling... oh, yes, I forgot to say that there's a fire in there... it's like a kiln for firing pots... but the dough sticks to the ceiling and cooks like that... then after a few minutes they get a couple of these spatulas and scrape them off the brickwork and bring them out...'

He holds up a piece of the wonderfully tasty naan style bread we are eating.

'... and that's how you get this.'

The atmosphere within our group is now sky high. There's a sense of family unity. The Afghan friendliness has raised our spirits. The girls feel free to wander around by themselves. Any prejudices about it being the Islamic religion that's responsible for creating intolerant attitudes to outsiders is being kicked into the long grass.

Putting on a theatrically strong southern American accent Tim drawls, 'How's about we just stay here for a while pardners.' He leans back in his chair, pushing his new hat to the back of his head. I guess he had a movie star in mind but which one I can't imagine. *James Dean? Gary Cooper? Lee van Cleef...*

'Let's put it to a vote then.' Phil interrupts my day-dreaming. 'Who thinks we should stay here a few more days, and who's for pushing on down to Kandahar later today?'

The vote goes: Tim, Theo and I want to stay in Herat for a while longer, Dick, Phil, Sarah, Dave and Odette want to push on. It's a close vote, but we happily eat up and return to the hotel to prepare for the next leg of our journey.

Chapter 35. The amazing American Kunst brothers

'What do you make of that, Phil.' I ask, as I peer through the windscreen.

Phil puts on his glasses and leans forward, as if it could make a difference. 'Mormons looking for Salt Lake City, by the look of it.'

We've been driving for a couple of hours across a dry, arid landscape with only sand-dunes and cactus to occupy our vision when, slap bang in the middle of this desert, we're looking at a covered wagon ahead of us in the distance. The shape is easily identifiable – it's a Prairie schooner – we've all been brought up watching "Rawhide" on TV.

As we approach we can make out some writing on a large board at the back of it.

It takes a while with us all guessing, until eventually we decipher the large writing proclaiming "First Walk Around The World".

Soon we can also make out two youngish guys walking in the mid-day heat, leading a horse that's pulling their wagon.

Drawing up we introduce ourselves. They look like they are in their 20's, fit and well-tanned, their hair lightened by constant sunshine. One of them says, 'Hi. We're Americans. My name's Dave Kunst, this is my brother John.'

Handshakes all round - we exchange names and greetings.

'I'm impressed. Are you really walking around the world?' Phil asks.

'Anywhere that's not water.' John smiles a friendly smile. 'We don't swim well with the wagon.'

Phil nods in appreciation. 'No cheating at all?'

'What do you mean?' asks American Dave.

'It's just that here we are, in the middle of the desert on a bloody hot day, and you're walking along. Isn't it a temptation to get some shade in the wagon and let the horse take you on occasionally?'

John and American Dave look at each other. John starts to speak but appears confused, 'But then it... it...'

'...wouldn't be the first walk around the world?' Sarah finishes the sentence for him.

Phil won't let it go. 'But nobody would know.'

'We would know,' they answer in unison.

Understanding my brother like I do, I know he's playing devil's advocate. He knows these two are genuine guys.

I interrupt the flow with, 'Phil, stop being so bloody mischievous. Sorry guys. My brother can be a bit of a pain in the arse, but it's just his sense of humour.'

Both the Americans chuckle. 'Okay, we get it,' says John.

Odette has been looking at the horse, and now comes around to where we are sitting by the road.

'What do you feed your horse on out here?' she asks.

John answers. 'You mean Williemakit? He's a mule. Compared to horses mules are a lot less fussy about what they eat. Most of the time he feeds himself, but in these situations we buy loads of straw or whatever we can get.'

He pauses, then adds, 'We also have to make sure he gets plenty of water, so we have these leather water bags.'

We look to where he's pointing under the wagon to see four or five heavy looking leather bags hanging down. Next to them is a wire cage in which a dog lies sleeping. It looks like a collie but we can't be sure.

John sees our bewildered expressions. 'That's Drifter Two.' He explains. 'Our original dog, Drifter One, was killed in Turkey – but, too late for us, we found this one doesn't like to walk, so we had to build him a mobile kennel.'

Just then Theo shouts. 'I'm brewing up – anyone interested?' We all are.

Scottish Dave rolls a joint. Dick fills the stone chillum, which he's smuggled through Iran in his underpants. He lights it and the smoke pours out of him. He resembles a tyre factory on fire.

American Dave looks at Dick for a moment and then turns to me. 'He likes his smoke doesn't he?'

'Yep,' I nod in agreement.

Theo, with Sarah's help, passes around tea and some of the cookies we stocked up with before leaving Herat. Sitting in a rough circle the inevitable barrage of questions begins.

'So where are you guys from?'

'Originally from Waseca, Minnesota State.'

'How long since you left home?'

'Two years ago, but we're making good progress.'

They told us their biggest problems so far had been blisters, and a slight miscalculation on how many calories they would need each day.'

'Yes, we were both getting really emaciated, but we're fine now.'

'We had to double our planned food intake to get some weight back on.'

At times when American Dave started a sentence John would finish it, or vice-versa - and they would both nod at the same time. In fact talking to American Dave and John and was not unlike talking to identical twins. They had similar hand gestures while they spoke, and would quickly help each other out if one of them had forgotten a name, place or a date. It was like listening to one person in stereo.

'All we can say is we are very pleased to be out of Iran for sure,' sighed John.

'Halleluiah!' We all nod our agreement at that sentiment.

We drink tea and talk for an hour while we listen to tales of incredible physical hardship. How difficult it had been to traverse the mountains in Turkey; how thankful they felt for the wonderful hospitality they had been shown by different nationalities on the way; how bureaucratic and difficult some borders were to cross – especially with their animals.

Dave adds, 'I'm sure they thought we were CIA spies at the Iranian border. This would be a pretty impressive cover to come up with, wouldn't it?' The image makes us all laugh.

Scottish Dave sips from his enamel cup and asks, 'So, how long do you think it's going to take to do the whole trip?'

American Dave and John shrug their shoulders in an identical way. It is obvious they have been asked this question many times before, even before they set off.

American Dave says, 'I just want to get back to America before my girlfriend gets fed up waiting and marries someone else.'

Although he laughs as he answers, I detect an element of anxiety in his voice.

Eventually, John stands up and says, 'I guess we better get on guys - long way to go.'

We had only stayed with them for an hour or so but we feel very close to these two heroic figures. Wishing them all the luck in the world we wave them goodbye.

Chapter 36. The French hippies and Mufi

The Yellow bus is still inspiring us with its willingness to cross mountains and deserts; but not without some cost. It has the look of a custom vehicle with deliberately lowered suspension, but that's the result of the two broken front springs. Frequent rain storms and sand storms have streaked the paint until no dominant colour remains. She is the Yellow Bus in name only. The prize fighter we had started out with has turned into a punch drunk pugilist with cauliflower ears and a broken nose – but, thankfully, still prepared to take on the next fight.

In London we would have been laughed at down King's Road or Carnaby Street, and pulled over by the police for driving such an obviously un-roadworthy vehicle, but in Afghanistan we don't particularly stand out.

***

Kandahar is a wonderful city with an array of fabulous mosques and wide parks full of blooms in various colours. There's a sense of tranquillity and history in every street. The boundaries of the city were originally mapped out by Alexander the Great who named the city Alexandria of Arachosia.

It's also one of the richest cities in Afghanistan. Sitting on a number of ancient trade routes it has great business advantages. Over the centuries it's traded in sheep, wool, cotton, silk, felt, food grains, both fresh and dried fruit, and tobacco. As in Herat, we walk around it with a feeling of total safety.

In the centre of the city we decide once again that the inexpensive hotels offer great value. Both the desire and need to camp out is deserting us, as we recognise just how cheap hotel rooms are. We book into a real budget hotel run by a young Afghan called Mahmoud, who is managing it while his father's away. He suggests a room price which we don't even bother to barter down.

Mahmoud's pride and joy is a beautiful dog called 'Mufi' which looks like a cross between a husky and a labrador. He lopes over to us as we book in and sniffs each of us in turn, as if registering us in his little library of smells for later reference, should he be required to locate us.

Everyone takes to their rooms to write, read, or do whatever else they couldn't do in a hot, noisy crowded bus. I want to sleep more than anything, so spend most of the day in bed, until Phil wakes me for dinner.

All sitting together in the room Phil and I share, everyone nurses a story they are bursting to tell. Odette is describing the market place that she and Dave had visited.

Her eyes are bright and her beautiful face animated, as she describes the range of edible sea creatures they have for sale.

'…and then, just as I have my face this close to the glass, trying to work out what it is, it opened one eye and looked at me…'

Tim, hardly waits until our laughter dies down. 'Hey everyone, I have a warning for you all.'

Our merriment stops stone dead.

'Well that got your attention.' He removes his new hat and throws it onto my bed.

'I was feeling really hot so went into that little café down towards the junction, and ordered a Fanta. The waiter came out with a glass and put it on the table, then turned slightly away from me to open the bottle. I heard a 'phiss' noise as he opened it. Then he poured a little out and walked away. But as soon as I picked it up I could see it was flat and gasless. It smelt foul and tasted like dry cleaner fluid. I was sitting there feeling pretty angry about it when a really big guy, a Norwegian I think, came in and ordered the same. This time, as the waiter turned away from him to open the bottle, he turned towards me and I saw him making the 'phiss' sound himself as he pretended to lever the cap.'

Tim looks around and pauses for dramatic effect.

'The waiter realises I have seen him and he looks a bit shocked for a second, but carries on like nothing's happened. The big Norwegian guy wasn't having any of it. He stood about two feet taller than the waiter and made the waiter drink some himself. I took the opportunity to join in too, and showed him my drink, which seemed to incense the Scandinavian even more. You should have seen the face of the waiter; he was terrified.

'So the little bugger should've been,' adds Dave.

Soon, the waiter runs into the back of the shop and comes out with two new bottles of Fanta and gives us the opener. These ones are the real McCoy. The Norwegian told me he already knew about this trick. They try to take the lids off new bottles without bending them so they can recycle the bottles filled with this locally made horrible 'liquid. It isn't even the same shade of orange as Fanta. It seems enough people don't complain so it makes it worth their while.'

Pleased with the telling of his tale he ends up triumphantly with, 'So, everyone be warned.'

At that moment there's a knock on the door. Odette jumps up to answer it and returns, followed by a stranger, a gaunt-looking man with long matted hair, dirty clothes and a plaited beard. He is very thin and barefoot, and he looks in desperate need of a shower. He speaks in English with a strong French accent.

'I am living across the landing. Perhaps you have some tobacco for me?' he says. He shifts from foot to foot and looks suspiciously from one face to another as if ready to run if startled by any of us.

There follows a pause as each of us looks for a reply. He steps forward a pace. 'I have some money. I can pay.' Pulling the leather satchel from his hip he rummages in it to display a couple of American Dollars. 'I can't go to the shops.'

'Why's that then fella?' asks Dave.

He points across to the open door to indicate his room. 'My friend is not well. I can't leave him.'

Now Phil speaks. 'What's wrong with him?' The French guy merely shrugs as if about to say he didn't know, but then says, 'amoebic dysentery.'

This woke us up. Most travellers at one time or another get ill. Usually a few days of good food and clean water and access to a toilet of some kind is enough. When I say 'a toilet', I mean anything that would do as well, such as the desert. But, amoebic dysentery? That's a different ball-game altogether. For travellers, this is one of the bad ones along with typhoid, cholera, malaria, hepatitis and a few others that can kill you

Phil and I jump up and start to herd the guy towards the doorway. 'Show me where he is,' Phil demands.

We are shown into a dark and dirty room. Over in one corner a figure lies on his bed; he looks dead. The French guy runs to him and kneels down by his bedside. 'Max, Max. Parle moi. C'est moi, Michel.' Max doesn't respond.

'Did you take him to the doctor?' I demand.

He nods, jumps up, goes to a table and shows me a bottle.

The medicine used for amoebic dysentery is crude; fundamentally it's a poison which, prescribed in exactly the right dosage, kills the amoeba without killing the patient. The problem is, as time passes it becomes ever easier to accidently kill the patient as they become weaker and weaker at a rapid rate.

Max is obviously very weak by now and we decide not to leave without making sure he gets some of this medicine into him. Without it we are convinced he is going to die. While I make it up Phil tries to get Max to respond, or invoke any semblance of consciousness, so he can drink.

Putting the glass of medicine on the floor I point it out to Phil and then start to question Michel to see what I can learn.

I sit with him at the small table by the window. 'How long has he been like this?'

''A week - maybe.' He puts his head in his hands and his sleeves fell back to reveal needle tracks in both his thin bony arms. 'He shakes his head. 'No, I really don't know.'

Phil comes over and sits with us. 'What's this bullshit? You don't know how long your pal has been ill for? You must have some idea.'

'Okay,' I say. 'How long have you been in this hotel?'

The total blankness of his expression says everything.

Some minutes pass with us trying unsuccessfully to get information from this skeletal French hippy before we all become aware of a lapping sound.

'What the hell?' I ask.

We turn to see Mahmoud's dog Mufi eagerly lapping the last of the medicine from the glass.

'No!' Phil and I shout. Both our chairs go crashing as we run towards it. The dog scoots out of the room in a flash.

'Merde!' Followed by a blank expression, is Michel's fatalistic contribution to the events.

After carefully washing the glass I make up another batch. Michel seems unable to say anything except, 'Le Chien – est mort no?'

This time we have more success getting Max to drink. We mix up another batch giving strict instructions to Michel when to give it. We put the glass high on a ledge before leaving.

The following day an anxious Mahmoud is asking if anyone has seen Mufi. 'It's not like him to disappear when breakfast's ready,' he bemoans.

It would have been of little use to explain what had happened; anyway we didn't really know of Mufi's fate. Perhaps he's just holing up somewhere, waiting for the bad feeling in his guts to go away. We don't see Mufi again, but the good news is, after a couple more days, Max is up on his feet and looking much stronger.

Chapter 37. Doctors good and bad

As we set off from our Kandahar hotel, Sarah leans over between Dave and me to put a tape into the cassette. It's one of the many tapes we've been carelessly throwing onto the dashboard to be baked by the ferocious mid-day sun.

It's meant to be 'Judy Blue Eyes'. When it starts it just whines and screeches. The tune is hardly discernible. It sounds like a cat's chorus and for fun we try to sing along with it, but after a couple of minutes we're all gritting our teeth. Dave, who's sitting in the passenger seat, ejects the Crosby, Stills and Nash tape from the player to applause.

By this time we have started negotiating the smaller roads to get onto the road to Kabul and have attracted a horde of children who are shouting and holding their hands out for some coins, or whatever. Casually, Dave tosses the distorted tape into their outstretched hands.

Such a whoop of joy goes up, and the lucky recipient holds it high, like they had won Olympic gold. That encourages the others to crowd dangerously close to our wheels. Dave, like a rich man distributing charity to the poor, throws out one cassette after another from the stash on the dashboard and a cry of joy accompanies each one.

'They'll no be so pleased when they play them, right enough.' He laughs.

Dick Miller, crouching behind us, adds, 'They'll just think they're supposed to sound that way. I bet if we come back in a couple of years they'll have formed a band and will be singing like it.' He bursts into a terrible distorted version of The Beatles 'Love Me Do.'

A couple of hours later, I look into the rear-view mirror and see Odette rocking with the movements of the bus. She has her hands clasped in her lap and, what the American soldiers in Vietnam call, 'The Thousand Yard Stare' in her eyes. This is where desperately fatigued soldiers can't even see the enemy walking up to them, even though they have their eyes fully open.

She's been getting worse for a couple of days now and is falling into bouts of fever.

I hear Sarah say, 'You're not looking so good, honey. Here, let me put this around you,' as she wraps a blanket around Odette's shoulders.

Odette smiles weakly, 'I'll be okay – just need to sleep I think.'

Odette and I are both doing what we can to play down the attraction we feel for each other. We smile at each other when no-one's looking; other than that we seem to know something emotionally that can't be put into words. I'm strangely unworried about this gap, in what I feel to be our relationship. There's no jealousy now in me that she's still sleeping with Dave, while I sleep alone. In some way I know our being together is inevitable; it's just a matter of time. I've tried to push the memory of our love making to the back of my mind, but now she's ill my feelings towards her are making themselves known. I feel a gut wrenching apprehension about her condition.

I keep the Yellow Bus at maximum cruising speed, which is now about forty- five miles per hour. The road surface is good and we're making steady progress. It's nightfall when we arrive in Kabul after seven hours of almost non-stop driving. Odette is visibly weak and unwell. We book into a hotel as fast as we can and, hiding her condition from the manager's eyes, are able to get Odette into her room unchallenged.

Early in the morning an urgent knock at the door wakes us. 'Get up everyone. We need some help here.' It's Dave shouting.

Grabbing our clothes as fast as possible we run out on the landing to find Dave, wearing only boxer shorts, pointing us towards his room.

'She's gonna die if we don't do something.' His already white face and body now resembled a trembling ghost.'

We burst into their room to see Odette, wearing her red Kutchi dress with the small mirrors sewn in, lying on her back and staring unblinkingly at the ceiling, looking like the painting of 'Ophelia in the Rushes' by Millais. I was struck by her beauty, and then suddenly, by the inappropriateness of what I was experiencing.

Tim and Theo both appear, fully dressed. Phil shouts at them. 'Tim, Theo, find a doctor. Ask the reception guy. Get him to come, immediately!'

Theo and Tim run out to find the doctor, while we try to make Odette as comfortable as possible. They return after twenty minutes or so, which seems like a long time to those of us waiting.

The doctor walks in behind them. He looks every inch a practicing doctor. In his late thirties or early forties, he sports a very neatly trimmed moustache and whiskers, and wears a good quality black coat, polished black shoes and carries a Gladstone bag. But for the little Muslim cap and the gown, he would pass for a country doctor in any rural part of England. He inspires confidence.

He quickly checks Odette's eyes and her breathing. She appears totally lethargic and unable to talk.

'Out. Out. Everybody,' he commands briskly.

Imagining this might mean there was a risk of contagion and just wanting to do the right thing, we all hastily withdraw. Congregating in Theo's room we wait nervously, too anxious to talk.

After ten or fifteen minutes a strange unease comes upon us. Something feels wrong but we don't know what. Dave looks at me with a quizzical expression and a slight shrug of the shoulders. I look at Tim and Phil. Then in a wordless agreement, we all return to the room.

We throw open the door and reveal a sight straight out of a 'What the Butler Saw' peep show. Odette's skirt is around her waist and the doctor is working her knickers down over her feet. He stops dead and we all stare at each other.

Perhaps I imagine it, but to me, a range of expressions cross his face. First, a stern look meaning, 'How dare you disobey my instructions,' but his survival instinct censors it almost immediately. The next fleeting expression is a slight smile, as if he is about to say, 'This may look odd, but in my country...,' wisely he ditches this reaction too. The last expression, and the one really consuming him, is his abject fear and embarrassment of having been caught red handed. He has good reason to be afraid. I am in no doubt the average Afghan man would think little of killing such an odious little creature caught in the act of rape. The Afghans are a kind people but they have an unflinching code of justice. This doctor is a very lucky man, we are almost speechless, and experiencing something we can't quite conceive.

Within these few stunned milliseconds the Doctor decides on his method of escape, and it works very well for him. With all the humility and grovelling body language of Uriah Heep, the character from David Copperfield, he grabs his bag, nods apologies vigorously to one and all and swiftly leaves with a stream of, 'I'm so sorry, I'm so sorry, I'm so sorry,' echoing behind him.

It seems unbelievable we do nothing to stop him, but the truth is, it takes a few moments to take in what we've just witnessed.

'What the fuck?' Dave says, about to give chase. 'I'm going after the wee fucker.'

'Dave. Stop!' Sarah's voice is so forceful Dave freezes. 'Forget him. We need to get Odette to hospital.'

With Dave and me heavily supporting her, Odette walks, tortuously slowly to the reception desk. We no longer care if they see her now. The guy at reception tells us that Kabul General Hospital is very close and gives us directions.

A swift taxi ride gets us there and we help Odette into the main entrance. The Hospital is an incredibly run down place. Some of the ceiling has collapsed and a pile of rubble lies in the centre of the main corridor. It's simply been pushed in a heap to allow the squeaking trolleys to get by. The walls are stained with marks that I don't want to think about. Everyone in the place seems to be working flat out.

An English speaking doctor promptly turns up to try to understand our needs. He's a breath of fresh air after the little rodent, posing as a doctor, we'd just been with, and he makes sure a bed is found for her immediately.

With the others back at the hotel, Dave and I sit in the small waiting room. This sparse room has a couple of wooden benches, four or five chairs and a table. There are none of the normal conveniences, like a coffee machine, magazines or even blinds at the window. The early morning sun streams relentlessly in, highlighting the dust motes in the air. We are the only two in the room.

'Why didn't we stop him? I ask.

'Who's that?'

'That doctor in the hotel. How did he just walk out while we stood there and did nothing?'

'Och, we canna worry about him now.'

He goes silent for a few seconds. 'It was like we were hypnotised by the wee scoundrel. He was a lucky man today alright.'

Just then an elderly man comes in with his rough fieldworkers garments soaked in blood all down his left side. A friend helps him to the bench and he sits down with difficulty. He must be in considerable pain. I can't imagine what's happened to create such a loss of blood, which I believe is his rather than an animal's, as it's still dripping from some hidden wound under his garments.

When, a couple of hours later, the doctor returns and says we can see Odette, the man is still patiently sitting there, next to a pool of congealed blood, waiting to be seen. His stoicism is impressive, but as I later learn, this is characteristic of many Afghans.

Odette is unconscious when we walk into her room. We speak in whispers. She has been wired up to a machine of some kind, the ones with a screen and a spiky line that that looks like a radar, that flat-lines when someone dies. It surprises me they have something so sophisticated in this hospital and my confidence in it rises.

The doctor gathers us together in one corner. 'It's very serious,' he whispers. 'She has typhoid and her fever is severe. We are giving her treatment, but we can't be sure we are in time.'

I look over at Odette. She resembles a child's doll that had been discarded. Her head down and sideways, her hair spread across the pillow, her arms slightly out from her sides. They have dressed her in a blue cotton gown. My heart aches at how vulnerable she looks.

'There is nothing more to be done,' continues the young doctor. 'It is all down to time now, and her will to survive, of course.' For some reason I find myself feeling pleased that Allah is not part of his answer.

Dave asks him some questions, but I am not listening to them, nor the answers. Odette's life is hanging by a thread, leaving it in the lap of the gods.

With heavy hearts we return to the hotel. The day seems to last for ever as none of us want to eat or sleep or wander about, but nobody has much to say either. We've been told to come back to check on her the following morning, so at first light Dave and I walk back to the hospital to see what the news is – good or bad?

The doctor's still on duty. He appears pleased. 'I think she is past the worst,' he announces, 'but it is still too early to be sure. We will continue to monitor her of course.'

'Can we see her?' asks Dave.

The doctor shakes his head. 'It's probably better to leave her to rest. She'll be exhausted. But it appears the fever has broken.'

In our optimism we take this to mean she is going to be okay, so we celebrate with a good breakfast of omelettes and toast at the hotel. Afterwards, I go to get some much needed sleep and don't wake until about 4pm when Dave, Tim & Theo burst into my room for a chat and to roll a few joints. The chat is, of course, about Odette and how she is doing, and how we'll need to hole up for a week or so before we can push on: that we may as well get to see all the sights of Kabul while we wait for her to get strong enough to travel.

Chapter 38. "Odette is dying!"

With great ceremony, I cut a substantial amount of dope from a big lump I have next to my bed and swallow it. 'I'm celebrating Odette's recovery by getting excessively stoned,' I declare.

Dave, Tim and Theo need no further encouragement and follow suit. Perhaps I have been a little too cavalier with such amazingly strong Afghan dope because by seven o'clock I can't talk. I am very, very stoned. It has been a lot of fun getting there and we'd all chatted and laughed ourselves silly for hours, but now I was starting to get hallucinations and I'm thinking I am just as stoned as I could ever want to be; maybe a little too much so.

We are sitting drinking tea that we've ordered up to our room when, all of a sudden, Phil comes in. He is visibly agitated and has something urgent on his mind. He needs to talk to me about items of great importance. He is gesticulating and trying to explain something I can't focus on. He paces around the room. His voice rises and falls like a police siren. I try to focus, to understand, but all I can hear are disjointed fragments of what he is saying, because I'm coming and going in and out of consciousness, like waves rolling and receding from the shore of intelligence.

'…in love with Sarah…'
'…Dick and Sarah … going to Nepal…'
'…can't say goodbye…'
'…. need to take money…'
'…you'll make out…'

'...I'm sure…..'

I stare at him, unblinking, with brain-sapping concentration. Trying to decipher what he's saying.

None of this makes any sense to me. My brother, Phil, seems to be asking me for a decision of some kind. But about what? I don't have a clue what he's after. At times he is my brother, and then he is a fish just pulled out of the water, comically gasping for breath.

Desperately, I need to try to communicate my condition. If I can explain to him what I'm experiencing surely everything will turn out okay? With immense single-mindedness and a ferocious act of will-power I gradually hone a sentence together, which I believe will explain everything, and at the same time be unequivocal. I put my finger to my lips to silence him, then slowly and with great gravity say:

'Phil, I am very, very stoned. Anything you say to me I probably won't understand the way you mean it. Anything I say to you will probably come out wrong, as I am not sure I can find the right words to express myself. It comes down to this; I don't understand what you are telling me, and I don't know how to say anything that makes sense to you. Either way we can't communicate anything sensible to each other at the moment. Let's talk tomorrow.'

Pleased with myself I fall onto my bed, exhausted from the effort. To my surprise Phil carries on talking. It's simply an irritating noise that I can't grasp the meaning of. He leaves, or at least the noise stops.

Time passes, the world spins. I watch cartoons play out behind my eyelids. Just as I am about to fall asleep someone comes banging on my door. Through the overwhelming haze I hear something that cuts through me. It's Theo's voice.

'Alan, Odette is dying. You must come at once. I can't find Dave anywhere.'

I leap up and am falling down the hotel stairs within seconds. Theo isn't there. Did I hallucinate this? The hospital is ten minutes' walk away, which is good, as I need both the air and the time, but the street seems totally different and I can't recognise anything. Which way did the taxi go earlier? The dope has such a strong hold on me I'm having both audio and visual hallucinations. Then I see a road sign with a picture of a hospital on it. But I can't make up my mind which road it's designating – why do they put signs up that confuse people? I realise I'm alone. Where is everyone? I try to rationalise the situation, but I can't tell whether I'm talking out loud or merely thinking.

'What am I doing here?'

'I'm going to see Odette in the hospital.'

'She's dying.'

'I know.'

'Look horses! I could get a horse-drawn taxi.'

'Those horses are well looked after.'

'I'd like to have a horse.'

'I'm too stoned to see Odette.'
Now I'm singing. 'Odette, pretty little girl Odette.'

'Shut the fuck up.'

'I'm too stoned to see Odette die.'

'I need to come down.'

Arriving at the hospital, knowing I'm still far too stoned to go in, I decide to walk around the building. I breathe deeply – in – out – in – out. Every time I begin to float away I bring myself back by reaching up and pulling at the shirt-tails of the hallucination and wrenching it down to the ground again. Every time the trees began to act oddly by melting or conspiratorially whispering together I search my brain for an appropriate piece of reality and roughly hammer it back in place. That reality is the memory of why I'm here.

'Dying's natural. Everyone dies. What's the big deal?'

'Dying for a pee. Really? Nobody's really dying for a pee.'

'Things we say, us human beings eh?'

'That's true.'

Then over and over, until the guardian at the gate of my sanity begins to return, I recite:

'I take refuge in the Buddha. I take refuge in the Dharma. I take refuge in the Sangha.'

By the time I have done a complete circuit of the building and have reached the front door again, I am completely clear, straight and sober.

Apparently, according to the same doctor, (God knows when or where he sleeps) she will either die tonight or get through the fever, which is now peaking.

'I thought that was last night.'

'So did I,' he replies kindly. 'Wait here and I will come for you as soon as there's any change. If you are religious, I suggest you pray.'

Sitting in the hospital all night is depressing. Where the ceiling has fallen in everyone has to climb over the rubble as a queue of trolleys with people waiting on them now blocks the way. Afghanis see hospitals and doctors as the last resort and usually exhaust every traditional type of cure before parting with much needed money. Many of the people who turn up here are close to death.

I ask for a jug of water and the nurse comes back with a litre, which I thankfully drain without pause.

As the sun begins to rise the same doctor beckons me to follow him. I have sat on the floor for some hours to free up a seat for those who really need them so strain to make my muscles work.

Odette is still unconscious but obviously better, even to my untrained eye.

'It's good news. The fever has broken. She is going to recover.' The doctor seems as happy as I am. His eyes twinkle as he speaks. I can see how tired he is behind the smile.

I embrace him and he seems taken aback. Maybe I'm still a little stoned. But he laughs and says, 'She will need a lot of rest but she is strong. Is she Afghani?'

'Turkish,' I reply. 'Well half Turkish, half English.'

'She looks Afghani.'

'Everywhere we travel people think of her as a native. She just has those looks.'

He starts to walk away but turns and says, 'She is lucky to have you.'

Not knowing what to think, but not wanting to explain myself to anyone, I head towards the river and walk along its banks for what seems hours just to clear my head. The day is beautiful without being too hot. A slight and welcome breeze cools my skin and I continue with an empty mind that's just too exhausted to process the events it's been experiencing.

When I begin to get clear of the city I decide to get some breakfast and have a shower back at the hotel. On the way back, the strange goings-on with Phil the night before, start to swirl in my brain. Bits of what has been said return to me; something about going to Nepal and being in love with Sarah, and there was something else - about money.

'Never mind, I can ask Phil about it this morning.' I think, unaware that whilst I had spent the night in hospital the world has moved on. Phil had indeed been faced with a big decision; the one he'd had so much difficulty in explaining to me.

Theo is sitting in the hotel's breakfast room. When I ask if he'd woken me the previous night to tell me about Odette, he shakes his head. 'It wasn't me.' I tell him the good news about Odette.

'That's fantastic! Everyone's as worried as hell.'

'That's a point, where is everybody?' I ask.

'That dope last night was awesome. I think everybody's still unconscious.'

'How about Phil and Sarah? They didn't eat any.'

Theo says nothing and appears reluctant to tell me something. 'What? What's happened?' I insist.

'Because of Odette being sick, Sarah and Dick decided to take a train to Islamabad and then go on to Nepal. Apparently, that's their ultimate destination anyway, so staying around in Kabul until she's better and then going on to Delhi is not really helping them. They can go directly to Nepal from there, so they've bought tickets.'

'So they've left for Nepal?' I feel shocked and saddened. 'How's Phil taking it?'

Theo shifts awkwardly in his seat. 'Well, that's the problem. That's what Phil was trying to explain to you last night.'

So, that's what Phil had been trying to tell me the night before. A sudden weight formed in my stomach. I look intently at Theo. 'He's gone with them, hasn't he?'

Theo slowly nods. 'I guess it was a crossroads moment for Phil. He was trying to explain it to you last night. You know, how much he loves Sarah. I guess he couldn't say goodbye to her.'

'Yes, yes of course,' I hear myself say, without any help from my feelings. A strange emotion sweeps over me and I feel small and very alone again. I murmur, 'I think I need to get some sleep,' and start upstairs to my room.

'Oh, and Phil says he's taken the money. He said you have the bus and that would be about evens,' calls Theo. 'Sorry Al.'

My parting shot to Theo is not kind or well meant. 'Jesus! What a fucking idiot. I don't even have enough to pay for the hotel room.'

Chapter 39. "It was a lurve thing."

Returning to our shared hotel room I'm struck by how empty it feels. Phil's rucksack and all other traces of Phil are gone, bar the maps he'd left on the table. The room is bare in a way that's deeply depressing.

In Kabul with no money, the emptiness in my heart is overwhelming. My nineteen years feels far too young, as I realise how much my sense of security relies on having my big brother next to me. Climbing into bed, I pull the blankets over myself and try, unsuccessfully, to sleep.

I thought I would be angrier with Phil for taking off than I am. As Barry White would have said in his deep bass voice, "It was a lurve thing." And who can stand in the way of love?

Frankly, I'm much more pissed off at Sarah and Dick for booking tickets at such a crucial time without being sure Odette is going to survive. With Phil, Sarah and Dick gone, not to mention all the money, I have to try figure out what to do next. In my wallet is only about five pounds in Afghanis, the national currency.

The first question is, do we go on or turn back? There's still Dave, Odette, Theo and Tim who've paid to go all the way to Delhi. I can't refund their money. I don't have it. But what *do* I have? Only the Yellow Bus – our broken down work-horse we'd saved from the breaker's yards of London. *What else? What else? What else?* Eventually, I fall asleep with these unhelpful thoughts running through my mind.

I sleep peacefully for about four hours before being swept up in a nightmare. In it I'm in an Arab medina being sold as a slave. I stand naked, with other naked men and women, in the market square, with dozens of shouting people prodding and poking and laughing at us. An old withered man grabs my beard roughly and pushes my head back to look at my teeth. He is screaming in Arabic. I wake up sweating and breathless, and realise I still have all my clothes on. Peeling them off, I get back in bed and return to sleep for a further eight hours.

Reluctantly I wake and try to go back to the blessed security of sleep again, preferably forever - but I can't. It's a day of decision-making and none of the obvious options appeal to me. I dress and sit in my room trying to think things through, without looking for the others.

Spreading a map on the bed I calculate it's still over fifteen hundred miles to Delhi; a quarter of the journey. If I advertise for a few more people to go on to India I can possibly get them, but it's difficult to compete on price with the ubiquitous Afghan buses. They stack people, goats and clucking birds up to, and on top of, the roof - and are cheap. Here, in Asia, sitting with chickens fluttering around your head or squatting on your backpack for hours on a bus is normal.

Can I compete?

Their buses can cram fifty people in, the Yellow Bus only eight. By my calculations I might not be able to charge enough to cover the petrol and running costs. And can the Yellow Bus even make it? I have already kept my concerns to myself about the damage and wear she's sustained; it had been asking a lot from such an elderly bus to do this journey. Without the question mark hanging over how many miles she still has in her, I would go – but it seems too risky now.

That leaves the option of going back; but then, how can I repay my existing travelling companions? Again, the fuel costs are higher to return. Are there enough people prepared to risk taking a small bus rather than have the security of one of the larger over-lander companies. It all feels hazy and very doubtful. The term 'between a rock and a hard place' comes to mind.

At that moment there comes a knock at the door. I hastily fold the map and put it in a draw, as if I'm a spy caught in someone else's room. It's too early to tell anyone what I am planning because I don't know myself. 'Come in,' I call. Theo, Tim, and Dave walk in and sit themselves down in my small room. Tim grabs the only chair, Dave and Theo sit on Phil's bed.

'How are you feeling Al?' asks Theo.

'I'm okay now. Boy, I needed that sleep.' It was then I realised that I *was* feeling okay. The fears of last night, and the terrible sense of vulnerability I had felt about Phil leaving was dissipating. 'Strange days eh?' And, as an afterthought I ask Dave, 'How's Odette getting on?'

Dave lights a cigarette and nods. 'She's doing well. We all went to see her this morning. We tried to find you, but you must have been out. She's talking. We even got a bit of a laugh from her. The doctor reckons a few more days rest and she'll be mobile again.'

'That's brilliant.'

'She sends her love.'

That confuses me. *Is Dave gently telling me he knows about us, or is it an innocent remark that anyone might say?* I don't know how to respond, and am grateful when Tim speaks.

'What's the plan, Al? Now Phil and Sarah have gone. Are we still going on, or what?

It's the question I dread, but there's no point in lying. 'To be honest guys, I don't know. Look, we're going to stay put for a few days until Odette gets out of hospital; why not park that decision until she comes back, then decide?'

Dave nods. 'It will give us a chance to see some of this wonderful city, that's for sure. I'm all for that.' Everyone concurred, and that becomes our plan.

We spend a leisurely hour in my room chatting about plans to visit the city. All of us want to see the National Museum, as it houses a huge amount of Afghan heritage. Tim is keen on seeing the Darul Man Palace, the former home of the King of Afghanistan.

A few days pass. I keep my thoughts to myself as we all enjoy wandering around Kabul taking in the sights. Theo and I go to Kabul Zoo, which is very run down and underfunded compared to London Zoo. There are hyenas and a lot of small reptiles. We're about to leave when we're surprised to see two huge Bengal Tigers. They're fabulous animals, or should be, both full grown males, with a downcast and hopeless look in their eyes. One paces restlessly back and forwards the length of the tiny cage; the other is lying down and morosely chewing the fur on its legs, which are in a dreadful state.

Leaving that depressing scene we go to see the gardens surrounding the tomb of the first Mughal, Emperor Babur. It's a popular park with Afghans for picnics and lazy afternoons. I look at the generous spreads of food they're enjoying. I don't eat anything but an apple on the second day as I'm determined to save the little money I have for emergencies.

Good news comes when I visit reception to check how much I owe. Thankfully, with some generous foresight, Phil has paid my room up until the end of the following week. It's an unexpected joy which I add to my mental list of positives. Another one to add is that we'd filled up with fuel when we entered Kabul; in the confusion that followed, I had forgotten. That makes me feel a lot more positive about the future!

Odette is out of hospital the following day, and spends a couple more days resting in her hotel room, with all of us going in to cheer her up at different times. I go with someone else each time, never alone, I don't know why that is. Probably, I have enough troubles on my mind and I know soon I will be having to say goodbye.

When she is strong enough to join us in the breakfast room, I tell everyone my plans.

Not knowing how to begin, I just dive in with the news. 'I'm sorry guys, but it's the end of the journey for us.' Total silence follows.

'Phil didn't leave me any money and the Yellow Bus is not going to make it across another fifteen hundred miles of bad roads. She's been incredible. Henry Ford would've been proud of her. But if she breaks down in a really remote place we're totally screwed. You've all paid for this trip, but I can't ask you to take on the cost of repairs to keep her going, that's not right. I'm really sorry, but it's the end of this expedition'

Dave broke the long sad silence. 'This has been an amazing journey Al. You did your best, man, we know that. It's no so far to Delhi anyway. And... and we won't have to listen to Tim singing any more, so that's a plus.' Tim gives him a grin, accompanied by a one-finger salute.

'We'll be fine taking the local bus, don't worry,' adds Odette gamely, although she looks too weak for a journey of any magnitude.

'What about you, Theo?' I ask.

Theo smiles, 'To be honest when I first saw the Yellow Bus I didn't think it would get across Belgium, so I'm impressed to be here. Hell, I wanted to give her a Viking burial back in Turkey. That was a memorable moment I'll never forget. We'll all have a reunion one day, all get stoned together and talk more of the excellent bullshit we do so well. I'll be fine Al, don't you worry about me.'

'Tim?'

'Not sure I agree with Theo's 'memorable moment', but I agree with him on everything else,' says Tim, 'The Yellow Bus has been amazing. Okay, it hasn't made India, but Kabul for fifty quid is pretty good.'

I feel overwhelmed by their optimistic good nature. Tears start to well in my eyes. And as I always do when feeling emotional, I become the pragmatic Englishman. 'All of you, please, let me know where you are when you get settled for any length of time. I'll send you a refund as soon as I can.' That fell on deaf ears. By now they've all turned into travellers capable of taking the rough with the smooth. They're more concerned with what I'm going to do than with themselves.

The very next day Tim and Theo leave on a bus heading towards Pakistan, and the morning after I wave goodbye to Dave and Odette. She's making a remarkable recovery. Wearing her new dress and looking every inch a Kuchi tribe member, she climbs on the bus. I stand and watch as Odette waves from the back seat of the overloaded Mercedes. Then she smiles and blows me a kiss that sends a shiver through my spine. It's a sad moment, like a family breaking up.

Walking back, I feel strange - both lonely and liberated; now I only have myself to worry about, and that's always so much easier than having responsibility for others.

Chapter 40. Zigi & Kati

In many ways I've matured and am far less worried about what the future holds for me. In England it's all about your future, or lack of it. How are you going to "pay your way", as my father would taunt. But I'm freer here with a few pounds in my pocket and a busted up old bus than I've ever felt back in Blighty. But how to keep afloat – that's the problem now.

As Kris Kristofferson wrote, *"Freedom is another word for nothing left to lose."*

Cleverer people than I have solved the problem of earning a living and staying in a foreign country; which is something I want more than anything. I've no real desire to go home, but the people I've met who had managed to stay, always had something to invest in the first place. They are tradespeople, professional people, people who've sold a business somewhere, or inherited money. None of these applies to me. I have no special skills to offer. My parents both work hard, but they have no savings whatsoever. There's no point in torturing myself with these thoughts, so on the way back from the bus station I buy a pack of postcards.

Over the next couple of days I hang about the Karmozan Cafe in Chicken Street, to talk to the ever changing motley bunches of travellers and listen to their tales. I pay a couple of Afganis to put a postcard on the notice-board.

'Yellow Bus to Istanbul for $20 US leaving Thursday 8th at 2pm'

Underneath I put my name, the hotel name, and my room number.

In this part of the world the American Dollar rules; it's the international currency, and universally accepted by every black marketer and racketeer in the world. Istanbul is my choice of destination for two reasons. Firstly, it's the funnel that feeds people from all over Europe into the 'Hippy Trail': secondly, I don't know how far the Yellow Bus still had left in her. I'm trying not to raise anyone's hopes. The departure date is for four days ahead as that's the last day my hotel room's paid for. I visit all the hotels and cafés travellers hang out in and pay a few Afghani's to put cards on their notice boards.

Then I wander around Kabul just taking in the fabulous mosques, museums, civic buildings and the friendly people. Trying to fix it all into my memory in case I can never return.

That evening, as I am reading the last pages of John Steinbeck's 'The Grapes of Wrath', there's a knock on my hotel door and a German couple enter and introduce themselves as Zigi and Kati. They are both very well-dressed, tall and striking as if they're film stars or models, both of them, I guessed, in their mid-twenties. They look very fit as if they work out every day.

'We have come in response to your cards. We want to get back to Germany,' Kati explains.

They both appear so clean and well-groomed, Zigi wearing a Panama suit and Kati in a black Spanish style lace dress. It's hard for me to see them as anything but first-class travellers. They certainly don't look capable of travelling rough. Zigi's face is a perfect blend of rugged and intellectual. The three day stubble on his cheeks gives him a sophisticated look, almost like a young, less dissolute Klaus Kinski. The same beard growth on me always makes me look like a hobo.

'Please sit down.' I clear my throat. 'It's a pretty basic way to travel. Just an old hippy bus really. No comforts at all…'

He lifts his hand to cut me off. 'Don't worry about us - we will be fine. We're comfortable with travelling rough'

We talk a little about Kabul and travelling in general. It's only then I discern a slight German accent under their good English. When I ask why they didn't try one of the professional overlanders, like Contiki or Sundowners, Kati laughs.

'No, we don't like big groups of people. Someone told us you had a small bus. That suits us better.'

I find it hard to look at Kati for fear I will stare and appear impolite; but it's a challenge not to. She's so attractive.

Realising this, I take the cowards way out and direct all my conversation to Zigi. I have no idea whether Kati thinks I am ignoring her. Perhaps, having recently waved goodbye to a girl that I had fallen in love with made me more sensitive to any beautiful girl. I don't know. What I did know was that this statuesque German girl was both elegant and stunning.

'We need to go home.' Zigi explains. 'It was purely on a whim we came east.'

'Just for a bit of fun really,' adds Kati.

As he talks Zigi slips a couple of notes from a sizeable roll he pulls out of his jacket pocket and passes them to me. I make a conscious effort not to appear to count them in case I look cheap. We chat for a while longer and I'm conscious of Kati sitting there, totally at ease, no emotion on her face, like a beautiful figurine. It's only been about fifteen minutes, but I become aware, when they walk out of the room, I'm as tense as a spring.

I look at the $40 Zigi has given me and, practical as always, go out for a much needed meal.

The next morning I'm stopped by a back packer as I leave the hotel.

'Are you the Alan dude who's driving to Istanbul?'

He introduces himself as Mike and tells me he is South African.

'I have a plane flight from London to Jo'burg next month so I think I'd better start heading home.'

We walk to a nearby café and have tea together.

Mike is a stocky looking man, dressed in khaki shorts and a shirt that looks military. He has legs like a Victorian grand piano and wrists as thick as my forearms. His body language is definite and challenging. He sits down and leans forward in a slightly intimidating way. With his hands on his knees he starts flexing his chest muscles like a gorilla chasing off a challenger. He also appears somehow chameleonic and I have real trouble trying to decipher him. Sometimes he stutters as if nervous, other times his face is set into a determined expression which becomes menacing. He tells me he's in his early 30's and, like me, can't stand his own country. I sympathise, although I shouldn't, for our reasons are totally different. He hates South Africa because, as he sees it, the white man is being beaten there, and the status quo is under threat. With me, I dislike the status quo in my own country and would welcome some kind of revolution.

With the very little I know about South Africa I'm inclined to put my sympathies with the downtrodden, but truthfully, I understand little about the awfulness of apartheid, or the struggle going on against it.

We are unlikely ever to see eye to eye so I steer the conversation away from politics. Sometimes, as we talk he seems to be trying to quell an inner violence. I try to tell myself I am misreading the situation. But, within a short time I realise, I don't like this guy very much. I tell him the price to Istanbul is $20 and he says, in his heavy South African accent, 'I'll pay you when I'm sitting on the bus.'

Chapter 41. Mike & Sandappa

I feel confident and happy because, with South African Mike, I have three passengers, and by my calculations, need only one more to be sure of covering the cost of getting to Istanbul - without breakdowns, of course.

The fourth passenger arrives later that night in the shape of Jon, an American. Calm and easy-going, He's in his early twenties, clean shaven and studious looking, and easy to talk to. He tells me he's writing a diary about his travels. 'Maybe I'll turn it into a book one day.' He smiles.

He's heading west, after having done a circuit taking in Nepal, Delhi, Amritsar, Goa and all the other hippy hangouts that were quickly becoming popular. I have to admire him for having seen so much. Now he's heading back to London where his journey had started. From there he would fly home to Washington.

I ask him what he does for a living. He replies, 'Oh bits and pieces – anything really.' He seems a kindred spirit to me, perhaps someone to whom travelling, no matter how rough it is, is better than low wages and an ever rising tally of dead-end jobs at home.

He'd seen the Yellow Bus parked up outside the hotel and asks me what I thought the odds were of us making it to Istanbul. I told him what I'd told Phil before we set off. 'It may not look much, but she has the heart of a lion – no worries. We'll make it okay.' I wish I felt as confident as I tried to sound. I'm not so naive now about the rough journey ahead of us.

We meet up at eight o'clock on a beautiful Saturday morning. As we are loading our luggage, our last passenger turns up out of the blue. A girl packing a rucksack, far too big and heavy for her, stands awkwardly on the pavement. She's tanned in the way you only get from being in a sunny country for a long time, her hair is pure blond and hangs in one long plait behind her.

'My name is Sandappa,' she says. 'I would like to join you, yes?'

'Do you have $20,' I ask, but immediately felt guilty for being so blunt.

There is a pause of about half a minute, and I am wondering if she's gone into a catatonic state, before she answers simply, 'Yes, I have.'

Her accent and her looks make me think she is Swedish or Norwegian but her name is clearly not. 'Where are you from originally?' I ask, wanting to know if my guess is right.

She shields her eyes with one hand and looks up at the cloudless sky for ten or more seconds before saying. 'It's a good day.'

'Yes, it is. Have you been in Kabul long?'

She explains that she had been in Amritsar for over a year studying in an Ashram. But she allows so much time to elapse between each word I fight the desire to finish her sentences just to get the conversion moving along. My Buddhist nature, aware of the requirements of mindfulness tries to slow down to match her. Unfortunately my circumstances are urgent and there's a lot for me to do.

Mentally, I remonstrate with myself for my lack of discipline – remind myself for the thousandth time that I will never gain enlightenment - and proceed to lash her pack to the roof with the others, pleased to get the extra money.

'Have you had breakfast, Sandappa?'

Ignoring my question she merely shrugs her shoulders and sighs. 'It has to be.' Engaging in small talk with such a low rate of production I find slightly irritating, so I move on to doing other things.

Over the next few days I find she has a strange way of making everyone around her feel like an annoying mosquito. But it's not her that does anything – we do it to ourselves.

Going in to say goodbye to the hotel manager and to thank him for his hospitality, I run into a man I know as Kevin. He's an elderly British journalist who loves Afghanistan. We had spent some hours chatting previously in the breakfast room. He's staying at the hotel whilst waiting for some people to catch up with him before travelling on to Pakistan.

'I see you're off, Alan.'

'Yes. I've just landed an extra passenger, which should give me a bit of financial breathing space. We'll be okay.'

'God willing, or Allah willing in these parts.' He grins. 'You remember those American chaps you met in the desert – the ones you told me were walking around the world?'

'Are they here?'

He looks down at the floor for a few seconds, the way people do who have something unpleasant to say.

'Seems like they upset someone they shouldn't. Their heads were left by the side of the road. A couple of travellers told me the story this morning.'

'Oh shit.' I feel sick. I remember the American brothers John and Dave; their beaming faces, so proud of their achievements; trying to be the first people to walk around the world. Memories of them and the good natured, optimistic conversation we'd shared in the desert, run through my mind.

'Yes, they must have been killed shortly after you ran into them; they were on the same stretch of road you met them on.'[ii]

'Oh, that's just crazy shit. Any ideas why...?'

'There was talk about one of the brothers trying it on with a girl from the mountain tribes, but that's just rumour; more likely they were killed for their horse. Times are hard for these people at the moment. There's a long running drought.'

'That'd explain why I saw a couple of tribespeople begging in the streets the other day.'

He nods. 'Drought for the last couple of years means little to eat for their goats. They're a dignified people. They don't beg unless people are dying.'

We talk a little more, but Kevin admits the stories about Dave and John are only hearsay passed along by the tribal drums, there's no real evidence. The roads are always buzzing with rumours, often completely untrue, but it's with a heavy heart I drive out of Kabul to head back towards Kandahar.

Chapter 42. What the hell is a credit card?

Travelling changes people. When I remember the excitement and joy of setting off from Thornton Heath, how we sang '10 Green Bottles' and played interminable games of 'I Spy,' I contrasted it with this quiet, efficient and purposeful band of passengers. Everyone has seen a lot of things, and learnt a lot about people – not all of it good either. Travelling alone can be a sobering experience because you walk around with your rucksack, declaring your vulnerability to everyone. You're saying to the world, 'I am all there is. I am my own army – there's no back-up, there are no relatives or friends to take revenge on how you treat me.' And, as John and Dave found out, sometimes no law to protect you either.

For women the risk is all the greater, and many women travellers have amazed me with their courage. No matter how much I love this part of the world it seems madness for a single girl to travel here without protection. But some of them do, and gain respect and support from people they meet. Many come away with fantastic memories.

In my stay in Kandahar, I met an Irish girl who hadn't been lucky in that respect, but had travelled all over the world. In our conversation she told me she had been raped six times in four years on the road. I was horrified.

'But,' she said calmly, 'I knew there were risks before I started this life style. I just keep thinking about the positive things.'

That conversation disturbed me, and I sometimes question the truth of it. I wanted to ask for more details. Her attitude was kind and gentle, so different from what I would have expected. Did she know these people? Which countries did they happen in? My prurient mind started to demand more information, but some part of me told me to shut up. How she had dealt with rape, and refused to let it destroy her attitude to men and life in general, I couldn't imagine. Her strength left me feeling humbled.

Turning in my seat and looking at my new passengers I see Kati, reading a book, and the solidly carved figure of South African Mike sitting next to her, the ever-worried looking Sandappa meditating, with American Jon already scribbling in his journal. Zigi has taken on Phil's role and sits in the passenger seat with the maps on his lap.

We head south, through the beautiful tree-lined avenues, away from Kabul. I listen intently to the sound of the engine. Tentatively changing into top gear, pushing hard on the accelerator to test the clutch, the engine note goes down as it struggles against the extra load, but it doesn't slip. A discernible amount of smoke comes from the noisy exhaust, particularly when first starting, but we still have some more oil on the roof.

Zigi says, 'Next stop Baraki Barak – about sixty miles'.

I nod. 'Let's stop for coffee there.'

But we don't stop there. It's as if the Yellow Bus has a 'use by' date and we have to get as much as we can from her before she expires. We keep going all day, well past Baraki Barak. We travel almost in silence. From the tight knit community we were on the way out, the atmosphere had now become reminiscent of commuters on a double-decker London bus; polite but compartmentalised.

The evenings are getting cold, and in the desert a chill wind creeps up at night-time. My lost sleeping bag has been replaced with a couple of thin blankets, which aren't so warm. The heater on the Yellow Bus has packed up long ago, so travelling after the sun goes down encourages everyone to get into sleeping bags I wrap both blankets around my shoulders. The gap where the door doesn't close sends a cold wind directly into my face and right shoulder which can feel quite numb after a while. The bus is still driving well and pulling us along at forty-five miles per hour, which is fast enough. For some reason it seems to go better in the cold.

Just beyond Qualat, we pull the bus up to make camp.

'Do you mind if Zigi and I sleep in the bus tonight, Alan,' purrs Kati, as I busy myself recording our mileage in my note-book. Something I did to calculate fuel stops, as the fuel gauge had also stopped working.

'No, of course not,' I say, without thinking. As soon as I do, I feel briefly uncomfortable but keep quiet. It will be colder for me.

The Yellow Bus

We're in the middle of the Afghan desert in absolute silence. Above us the sky is inky black, overwhelmingly beautiful, and so dotted with stars there doesn't seem to be room for another one. *It's a pity we don't see skies like that in England.* We brew tea and chat small talk for a while. Then I pull my blankets over me and lay down near Jon who's sitting up in his sleeping bag, leaning against the front wheel on the driver's side.

Mike is some yards off with a very warm looking bag. He says it is 'tog 30' or something, which means it's very warm. I'm not too familiar with togs. He's stripped naked and is standing in that peculiar pose male nudists often strike at nudist beaches, both hands on hips, far away stare into the horizon, buttocks clenched, chest inflated, and genitals in profile. After a minute or so he climbs into his sleeping bag.

'Cold, isn't it, Jon?' I say, shivering and trying to pull my thin blankets where they can do most good.

'Sure is. Can't say I like it much either.'

Just then we see a shooting star streaking across the heavens like an old biblical portent; but of what we don't know. We decide its good luck – well why not? As I start to doze Jon speaks very quietly in his slow American accent.

'You know Al, I've been thinking when we hit Herat, I might just use my card and fly to Turkey.'

That woke me up a bit. 'What do you mean Jon, use your card?'

'My credit card.'

I have no idea what this 'credit card' is he speaks about, and I tell him so.

'It's a plastic card that allows me to go into a bank and withdraw money.'

'Any bank?'

'Pretty well.'
'Wow.'

'I've had enough of all this hardship.'

Hardship? We've only been on the road for a day and I think things are going really well.

'So, how do you go about getting one of these cards then?'

'My dad gave it to me before I left.'

'Christ, how much can you get out?'

'It's a gold card. I'm not sure there's a limit.'

'What's he do for a living?'

'Who?'

'Your dad.'

'He's an executive with the Coca-Cola Company.'

There's a long silence. I lie there thinking about what it must be like to travel with such a safety net – it's too astonishing for me to get my head around. The idea that whatever scrapes you get into, you just play your 'Get Out of Jail Free' card and make everything all right! I thought about his diary and how it would probably talk of cheap hotels and drug taking hippies, and travelling across the plains of India in a 3rd class carriages and eating street food. Would his gold credit card get any mention in it? I don't think so.

'You asleep Al?'

I pretended I was.

In reality I was internally fighting on an emotional level, *'The politics of envy.'* That's a phrase I've heard used a lot in conversations. It's even one I've said myself when people banged on about how easy life was for people with money. 'That's just the politics of envy,' I would declare, as if I had just thought it up, but now I'm in the grip of it, and it hurts. I was happy for Jon to have what he had – it's just that I wanted some too.

It's only when the morning sun streaks across the desert sands, I realise I've been awake all night.

Chapter 43. The next level of consciousness

Parking outside the Kamina Hotel in Kandahar again is a frustrating experience tinged with a sense of failure. It reminds me of how full of enthusiasm I'd been on the way out. My brother and our original passengers have gone, heading east on to, God only knows what fantastic adventures.

The challenge for me now is to get home, solely on the money I can make from the Yellow Bus. I miss having Phil alongside me; someone I can always share my worries with, and receive sage advice and friendly insults. With some effort I throw off this creeping feeling of disappointment and remind myself that adventures can lie in more than one direction. India can wait.

Feeling savvier with the ways of the world now, I stride confidently into the hotel. 'We are five people looking to stay the night. If you give me a free room we'll stay here; if not we'll go elsewhere.' It works. I get my free room.

I carry Sandappa's huge rucksack up to her room for her. She's said very little since we set off, often sitting in a lotus position in the seat behind me, meditating and droning mantras. She has a wonderful smell of a soft blend of sandalwood and patchouli oil about her which I like. She's a walking incense stick that perfumes her surroundings.

'This is a nice room,' I say, trying to make conversation. 'You'll be comfortable here.'

She looks at me for few seconds, with no expression on her face. By now I have given up expecting quick replies to anything.

Unexpectedly, she starts to cry.

'What's wrong, girl?' I put my arm around her shoulders.

'Nothing, nothing, I am alright,' she sniffs.

I wait. Anything you do around Sandappa has to be done slowly for fear of alarming her. I release her and start for the door. She sinks down onto the floor in a lotus position and starts to dab her tears with a hanky. My exit is halted by her saying,' I have been sent away. I'm not handling it properly, not the way I have to.'

'Sent away? Who sent you away?'

'Baba Mia.' As she says this name she places her hands together and bows in respect.

I wait.

'My guru.'

The only thing I can think to say is, 'Why?'

After the usual long wait, and shortly before I'm about to repeat my question, she answers. 'He said my next level of consciousness lay at home. That I couldn't move up if I remain with him'. She cries into her hanky some more before continuing. 'But I wanted so much to stay with him.'

This was followed by a large blow into the hanky.

'He said I couldn't get to the seventh level of consciousness unless I went back home. I have to do it from there.' She puts her face in her hands and sighs. 'It's too complicated to explain. He said, I could go back to him afterwards.' She speaks in a controlled way, as if holding back an earthquake which was threatening to shake her to pieces.

'What's your name at home, Sandappa?' I ask gently.

'Baba Mia (she bows at his name again) gave me the name Sandappa. That's my name. Sandappa means…..'

'No, no,' I interrupt. 'What were you Christened, or whatever...? What did your parents call you? And where do you come from?'

I've had plenty of similar conversations, frequently with Hare Krishna followers, who take a delight in explaining the meaning of their exotic teacher-given name, but become embarrassed to reveal they used to be called Jim or Susan. I remember it amused me to learn the great Italian composer Giuseppe Verdi's name is simply 'Joe Green' in English. Now to my ears, 'exotic' usually just means 'different.'

Sandappa thinks for a while. She appears to be deciding whether or not to divulge personal information. I half expect the quasi-mystical response of, 'There is only the 'now' - and now, I am Sandappa,' or 'Who is anyone? What do you mean when you say 'you'? Head games bore the hell out me, and I usually move on whenever they start. Instead she surprises me by saying. 'My name is Ingrid and my parents live in Stockholm.'

'Ingrid could I ask you a personal question?'

She nods.

'Were you sleeping with this Baba Mia?'

'We are twins in body and soul, night and day,' she says proudly.

'That's very beautifully put. And is there anyone else he was... erm... helping in the same way?'

She stiffens, and I realise I've hit a nerve. She starts to cry again. This time she recites a mantra until her breathing subsides a little.

'This is my fight for the next level of consciousness. I need to see the truth, but I am still too weak. I hate her. I know that's wrong. This is holding me back – this animal jealousy that needs to be erased.'

She looks up at me so pathetically, I feel sorry for her.

'Baba Mia wants me to return when I have conquered the illusion of jealousy,' she sobs.

'Where is this other girl from?'

'She's Chinese. He gave her the name of 'Kara.' Her eyes narrow.

'Look Ingrid, 'I say as mildly as I can. 'It seems to me, it's not about levels of consciousness or erasing jealousy. It looks like good old-fashioned abuse of power. This guru of yours, Baba Mia, is in a position where girls are asking to sleep with him because he's told them it'll raise their level of consciousness.'

She stares at me as I continue.

Stupidly, I follow this with, 'Some people would think the guy's a genius…' I let my voice trail away into silence. *'These are all the wrong words.'* I'm thinking. My attempt at being subtle is as subtle as a slap in the face. Macho clumsiness isn't helping her at all.

'Go away please,' she hisses. 'I must centre myself, I must centre myself,' she repeats over and over as I slink off, feeling I hadn't handled the situation very well. *'I think maybe a woman would have done a whole lot better.'*

Feeling depressed, I go to pay a visit on Zigi and Kati. They have an open bottle of Irish whiskey. Zigi pushes a glass towards me as soon as I enter.

Kati has washed her hair and wears a white towel wrapped, like a turban, around her head. It cheers me up to be back in a decadent setting, something I understand and feel comfortable in. We smoke a couple of cigarettes and indulge in small talk for an hour before I return to my bed to sleep.

Chapter 44. A real Desert Storm

Early the next afternoon we're driving in the southern plateau area of Afghanistan and heading north to Herat. This area is about 3500 feet above sea level, very dry and barren, the view breathtakingly wide. Over to our right we pass a large group of Kuchi nomads moving south for the winter. These people are on the United Nations most vulnerable list.

Like nomadic people everywhere they frequently come up against their settled competitors in their fight for grazing rights and water.

Hundreds of camels, goats and heavily-laden donkeys form a long straggling line. Small children and the elderly are wrapped up in blankets and tied to the camel's backs, while everyone else walks. The women, unlike their burka-clad counterparts from other ethnic groups, wear brightly coloured embroidered dresses and baggy pants, and normally leave their faces uncovered. Although now, because of the sand-lifting winds, most have wrapped scarves around their faces for protection. It's a timeless sight.

I know, given the choice, I would rather be a nomad than a settler, but also know as human populations grow there's less uninhabited land available to move animals on to graze. There can only be one winner.

Every now and then we watch small swirling chimneys of sand form, whipped up by the wind, race across the desert floor for a couple of hundred yards, and then dissipate and sink back down exhausted. Some of them are only knee-high and last a few seconds. We look out for them and call attention to each one. Occasionally they run along the edge of the roadway and we try racing them. The wind is definitely getting stronger.

It's Kati's turn to be in the passenger seat and she sits with bare feet up on the dashboard, her long jet-black hair held up by a couple of Japanese-style wooden sticks. She asks Zigi to pass her a bottle of water, takes a swig and passes it to me. 'They are getting bigger, I think.' She says, referring to the whirlpools of sand.

'There's one,' announces Mike, 'a big bastard too.'

Where Mike is pointing we see a tube of swirling sand about the diameter of Yellow Bus coming straight towards us. It rocks the bus when it hits us and we all shout and laugh. 'Wow, I could feel that through the steering,' I call.

In fact, the wind is starting to rock the bus around violently and it's only by constantly turning the wheel left and right can I keep it in a straight line. Some of the movement I put down to steering wear, as well as the weather.

We are hit a few more like that before Mike speaks again, but this time his voice is more serious. 'Stop the bus.'

'What?'

'Look what's coming.'

This time there's a tornado about the diameter of a football field travelling towards us at speed. I stop the bus and put the useless handbrake on. We stare at the oncoming wall of sand with disbelief. It seems demonic as if someone has pulled the plug and all the sand in the desert was swirling down the sink, taking everything it met with it. When it hits us we are forced up on two wheels for a second or two, before crashing back down. A couple of times we thought we are going over. I start the engine again and drive the bus head-on to the wind to lessen the chances.

As we sit totally enveloped in this buffeting wind Zigi shouts, 'We have to go out in it.'

Everyone stares at him.

'Come on we have to see what it's like.' He wraps a spare shirt around his head leaving only his eyes exposed then slips on a pair of sunglasses. He reminds me of the invisible man on TV. Kati and I rush to follow suit.

Mike sits unmoved and just swears at us for our stupidity. Sandappa and Jon merely shake their head when I look at them. Kati tries to open the passenger door but doesn't have the strength against the wind.

'Out the back,' I shout.

Zigi climbs out and is immediately blown over. Pulling himself upright, he staggers sideways trying not to fall. Kati follows and the moment she moves a couple of feet away from the bus I see the two sticks holding her hair in place fly off into the distance, and her hair streaks horizontally out.

It's a strange feeling trying to walk against the force of the sand storm. Progress is slow as we have to shuffle our feet to retain any balance. The wind is not steady but gusty and angry as if dozens of hands were grabbing and trying to pull us in all different directions. The sand rubs on any exposed skin like sandpaper.

We hold hands— Kati in the middle, me to her right and Zigi on her left. Together we lift our arms, and look for all the world like a triumvirate of King Canutes. We tell the wind to stop blowing. We try leaning on the wind but it's too gusty. My shirt blows open as the buttons give up their fight to hold together. Even shouting close to each other's ears is useless. The roar of the wind is so loud it snatches the words away. I don't have sunglasses so can't face the wind with my eyes open. Zigi lends me his for a minute. It's better, although there's still nothing that can be seen through the wall of frenzied sand. Suddenly there's a lull, and I catch a glimpse of the horizon. A vast dark weather front is coming towards us. We are going to be here for a while.

I think about the nomadic tribe we have recently passed. In a sand storm the desert people get behind their prone animals and let them take the brunt of it. We are more fortunate, having a sturdy metal box to hide in, and that's what we quickly retreat to. Grinning and shouting like baboons we clamber into the safety of the bus.

'Well,' I say cheerfully, fired-up on adrenaline, 'there's nothing we can do but wait it out. I can't see a damn thing in front of me so we can't go anywhere.' To myself I mutter,' *Let's hope we don't get turned over again Yellow Bus.*'

'I'll make some tea,' volunteers Sandappa, and we all get ourselves comfortable for a long wait. The bus is being constantly rocked as if a toy in a giant's hand. The sense of apprehension in the bus is tangible. Jon is busy struggling to write in his diary. I assume it's about the present storm.

Zigi unties his shirt from his head and shakes the sand from it. He lights a cigarette and passes the pack around. 'So, where are you from Mike?' he asks.

'Johannesburg, South Africa,' is the accented reply.

'And what's it like there at the moment?'

Mike's solid features seem to harden. Some faces have the appearance of growing organically whilst others look carved out – Mike had one of those carved faces. 'It's all changing.' His voice is morose.

Zigi isn't being put off by Mike's apparent reluctance to add detail. He follows up on his questioning. 'For better or for worse?'

Mike looks at him, as if in disbelief that anyone wouldn't know what's happening in his country.

'For the worse, my friend, very much for the worse.' Mike adopts the same gorilla-like posture he had with me when we first met; hands on knees, chest out, head thrust forward.
Zigi keeps quiet as if he has detected Mike's desire to continue without needing more provocation.

'I mean it's not as if we haven't been good to them...'

'What do you mean 'them?' Interrupts Kati, in feigned ignorance.

Mike answers unemotionally, as if he is talking about commodities, such as the rise in the price of bread. 'The blacks of course. They do all right by us.' He looks at us and shakes his head.

'I know what you people think - but you don't know South Africa as I do. I know what the papers report in England and Germany and…' He turns to look at Sandappa but can't put a country to her, so continues. 'Well unless you live there, been brought up there, and worked like a dog to get what you have, you can't know what's going on. We've been there for four generations – it's our land. They weren't doing anything with it.'

When Kati talks I can sense a steely edge in her voice. She speaks directly, unafraid of the consequences. 'If the scientists are right and all human beings started in Africa then four or five generations is like the day before yesterday to *them*. And when you say they weren't 'doing anything with it' you mean they weren't building motorways and skyscrapers, so they don't deserve it. Is that It?'

Mike doesn't seem to be offended at all. 'But the blacks are very lazy; and they're dishonest. The white man makes everything but the black man wants half for doing nothing. You can't leave anything lying around without some native boy running off with it, whether he knows what it is or not.' Mike is now warming to his subject.

'I'll give you an example. When I was a boy I had a black maid called Bokamoso. I'd help her with household chores. She taught me to chop wood, kill chickens, cook sweet potatoes for dinner – that kind of thing.'

'When I was about five I broke a window; threw a rock at a pig and missed, and smashed the kitchen window where Bokamoso was washing up. To stop me getting a beating from my father she said she'd broken it. So he made her pay for it. Stopped it out her wages. Nothing I could do. I was just five years old.'

'Then one day when I was twelve or thirteen, my mother decided to test Bokamoso's honesty. She left a small ruby ring on the carpet in the bathroom. She must have been getting on by then. I guess she was in her late 60s. Well, sure enough it disappeared. Bokamoso took it, as my parents thought she would.' Mike sighs like a world-weary man who has once again been proven right.

'What happened?' This time Sandappa has spoken – without the customary pause.

Mike looks at her as if surprised. 'She had to go of course. I was unhappy about it. She was like a mother to me. I argued with my father. But he said he wouldn't have a thief in the house. We couldn't rest easy, and anything else could be stolen.'

Then, as if to sum up the moral of the story, he adds, 'And so there's the trouble; the blacks are basically dishonest. You can't trust them even after you have given them everything, including your love. Apartheid worked for a long time, but now all the do-gooders think they know better.'

Kati looks at Zigi and Zigi shakes his head fractionally as if to say, 'Leave it'.

I become interested in the sand storm still raging outside. Sandappa busies herself with sharing out the tea. Jon, who has not spoken a word throughout, is still writing for all he is worth. Nobody speaks at all for a while, and we sit out the storm in an awkward silence.

Chapter 45. A cruel joke

We drive towards a cluster of armed Iranian border guards. A couple of them appear fidgety and swing their automatic weapons in front of them. Back into Iran again – my heart sinks.

I speak, in a quiet conspiratorial tone but loud enough that they can all hear, 'I don't want to worry anyone but I feel you guys ought to know. There's twenty kilos of Afghan hash in one of the spare wheels on the roof.' I wait for a couple of seconds to let this sink in, before adding, 'But don't worry. No way will they find it.'

Before anyone can say another word we're being flagged to stop and the inevitable thorough search begins. Passports are checked. Guarded closely and lined up against a wall, we're all roughly patted down. Drug-sniffing dogs are led onto the bus and all our belongings are hurled off the roof with no respect for what might be in them.

After our personal bags come the jerry cans and finally the spare wheels. Thrown from the height of the roof, the first tyre hits the ground and bounces about four feet off the ground, it's allowed to bounce and roll until it loses momentum. The second hits the ground with a dull thud instead of the expected energetic rebound. Immediately a lot of pointing and shouting breaks out from the guards.

Zigi, Kati, Sandappa, Jon and Mike are frozen to the spot with astonishment written on their faces. They remind me of the game of 'statues' people play at parties.

They are staring at me like I'm a dead man.

One dog is pulled out of the bus and dragged over to the suspect wheel. A guard pushes the dog's head over the valve and releases some of the air for it to smell. The dog shakes its head vigorously at the unpleasant experience, and pulls away. The guard, not satisfied, pulls it back and tries again with the same result. I let out a giant sigh of relief.

With a senior uniformed official brought out from his office, they try it a third time. Lots of shouting is exchanged – the official seems annoyed at having been disturbed. The guards walk away without a word to us. Nobody informs us of anything, so we spend an hour replacing everything, climb on-board and pull away.

We sit in stony silence, as if scared the customs people had secretly bugged the bus, until we pull over at the sun-shades and plastic chairs of the nearest roadside café. 'I told you they wouldn't find it, didn't I?' I say coolly, when we're safely off the road.

'Shouldn't we keep going?' Jon suggests, his voice a little nervous. 'I mean, they might have second thoughts and come after us.'

Kati laughs, 'You're one brave son of a bitch, Alan.'

As I would have been, if the spare tyre genuinely held twenty kilos of hash.

With her beautiful compliment ringing in my ears I hardly want to spoil the illusion by telling the truth, but when we all have sat and ordered tea, I feel I have to. Feeling pleased with my successful joke I go into confession mode. 'There was no danger guys, honestly. That wheel that didn't bounce was repaired in Kabul in an Afghan garage. They have a method of inserting another tread under the first one. So, when the tyre starts to wear out you have another tread underneath to run on. I wouldn't have put you guys at any risk.'

Zigi, Kati, Jon and Sandappa laugh heartily but Mike's face screws up and turns red. He screams 'You Bastard!' at me loud enough for the waiter to come to the door to see what's happening 'I thought I was going to spend years in prison, you English bastard!' He stands up in one of his gorilla postures. 'I'll kill you, you English Bastard!'

He tries to hit me across the table but only succeeds in spilling everyone's tea. I move back to avoid his fist. He starts to come around towards me, all the time shouting about how he is going to murder me.

He isn't joking either. An empty chair is sent flying as he kicks it out of his way; his face glows red and veined. I'm amazed that I feel no fear of this man at all. It takes some minutes of fast footwork running around the bus, laughing until I can hardly breathe, to keep myself in one piece.

He's strong, but he isn't fast. The others all cheer as I outpace him and keep him at a safe distance. All the time Mike is panting and cursing me ferociously in a language I don't understand.

It takes the others ten minutes or so to calm him down. I stay on my feet ready to run until I am sure Mike's understands it was just an innocent joke. Not being fast enough on his feet to catch me I've little to fear from him in a chase, but I keep an eye on him as we climb aboard the bus again. He sits scowling. But my real fear at the moment isn't Mike; it's of having a fatal breakdown in Iran. In this part of the world your passport gets stamped with the details of the vehicle, sometimes with details of watches, cameras, just about anything a decadent westerner could sell to a poor Arab. If you turn up at the exit border post without it they won't let you out of the country — simple as that.

I don't know what happens to you after that - and I don't want to find out either

In the Khorasan Province, nowhere near any other dwellings, we stop at a roadside garage and café. As we pull up the owner rushes out and beams. 'Come in. Come in my friends.'

Pictures of the Shah and his family adorn the walls of his spotless cafe. In them the Persian Royal Family appear to share the same public relations company with the British one. There's lots of pictures of the Shah wearing full military uniform bedecked with medals, in much the same poses as our Prince Phillip.

He is staring purposely into the horizon, hand on sword ready to defeat the common enemy. I wondered how these people had the temerity to award themselves so many medals: the most dangerous part of their lives being drinking too much and falling off their polo ponies. And, of course, the Shah plays polo, judging by the flattering photos of this 'all action' man.

His wife stands with him in bejewelled dresses - about half a dozen different ones. Of course, there's a photograph of their son at the controls of a helicopter, grinning away, obviously trying to convey the same image as we attempt back home for our royal princes – a chip off the royal block, a born leader of men.

The Yellow Bus

It all seems a bit sad to me, but I'm a cynical working-class Englishman, whereas he is a committed Shahist. He is also a really pleasant man. It feels such a relief to talk to an Iranian without seeing contempt in his face. He brings us tea and some tasty cookies then relates his travels to us. How he had worked for Ford's in Cologne for four years, and spoke fluent German. Zigi tested him with a couple of sentences and nodded with approval.

'Ja, es stimmt, Sie sprechen Deutsch sehr gut.' Seeing my blank expression, Zigi explains, 'I am complimenting him on his German.'

This exuberant man continues. 'Then I went to England and lived in Oxford, where I studied. There I worked as a radiologist. Oh yes, I worked in Edinburgh for two years as well. Och Aye the noo. wid yee pass me sum haggis lassie?' I wish Scottish Dave had heard him. This man is a natural comedian. He talks as much with his hands and face as his voice.

He tells us about going down to London but not liking it much, 'No, too, too busy. I don't like people rushing and pushing all the time.'

'Well, you have all the peace and quiet you need here,' suggests Jon. Our host raises his opened hands in a typical Arab gesture when invoking Allah.

'Inshallah. I am a slave to my own name,' he says in a weary comic way.

'Go on. Why's that?' Jon encourages.

His eyes twinkle as it's obviously the reply he hoped for. 'My name is Jashmid. In Farsi it means 'Handsome'. It's why I have thirteen children. My wife cannot leave me alone.' His smile is mischievous - and infectious. We spend an hour being entertained by this humorous man, with a string of amusing tales.

Jashmid makes me re-evaluate Iranian people and reminds me that people everywhere are only as good as they are allowed to be. True everywhere – in every community. There is genuine good feelings between us all as we take our leave.

Chapter 46. Stealing the German flag

At the border of Turkey we breathe a communal sigh of relief. I feel proud of the Yellow Bus for having come so far, and the mere fact I get my passport stamped gives me joy. Now I don't care if or where we break down, because I will be able to handle it.

We were driving with the beautiful Lake Van on our right, when Zigi calls out. 'Look over there, Alan.'

Set back from the road is a large sports stadium with a long track leading up to it.

'You want to go running, Zigi?'

'No. I want the German flag,' is his excited reply. 'Turn off the road further down.'

I see what he means. All around the periphery of this huge stadium are flags from every country fluttering in the breeze. With the Yellow Bus safely parked some distance from the road, Zigi and I walk back. There's no-one in sight as we sneak across a field of long grass until we arrive at its perimeter.

We keep low, our eyes focused on the building at the opposite side, looking for movement, and we run until we are underneath the German flag. The knot on the pulley is too tight for me to loosen. Zigi pulls out a pocket knife and cuts through the nylon cords. Then, together, we start lowering it. The flag's about half way down when we hear a distant shout and look over to see two large men on the far side of the stadium sprinting towards a small white Peugeot van.

We work faster. It's been an optical illusion – the flagpoles are higher than they first looked. It takes an age to get the damned thing down. This wonderful German flag, that looked no bigger than a tablecloth up high, is bloody huge. It takes both of us to bundle it up and carry it between us. The Peugeot van has disappeared from sight, but we know it will be on us soon. Zigi makes as if to run back to the bus, but I pull my part of the bundle to stop him dead.

'We will never get away if they see the bus – let's go across the fields.'

So, bound together by this enormous flag we set off like competitors in a three legged race, trying to match our pace to each other. We are both laughing like loons as we run.

'I bet those two guys behind us are Olympic champions at cross country running,' he shouts.

'Yes, but we are the combined English and German flag stealing champions of the world. They don't stand a chance,' I gasp.

We look back. The white Peugeot van is now parked near the flag post we'd ransacked and two very large men were tumbling out of it. They're obviously not risking driving across the rough fields in it.

'They don't look like runners – more like weight lifters,' I laugh, but that's to hide the sense of impending doom I feel if we don't get lucky pretty soon.

Deep down I suspect, whatever discipline they follow, if they are any kind of athletes they will be able to overtake us. Our pace isn't bad, but it's been years since I last ran any serious distance so I assume that's because of the adrenaline kicking in. Zigi is one of those naturally athletic types so I'm pleased to be keeping close by him.

Zigi points. 'Look, a train tunnel. Let's make for that.'

A few hundred yards from us is a black hole in the side of the hill. We run in, but it's like going instantly blind. We keep going but at a much reduced rate. I have my free hand out in front of me expecting to run into a brick wall at any moment.

We look back but can't see any silhouettes against the light behind us. We keep going for a few more minutes until the tunnel curves and we can't see any light behind or in front of us. We are in utter pitch blackness. Neither of us speak. A few minutes of slow walking brings us a welcome sight; some distance away but definitely visible is the proverbial light at the end of the tunnel. Zigi has a good idea.

I can hear how much he's panting when he says, 'Let's bury the flag and come back for it later.'

It makes sense, as it's difficult to run fast carrying this great bundle between us, and we can't be sure if more running is going to be on our agenda. We can't actually bury it, it's too big for that, but we throw stones over it to stop it blowing about and keep it fairly hidden. While doing this I become more aware of our situation. The tunnel is a narrow one with only one track. There isn't room for a train and people in this tunnel at the same time.

My thinking now is simple, *Trains are big, heavy and fast. They take a long time to stop. Humans are soft and easily injured - and die when badly damaged. That's enough thinking about this subject.* I listen intently for any sound, and then, remembering my education at Saturday morning cinema, I put my ear to one of the rails – nothing.

It impresses Zigi, whose eyes are starting to adjust to the darkness. 'I bet you got it from the movies, Ja?'

I smile. There's no sign of our pursuers, but now we're not sure of our next move. Zigi knows exactly what I'm wondering.

'Which way do you think?' he looks up and down the tunnel in a hopeless search for a clue.

The thought of committing ourselves to walking its whole length is not a pleasant one. It all depends on guessing correctly what our athletic followers have planned.

'They may have given up,' I suggest optimistically.

'Or they may be hiding, waiting for us to come out again,' comes Zigi's sobering reply.

We both understand the other option: If our pursuers are local people who know where the tunnel comes out maybe they can drive there a lot faster than we can walk. They could already be there waiting at the far end - to make hippy shish-kebab of us both. One thing's for sure – we can't stay where we are for much longer. We creep slowly and quietly back in the direction we'd come. It's with great apprehension we nervously peer out of the tunnel again. Expecting to be ambushed at any time, we look for the white Peugeot van, but it isn't in sight.

Whether they'd raced to the other end of the tunnel we never found out. Perhaps they aren't even athletes, but a couple of overweight caretakers who had given up and gone home. Without the flag, we scramble cautiously back to the Yellow Bus by a circuitous route via some trees, to make sure we aren't seen.

Kati kisses Zigi passionately and hugs me tightly when we return. I feel like I've won second prize in a competition – happy, but envious of the winner.

Sandappa looks at our grimy faces and asks if we're okay. She has a genuinely caring attitude, and we are all warming to her now. Jon wants to know all the details and Mike ignores us completely.

'Can we get going now?' he scowls.

Zigi explains the situation with the buried flag.

'We need to wait a few hours before we can go back for the flag. They may phone the police.'

'You two pricks have jeopardised this whole trip,' Mike fumes, 'I should have gone with a professional organisation.'

I suggest we find a café to while away some time, so we drive into the outskirts of a town called Edremit and stop at the first likely place. I turn to everyone. 'Zigi and I will go back to get the flag alone. There's no point in anyone else coming as we have to come back this way. It gives everyone a chance to stretch their leg, do some window shopping and sightseeing. Get back here for 9 o'clock and we'll leave then.'

At 8.30 Zigi and I got into the bus and headed back to the tunnel. 'You have a torch?' he asks.

'No.'

This time we park closer but drive the last few hundred yards with our lights turned off. We both sit in the cab looking intently into the darkness for signs of anyone. Suddenly Zigi breaks the tension.

'It's only a bloody flag after all. I feel like I'm robbing a church.'

We both regain our composure and laugh.

For an unknown reason I go back in time to when I was a kid reading War Picture Library comic books. All the German characters spoke in clipped sentences that were theatrical. 'You can say zat but I bet it iz high treason to steal ze German flag. Zey will probably execute you for zis.' And from a bad German accent I switch to a bad upper class British one. 'And for stealing a German flag the boys back in Blighty will give me the Victoria Cross for actions against the Bosche.' I salute pompously. Childish humour, but it cracks Zigi up and lightens the mood.

Cheered up, we make our way under the darkening sky back to the tunnel. We enter and walk cautiously along. This time there's no bright little circle of light behind to help us. Disorientated by the absolute blackness we stumble along until we estimate we're at the place the flag should be. We walk about feeling for it with our feet and then on our hands and knees.

'Perhaps they followed us in and found it,' Zigi suggests. 'Wait, I have some matches.'

He lights a match and I laugh at how dirty his face is. His reaction at seeing mine is the same. We peer around us but can't see the flag.

'I think we were further along the tunnel,' I suggest.

'I agree, but I have only 3 more matches so we must use them carefully.'

We walk on using two of our matches to light our way but still can't see any sign of our little stone burial ground.

'Last one,' Zigi says.

As it flares I see a little bit of red material reflect in the light a short way up. 'There it is,' I point. Overjoyed we throw the stones off and liberate our stolen goods. Zigi starts to sing the German National anthem. 'Duechland Duechland uber alles…'

'Shut up, Zigi.'

'What is it?'

'I thought I heard something.' We both listen in silence. Once again I place my ear to a rail but this time I think I can feel a vibration.

'I think there's a train coming.'

'Scheisse. Which way?'

'How do I know? Let's get out of here.'

'But, which way?'

The noise is now pronounced and the rails are ringing with the vibrations.

'The fucking shortest – I don't know!'

If there is a medal to be won for synchronised running in pitch blackness we would have won gold. The noise behind us is growing to a roar. And we can see a small light heading for us like a torch-beam in the distance. Shouting encouragements to each other we stumble and fall and pick ourselves up again, over and over. Refusing to relinquish our flag we fly out of the tunnel and burst into the dusky light outside. Throwing ourselves over a fence we roll, tangling ourselves in the vast swathes of material, and land in a watery ditch, just as the train comes bursting through the tunnel. It's an ugly squat diesel train with eight carriages full of coal behind it.

Still lying on our backs in the cold water, we watch as carriage after carriage thunders past – followed by an eerie silence as the rear lights disappear along the track.

'That was close,' I say.

'Is that what they call an English understatement?' Zigi chuckles.

Then we start laughing with relief and sheer joy. We stand up, untangle ourselves from the wet flag and hug each other. We know we have created a bond, a memory between us that will be remembered forever.

Like children, we run back to the Yellow Bus and bundle the dripping flag into the back of it.

'It's a lot bigger than I thought,' said Zigi. 'I think you could wrap the Yellow Bus up in it.'

He was right.

Jumping into the cab Zigi casually flicked a cigarette into his mouth and offered me one. I took it - I needed it. He patted his pockets. 'Do we have a light?'

We didn't, of course.

Chapter 47. We lose a passenger

When Zigi and I return to the café, everyone is there except Mike.

'Anyone seen him? ' I ask. Everyone shakes their heads. 'He didn't say where he was going?' More shaking of heads.

I try to be philosophical. 'Well, it's not unusual to miss a deadline when travelling. Maybe he's got himself lost in the unfamiliar streets, or simply forgotten the time. We'll give him a while.'

'I think he's gone,' suggests Jon.

'He is a very unhappy man,' adds Sandappa. 'He has so much violence in his soul. He must have done bad things in his previous lifetimes.'

Jon adds, 'He was swearing a lot about having to wait for you guys, then he grabbed his stuff and walked away in a temper.'

'You're sure he took his rucksack?'

Jon looked at Sandappa for confirmation before saying, 'I think so.'

'I'll check. Then we'll wait for an hour. If he hasn't we'll have to wait longer.'

11 o'clock comes and goes without Mike turning up and we get bored, so we board the bus and take off through the city centre. I feel bad, but there isn't much else we can do. Enquiring with the local police is not a possibility after the night's adventure.

With us still carrying the German flag we've stolen the local police are not high on my list of people I want to spend time with. What if he is injured in a hospital somewhere? I console myself with the thought that Mike's an experienced traveller and hasn't left anything behind.

Kati asks gently, 'Alan, would you have waited longer if Mike hadn't been such a little shit?'

'No, I don't think so, Kati.'

As I drive I'm thinking about a guy called Greg Williams who I'd run into in a small town in Southern Afghanistan. He owned the Magic Bus, a British-built over-lander painted by Pakistani artists. It was covered with images of peacocks, lions, and all kinds of tropical looking vegetation in primary colours. Greg said It was named as a tribute to the Magic Bus of Ken Kesey and the Merry Pranksters of California.

He was about to leave one of his passengers behind because they were 15 minutes late. I took the keys out of the ignition, refusing to give them back unless he gave the guy another half hour. We had an argument which got heated, but I still refused to give him his keys. With Greg threatening to fight me, and me explaining that a few minutes is not important enough to ditch someone in a foreign land, the guy turned up, apologised, and got on board. Greg didn't have the hippy spirit as far as I was concerned.

There's no doubt in my mind, so I finish off with, 'I think we did okay by Mike.'

Kati considers this for a few moments before saying, 'Nevertheless, he *was* a little shit.'

Twilight begins to colour the horizon with pinks and purples. We find a patch of land to camp on so we can drive into Istanbul in daylight. The beautiful skyline of the city is ahead of us. The great domed mosques and the soaring minarets are outlined by the setting sun in a fairy-tale way. I hadn't expected to see it again so soon, but it thrilled me anyway. And the sense of relief that we'd made the first leg of the journey back was the icing on the cake.

Chapter 48. "What do you know about Baadar-Meinhof?"

The following morning we start early, and drive into the already bustling streets of Istanbul. I park outside The Pudding Shop on Divan Yolu to say goodbye to my passengers. First off is Sandappa. Zigi takes hold of her heavy yellow canvas rucksack as I lower it from the roof. Then I climb down and help her on with it. We look at each other for a moment or two. I'm no longer in a hurry and wait for her to say something, but she surprises me by hugging me and kissing me on the cheek.

'Bon voyage, Sandappa,' I say.

She shakes her head and says, 'Ingrid. My name is Ingrid.' And with a big smile adds, 'Thank you, Alan.' She waves goodbye and walks confidently off, a small figure almost dwarfed by her rucksack. A feeling of sadness comes over me. She had a calming influence on everyone except Mike, and is absolutely no trouble to travel with; the furthest thing from trouble if anything. I feel my heart sending her my best wishes as I watch her go.

Jon is next.

'I'm going to try for London in a couple of days,' I tell him. 'To be really honest we probably won't make it, but I'm going to try anyway. You're welcome if you want to give it a shot.'

'Where are you going to stay?' He asks.

'Probably at the Turk Hotel, down the end of Divan Yolu Street and turn left. It's just a few yards up the road.'

'When will you leave?'

'Maybe in two or three days, I suppose. It depends on when I can get some passengers.'

Jon strokes his three day old beard a couple of times. 'Let me think about it and I'll let you know.'

'Okay, can't ask more than that.' We shake hands and as I watch him wander off I'm fighting that overwhelming feeling of loss that's such an integral part of being on the road.

Zigi, Kati and I go into The Pudding Shop. They order coffee and I treat myself to a peach Mey Su, fruit drinks that are fantastic but pricey. I need a treat.

We sit out back in the garden that's beginning to heat up in the rising sun; there are only a couple of other people there. It's a beautiful morning, we all light cigarettes and watch the light fluffy clouds overhead. Suddenly, Zigi says in a serious tone that demands attention, 'Alan. Kati and I have decided to let you into our secret.' He pauses as our drinks arrive.

'Looking around to make sure there's no-one within earshot he continues. 'The truth is, we are wanted by the police in Germany, perhaps by Interpol.'

He now has my complete attention. 'Right. Okay. What for?'

He doesn't answer my question, but draws on his cigarette and blows out a smoke-ring before asking, 'What do you know about Baadar-Meinhof?'

Everyone's heard of the Baadar-Meinhof Group unless they've been living in a convent. Certainly I've heard of them - but not with any connection to charity work. They're depicted by all the media as anarchists and terrorists. Instinctively, I know neither of those words would be appropriate in my answer. Some of our previous scraps of conversation were now starting to make sense.

'Yes - also known as The Red Army Faction - I've heard of them,' I reply cautiously.

Zigi looks around again then leans forward in his wicker chair and looks intently into my eyes. 'Kati and I like you, Alan. You have integrity. I know we disagree on politics but not fundamentally, only on methods, and that's not so important. What's important is we feel we can trust you. You see, Kati and I work with Andreas Baader and Ulrike Meinhof. We are wanted for a number of political actions, including robbing a bank.'

He pauses to allow me to take this all in. It's on the tip of my tongue to question how robbing a bank is a political crime, but think I already know how Zigi will answer it, and don't need to hear him say it.

'That's why we headed to Asia,' he continues. 'Things were getting too hot for us back home.'

'And that's why you chose to come back in my beaten-up bus rather than a regular overlander? Kati and Zigi both nod to confirm my guess.

They give me time to weigh up what I know and feel about both of them. Then compare that with the little I think I know about the Baadar-Meinhof group. My instinct is always against violence and theft. On the other hand, I believe more in human collaboration than in a capitalistic 'winner takes all' society,' particularly when the 'winners' are usually in that position by accidents of birth. In my heart I understand the revolutionary spirit.

Eventually I reply. 'As far as I can see Zigi, you and Kati are friends of mine. You've done nothing to upset me. We've enjoyed each other's company. As you know, I am no lover of the status quo. Maybe I don't have the courage for the kind of actions you guys advocate; perhaps even with that courage I'd choose non-violence, but I'll do whatever I can to help you. You know that don't you?'

Kati let out a squeal of delight and says something to Zigi in German.

'What did you say Kati?' I ask.

Zigi responds. 'She said, she told me so. That she feels very close to you and knows you can be trusted.'

'Feels close to me? ' It takes a second or two before I realise not to take Zigi's translation literally. She probably said 'she understood me well' or something like that. Zigi and Kati were definitely besotted with each other. I'm amazed that on discovering she's an activist, anarchist, or even a terrorist, it does nothing to reduce my feelings for her. She could kick a dog in the street and I'd somehow think it sexy. I feel idiotically juvenile with this fascination and want to shake it off. They've obviously shared a lot together, rioting, marches, even robbing a bank together. Not something I feel entirely necessary on a date night. But I feel very suburban and parochial, and emotionally out of my depth.

Zigi continues. 'At the moment we're not sure how big the net is they have out for us. In Germany it'll be different as we have a lot of friends who will help us. But we heard you speaking to Jon about going on to London. We feel it would be safer for us to travel with you as hippies coming back from the east rather than to fly or travel by train. Our photographs will be in newspapers - and we may have to show identity papers.'

'Okay,' I say. 'How far do you want to come?'

'Anywhere within Germany will do us fine,' says Kati as she blows a stream of cigarette smoke into the air.

I think for a while. 'It's a risk, of course.'

'Life is a risk,' says Zigi philosophically. 'We understand the bus might not make it. God only knows what's keeping it going. But if you're willing to help us, we are happy to take that risk.'

'Of course I am.' I smile, and add flippantly, 'Life's been a bit boring lately, anyway.'

After chatting for a while about which hotel to stay in, I check with someone what day it is; Monday I'm told. We arrange to meet back at The Pudding Shop at 3 pm on Friday.

I immediately go and buy a packet of ten postcards and write on each of them:

Yellow Bus to London - leaves Friday 14th $25.

I'll be in The Pudding Shop every day from 3pm – 6pm wearing a green Indian cotton shirt. Ask for Alan.

Walking around the local hotels where low-budget travellers stay, I place postcards on all their notice-boards, then go in search of a hotel for the night. Luckily I get a nice room in the Hotel Turk with a double bed.

Chapter 49. An offer you can refuse

The next night, after lounging in bed most of the day reading Huxley's, 'Eyeless in Gaza', and dozing. I return to The Pudding Shop for 3 o'clock. As stated on the postcards I wear my green open-necked Indian cotton shirt. It only has one very small oil stain from the bus turning-over incident in the Turkish mountains, so is still quite presentable.

The Pudding Shop makes some mouth-watering dishes. It's the only place in Istanbul you can buy genuine Wiener-schnitzel with authentic potato salad as they serve in good German restaurants. However, I limit myself to a large coffee and sit in the garden and wait.

The Pudding Shop is always busy, so I sit for a while, just reading my book, making sure my body language is not inviting passers-by to relate travel stories or make small talk with me. My coffee goes cold and still no one approaches in answer to my advertisement. *It's going to be a long wait.* I sip ever so slightly on my cold coffee every now and then, and crunch on the luxurious brown sugar cubes that come with it. I look around for likely customers.

There's the usual mix of all types, from scraggy thin-faced heroin users to fresh-faced kids, probably from a range of European colleges and universities. There are haggard veteran travellers and patient looking businessmen attempting to identify customers in whatever field, legal or illegal, they make their money. Missing are the hotel-wallahs trying to badger tourists to stay in the hotels that pay them commission. The boss is good at discouraging hustlers from annoying the customers – that's what makes The Pudding Shop such an oasis from regular street life; that and a full and comprehensive notice board which sells and tells everything a traveller might need.

I'm running the earlier conversation with Zigi and Kati through my head and exploring how their revelations, or maybe confessions, make me feel. Even at my tender age I've already mixed with a wide range of people – often people who are ducking and diving to make ends meet. So, outrage is not one of my traits – a fact that always surprises me.

Discussing life with people sometimes brings indignant pronouncements from others on the morality of the actors in a story. I rarely feel that unless it involves really innocent people – oh, yes, animals too. On the other hand I know Baader-Meinhoff is not one of your regular criminal enterprises… when my thoughts are interrupted.

'Can I sit here? I look up at a thin Indian looking man, dressed immaculately in a well-made white suit, shiny tan brogues, and with a panama hat upon his head. In one hand he holds a walking cane with a carved dog's head as the handle.

'Certainly,' I reply, as I move to give him some room.

He sits with some care after examining the wicker chair for dirt, and then the table, before placing his hat on it.

I look intently at the pages of my book. 'My name is Arvind,' he introduces himself with a smile. My heart sinks. Making small talk with strangers is not in my plans. *Obviously my body language needs a refresher course.*

Without waiting for encouragement he continues. 'I have a friend who holds a senior manager's position with Arco's – you have heard of them, perhaps?'

I shake my head and try to show how intently I am reading my book. He is not discouraged. 'Arco's is one of Turkey's largest mining operations. They only mine for one thing though – diamonds.'

At this, he reaches into his inside jacket pocket and pulls out a small red velvet bag and gently teases the gold thread holding its mouth shut, until it opens. Tipping it slowly, a large diamond drops into the palm of his left hand. Whilst doing this he leans forward to block anyone else's view. I take a look at it. It's an impressive stone. Although only a fraction of the size of the incredible 'Spoonmaker's Diamond' in the Topkapi Museum, it's still enough to raise eyebrows. It appears perfectly flawless and beautifully cut to my untrained eye.

'My friend had the opportunity to smuggle this out of the mine one day. There is no tax to pay. That is why he can sell it so cheaply – just £300.'

I say nothing. The thought of having £300 at the moment would be a dream come true. My silence obviously makes the man feel uncomfortable. His voice takes on a more intense tone. '£300 is very cheap, my friend. He needs to get rid of it quickly before someone sees it. The longer he keeps it the more chance he will be caught. Therefore, my friend, I offer you this bargain, so you can take it back to your own country and realise a small fortune.'

He studies me intently as he transfers the stone from his hand to mine. I felt its weight and move to hold it to the light.

'Be careful.' His hand grasps my arm.

I keep it low and study it. It's a nice piece alright. In fact, it's one of the best cut pieces of glass I have ever seen.

'Of course, I will need to get someone to authenticate it as genuine,' I tell him.

He takes on a more earnest posture and leans closer to me and whispers. 'My friend you don't seem to understand. Even now I am taking a huge risk showing this to you. Nobody else must know about it.'

'So, you want me to give you £300, but I can't find out whether this is a genuine diamond or not?'

'Just look at it,' he urges. 'And anyway, you have my word as a gentleman.'

Perhaps, because I was whiling away time, or felt annoyed at being interrupted, I played along with him.

'My brother is in the jewellery trade. He's in Hotel Turk right now, around the corner. Let's go and show it to him. Besides he carries all our money. I would have to get the cash from him anyway.' I try to sound sincere.

His expression changes and I see the irritation pass across his eyes for a second. He reaches forward for the 'diamond' but I clasp my hand around it.

'My friend, I must have the money today. I can't leave this place carrying such a diamond. There are robbers in the streets. I must sell it today. My friend needs the money desperately. I get nothing from this sale – it is just a favour I am doing.'

'This is the same friend who's a senior manager in one of Turkey's largest diamond mines?'

Arvind, if that is his name, can see this sale unravelling at a rate of knots. He keeps reaching across for the 'diamond' but I hold on to it.

'It looks to me, Arvind you're in a difficult position. You can't call the police because if you're telling the truth, and this is a stolen diamond, they will lock you up. On the other hand if it's just a piece of glass that you've been trying to sell as a diamond then….well, I suppose they'll still lock you up, won't they? I let him sweat for a few moments.

'So, which is it? If you tell me the truth you can have it back, but if you lie to me I will keep it. Is it glass?'

The once dapper man was now agitated and perspiring.

'Is it glass?' I repeat.

He holds out his hand and nods. I drop the stone into his open palm. Without looking at me or saying another word he retrieves his hat and cane and swiftly leaves. As I watch him go, I feel cruel for the trick I've just played, but reassure myself it's only the same game he is playing on tourists. Perhaps I should have told him I'd already been approached twice in Afghanistan by dapper gents, with exactly the same story.

Chapter 50. A meal in uncomfortable luxury

The next day at The Pudding Shop, I check my card's still on the notice board. There's a piece of folded paper pinned to it.

The note says, 'Alan. Come for a meal tonight and we will treat you. 10 pm – don't be late. Hotel Sultania. Old City Sultanahmet - Room 117. Love Kati'

The address surprises me because it seems an unlikely place to find cheap hotels, just north of the Topkapi Palace. But then I thought, *'It's Zigi and Kati, the mysterious couple – anything's possible.'*

So, that night I walk across the old city. The moon is full as I pass through deep shadows, cast by the intricately sculpted portals of some of the large houses. In this deserted street, any shadow could hide a robber – a perfect place for muggers.

Two nights previously, I'd woken from a dream where I'd been running from robbers down the ancient narrow streets of Istanbul, just like these. Even as I ran, I was aware of the enormous studded doors and intricately designed arches, such as the ones I was passing now. In my dream, I had been stabbed. The feeling of the blade going into my chest woke me, soaked with sweat. People say you're never die in a dream, but I certainly felt close. It was sharp and vivid to me and I had felt my life fading away.

Later that day I overheard people at the Hotel Turk talking about how the body of an English traveller had been pulled out of the Bosporus. He had been stabbed and robbed. I couldn't shake off the feeling I'd become somehow psychically linked to this unknown person, and experienced his last moments with him.

Needless to say, my senses are alert as I walk in the dark. Upon seeing the grandeur of Hotel Sultania it surprises me; a modern looking building that takes up a whole block. '*Well, they did tell me they'd robbed a bank,*' I think, as I take the gold-painted lift to the first floor. The carpets in the corridor are bright red and plush underfoot.

I find room number 117 Zigi and Kati both greet me when the door opens.

Zigi waves me in. 'Very good, Alan. Did you have any trouble finding us?'

'Let me get you a drink,' Kati says.

Both of them have now changed from their usual travelling clothes into altogether different attire. Kati sports a new jet-black dress with a beaded pattern across her shoulders resembling a cobweb. Beads cover the whole dress; they shimmer and move independently from her. Perhaps it's the slight delay caused by the weight of them but it creates a hypnotic movement. Zigi has gone for an Arabian pyjama look. His loose cotton pants are striped, and he wears an open waistcoat, like something from an Ali Baba film. They have already started on a bottle of Johnny Walker Black Label and offer me a glass. Not wanting to get drunk, I ask if there's any tonic or lemonade to put in it.'

'No, no Alan. You will ruin the taste,' groans Zigi from the ornate quilted bed he had thrown himself onto.

I look around the room, taking in the gilt-framed picture of Ataturk next to the fine quality hangings with beautiful calligraphy, which I assume is from the Qur'an. This hotel is both secular and religious. *Belt and braces,*' I think.

Zigi sees my curiosity. 'Have a look around.' He waves his hand in an arc, careful not to spill the whiskey.

At one end of the room heavily carpeted steps lead to a raised dais surrounded by a classically Persian carved wooden archway. Beyond is the en-suite bathroom with gold taps and shower. The sink looks as if it's carved from a single chunk of onyx. There's also a luxurious deep bath with matching gold taps. The floor in the main room is of highly polished plain wood, which is a nice contrast to the intricately patterned wall hangings.

'Here, Alan, there was tonic in the fridge.' Kati hands me a large whiskey glass.

Once again, I steel myself for the effect I know she'll have on me. I look at her reflection in the large wall mirror. *Well, she isn't a vampire or one of the undead - she has a reflection.*

'You like the hotel?' Zigi asks.

'Very nice. Too expensive for me.'

'No. It's not so expensive.'

We exchange small talk for a while about what we've been up to that day. Zigi proudly shows me an antique silver Turkish dagger he's purchased, and a couple of Turkish military medals. He motions to me to sit on a blue- velvet covered chair so I can study them.

Holding them one at a time to the light, I say, 'These are impressive. Do you know what they signify?'

Zigi shakes his head. 'The man in the shop told me some story about them coming from a well-known Turkish hero. He probably single-handedly liberated an entire city. You know what Turkish shop-keepers are like. I'll research them when I get back. I just liked them.'

The whiskey tastes sublime, even with the tonic added. Some sense of mischief drives my next comment.

'When you think about it, my father fought your father in the last war. It got him some medals. He said they didn't mean anything to him. I asked him what happened to them. He told me that my older brother had cut his teeth on them, and must have thrown them out of the pram. He wasn't bothered.'

Kati, sitting elegantly on a leather poufy, sips her neat whiskey. 'What did your father do, Alan? Was he a pilot or something?'

I shake my head. 'No, he was a sailor. I think he was off Okinawa at some point. I remember him telling me about Kamikaze planes attacking his ship, oh yes, and he was also on the Russian runs. He was torpedoed and sunk in the Mediterranean on board the HMS Ulster or was it the HMS Medway? In fact, I'm pretty sure it was both.'

Kati smiles and says, 'He had a busy war by the sound of it. Well, obviously he didn't die because you're not old enough. Was he injured?'

'No, he got out without a scratch. After one of the sinkings, he was picked up, after floating in the sea for a few hours, then taken down to South Africa to recuperate.'

'That's a long way from home. Why South Africa?'

I shrug my shoulders. 'He told me that he went horse riding with the daughter of De Beers and they ended up having an argument and her storming off; so I was never sure if his stories were true.

She has a way of probing with her questions in a fluid manner. It's those beautiful green eyes. But it's likely to prove a one way street. Experience has shown me Kati is a closed book when she wants to be. Those large, cat-like eyes of hers could be welcoming, but can equally shut you out as securely as a bank vault.

I sip at my drink again. It has more whiskey than tonic by a country mile.

Zigi glances at Kati. I feel it to be a conspiratorial look. I avert my gaze. An atmosphere I can't grasp is building. I don't feel comfortable and the whisky isn't helping. For a moment I wonder whether I'm in any danger, but shrug the thought off as ridiculous.

At length, Zigi breaks the silence, 'But, nobody wins a war, Alan. You know that. Kati's uncle was in the Luftwaffe. He was shot down and killed over Britain. My father was on leave visiting our family in Dresden when the British bombers came. My parents survived, by some miracle, but my older brother, a baby then who I never met, and both my grandparents, were killed. My mother told me she saw her parents sitting opposite each other, still sitting at a table on the 4th floor of an apartment building. The whole side of the building had been torn away. There they were, in full view of the street, both dead.' He paused to let that image sink in before continuing. 'Dreadful things – wars.'

There followed another period of uncomfortable silence before I venture to break it. 'I feel like I've pissed on the parade a bit. We're supposed to be having fun tonight. The war was a long time ago. Let's have another drink and get something to eat?'

My head is spinning a bit and I'm not sure another drink is what I need. I realise then why the alcohol is affecting me so strongly. The only thing I've eaten all day are some sugar lumps with my coffee at The Pudding Shop restaurant.

Now it's Kati's turn to talk, but at least she changes the subject away from the war – although, not to a lighter subject.
'You remember, Alan, when we told you we were with Baadar-Meinhof? We wondered at your reaction. Are you really as easy going as you seem? Are you sympathetic perhaps? Zigi and I decided to have a private chat with you to find out more.'

She gets up and takes the empty glass out of my hand and leaves to make more drinks. As I watch the beaded dress swing slowly from side to side I feel like a secret agent in a black and white movie. All I need is the comforting feeling of a Smith & Wesson in my inside pocket to complete the picture. It's a silly thought and I dismiss it. I laugh to release the tension.

Zigi and I say nothing until she returns with the refreshed glasses.

Then I break the silence. 'I think the first thing to say is, all I know about Baader-Meinhof will take about one minute, and then you can judge for yourself. I don't believe in the integrity of the British press, and as they are my only source of information it makes everything that follows a trifle suspect.' *'Trifle suspect?' I'm even talking like a stereotypical war-time secret agent!*

'So, what *do* the British newspapers say about us?' asks Zigi eagerly.

'They say Baader and Meinhof are a couple, like Bonny and Clyde, I suppose. They rob banks and murder people for political reasons. They help German and French students riot, preach anarchy, that kind of thing.'

Kati hands me my refreshed glass. 'But you don't believe it? Or you believe some but not all?' She looks directly into my eyes. What is it you believe, Alan?'

This conversation is getting serious, and I don't want to jabber nonsense because of the whiskey. I try to concentrate on my reply.

'It's difficult to know what to believe if you don't trust your own media. George Orwell was a journalist. He wrote in depth about the iron-fist that controls everything printed in our national newspapers. I had a friend, a Canadian journalist who worked in turn for three British national papers. He told me that he never read a single contribution reported the way he wrote it. The editors always put a slant on it, left things out or put things in, to fit the agenda of the newspaper's owner. He returned to Ottawa in disgust.'

At that moment, Zigi interjects, 'But people are queuing up to live in the UK. How can it be so bad when you have people from all over the Empire wanting to live in the 'Mother Country'?'

Aware that my strings are being pulled, but unable to refuse the challenge, I pick up on the thread. 'People who migrated to Britain from the Caribbean were astonished when they saw poor white people. They couldn't believe we lived in run-down tenement blocks or swept the roads for a living. They thought all British people were wealthy. The literature was written by the upper classes to get cheap labour for their factories. The photographs they saw were all taken in the height of summer – they couldn't imagine just how cold Britain is in the winter – and nobody was going to tell them. It was only the letters coming back from the first wave of immigrants that put a brake on things.'

Putting her drink down on a small carved table next to her Kati asks, 'Yet thousands of people from the Indian sub-continent are queuing up to get into Britain. I read that in the papers. Why are they still so keen?

'It's interesting that it didn't affect the Indian people the same way. It's because the British and India social systems are so close. The Hindu 'caste system' and the 'class system' are identical in spirit. You are born into a situation and that's it, until you die.'

I ended with, 'In short, Britain is a stagnant pond with the least social mobility of any country in the world. It needs a revolution—and that's what's happening now.'

Zigi had stood up while I was talking and is now walking up and down the carpet. I can see he wants to interrupt and is forcing himself not to. Finally, he says, 'Tell us about this revolution in England, Alan?'

I describe the vibrant music scene, the festivals, the underground magazines, fringe theatres poking fun at the establishment, the drug-taking among the young, and the heightened sense of political awareness. Here I flounder a bit as I add some things without really considering their truth. Are we not just having a revolution in hedonism? Isn't my lack of political awareness the norm for working-class people like myself? My hesitation is picked up by Zigi, whose tone is taunting.

'So, how long do you think it will be before the British authorities relent under the pressure of the Rolling Stone's music or Oz magazine's cartoons, and allow you a fairer society? Can you see a day when members of your House of Lords, after listening to the latest Beatles record, declare they have far more wealth than they can possibly use and wish to share it with the workers?'

I make a futile attempt at humour. 'The Beatles aren't going to make any more records they say—but—unlikely,' I agree, noting as Zigi's passion rises, his excellent English becomes tinted with a definite German accent. He has starts to pronounce 'wealth' as 'vealth'

'So if there is nothing you can say to them that will change society - and all you do is talk – what kind of revolution is that?'

'A failed one,' Kati finished his thoughts, dejectedly.
I feel angry at being mocked and I shake my head. 'If you're saying only a violent revolution can work, then I disagree. What about Mahatma Ghandi? His non-violent struggle won India independence from the British.'

Now it's Kati's turn to get passionate. 'The Indian people had a political goal, a common need. Your 'revolution' in Britain has no goals. People want to get stoned, play music, work less for more money, have more sex with more people, but it has no real goals. Because of that, the authorities will play along, sell you hippy wigs and herbal alternatives for your hookahs; and all the time, they make it all fall to bits like a piece of rotten fruit. It isn't a revolution at all.' She sips her drink and lowers her voice. 'Just children shouting they want more sweeties, that's all.'

Feeling I'm playing the role of a naive child irritates me, but I only have myself to blame.

After we finish our drinks we go upstairs to the restaurant and bar, on the roof. As I hesitate over what to order Zigi says, 'It's our treat, order anything at all.' When the smartly dressed waiter comes over, I ask for Adana kebab on pita flatbread, with green salad, grilled tomatoes, and peppers. 'And a glass of ayran please,' I add, thinking that the yoghurt based drink may help dilute the effects of the Johnny Walker.

'I'll have the Kuzu Güveç. No starter,' Zigi says.

'For me, the vegetarian eggplant salad with fasulye beans,' Kati adds.

Our conversation on the terrace is more subdued. There are a number of guests who could overhear us.
'Let me explain the situation in Germany today, Alan.' Kati says quietly. 'After the last war ended the allies didn't know what to do. But the fools had already experienced what happens if you make a country go broke. They did it to Germany in 1918. They allowed the economy to crumble whilst demanding reparation payments from the German people, who had no ability to pay. The harsh conditions between the wars bred fascism and racial hatred, and the rise of Hitler.'

'And the Nazi Party.' I offered.

'Amongst others, yes. But not everyone on the far right would necessarily call themselves a Nazi. That's too much like declaring... what do you say about 'nailing a flag to the mast,' – something like that?

'You mean, nailing your colours to the mast?' I suggest, surprised how good Kati's English is at remembering such a little-used idiom.

'Yes, that's it.

Realising she's raising her voice Kati looks around to assure herself nobody is listening, before continuing in a lowered tone.

'Now we all like to pretend it was only a few misguided people who believed in Hitler and the Nazi party. In German schools, we're told the majority of people were against him. If you talk to older people in Köln or Dusseldorf today, you will find plenty who say, 'I wasn't fooled. I didn't follow Hitler - I knew he was no good for Germany. They are all liars. The truth is, his rallies were packed, and there were no stadiums big enough to hold the crowds. Everywhere the man went, he was besieged like royalty - no, more like Jesus. Flowers were strewn in his path by schoolchildren.'

So far, I haven't really learnt much I don't already know, but it's a joy to see Kati talking with real emotion and commitment. She reminds me of a tigress, capable of long periods of inactivity, but then ferocious and direct when provoked.

'All the banks were controlled by Jews before the war. Hitler sent them to the concentration camps and gave the banks to Nazi backers in the establishment. Our banks became unofficial hiding places for much of the loot 'liberated' from other countries. You had bankers hiding Nazi loot in the German banks where there was no official record of that wealth being there at all. After the war, they used it to buy vast amounts of land and property for themselves both in Germany and South America, even as the German people starved.'

I interrupt. 'Surely after the war, there were a number of war crimes trials. Didn't this all come out?'

'Of course, but the Americans and British are not bothered by corruption at high levels, it's like expecting a burglar to be offended by a shoplifter. They didn't know what else to do but return everything to normal, and as fast as possible. Normal, wasn't what the German people needed. They had suffered badly but The Allies weren't interested in social justice, only in returning the status quo. They hoped to prevent another cycle of unrest from fuelling further conflict. The poor could carry on eating dogs as far as they were concerned. Rich bankers from America colluded with rich bankers in Germany to establish security for the elite – and allowed them to keep their plunder.'

The waiter comes with our drinks and Kati pauses until he leaves. 'We are going to bring this situation to the attention of the public. For us, this is part of our goal. How can we live in a country when all the wealth of the people is still in the hands of Nazi's?'

Sipping my cool ayran, I try to take this in. This is something I haven't any previous idea of. I know that famous Nazi scientists like Von Braun had been given well-paid jobs in America. That seemed strange to me when I first heard about it, but this was in a different league. And it sounded very plausible.

Now Zigi takes up the story. 'Alan, perhaps you can see why your hippy 'revolution' with long hair, water pipes and rock and roll isn't quite what we need in Germany? Our police are armed, unlike yours. We have to be more militant, and use whatever tactics we can to change the status quo.'

'Like robbing banks?' I suggest.

Zigi nods. 'There will be more. We're growing fast and a lot of people are joining us from both inside and outside Germany. Who knows, perhaps one day we'll wake up the stoned hippies in England and America and get them to see what's really happening?'

We spend the rest of the evening eating and drinking but, thankfully talking about lighter topics. I learn that they both play tennis to a high standard and that Zigi hopes to become a professional one day. It's in the early hours of the morning I stagger back to Hotel Turk. My mind troubled and whirling, I fall asleep and lie unconscious until mid-day.

Chapter 51. The joy of Chris & Liam

Once again, I'm sipping on my single cup of coffee in The Pudding Shop. Come 6:30 nobody has approached, so I decide to find a cheaper restaurant to eat at and try again tomorrow. Making my way up Divan Yolu, I head north towards some of the smaller streets away from the tourist attractions, and find a place where ordinary working Turks eat.

In a dark candle lit place full of local people, I order rice and chicken and sit in thought to consider the options. This is Wednesday night and there are no confirmed passengers yet except Zigi, Kati, and perhaps Jon. There still remains the possibility of selling the Yellow Bus and hitching home.

The Yellow Bus looks like a beaten up piece of paint-streaked junk. The driver's door is bent out at a severe angle from the middle and lets rain in over the driver's right side. It blows out clouds of smoke on starting. The handbrake doesn't work and the electrics are a mess. Luckily, there's no vehicle fitness test in Afghanistan – at least not one I'm aware of, so I assume it's legal to drive, but I know I won't get much for it.

If I do manage to sell it I'll need to buy a coat of some sort, maybe a sleeping bag as well, for the nights are getting chilly. Another possibility is to fly home. That would require me to get to the British Embassy, declare myself destitute and ask for repatriation; it's not something I want to do as long as Yellow Bus can run. My sense of pride tells me there's still a chance of making it back under our own steam.

The next evening, back at The Pudding Shop, I buy my large coffee and look for a place in the garden to sit. As I head towards a vacant seat, a slightly built man in his early twenties and dressed in a light blue cowboy shirt stops me.

'Are you Alan?' he asks. He sounds like a New Yorker, as far as I can guess.

He invites me to join him and guides me towards a table inside. There sits a large bear-shaped man wearing a thick roll neck sweater.

This man looks a little older, perhaps in his early thirties, and has eaten nothing but pies all his life. As I get close he stands up, towering over me, and holds out a large hand. Mine feels like a child's in his as I shake it. Although he is built like a bear, it's an overweight teddy-bear he puts me in mind of rather than the menacing black grizzly version.

Everything about him is large. His face is heavily featured for nature has painted him with a generous brush. His small eyes disappear when he smiles.

His voice is higher than I expect 'Nice to meet you Alan. I'm Christopher and this is Liam.' No booming voice rumbles from this cavernous chest; it comes high pitched, but with a friendly tone to it.

'Do sit down. We saw your card this morning. We're hoping to join you on Friday. We're heading for London. Do you have room for two small ones?' He chuckles gleefully at the reference to his own size and his eyes disappear again.

Liam, keeps his cowboy hat on. He reminds me of the lead singer of The Who, Roger Daltrey, slim with curly hair down to his shoulders and a blue-eyed innocent expression. Noticing his beautiful pair of Afghan carpet-boots I remember how I'd promised myself a pair; that was before Phil had taken off with our money.

Christopher is exactly the opposite of Liam in every way. He has short black hair growing in tiny curls across his head as if drawn on with a permanent marker. He has no neck, so his extremely large head rests squarely on his wide shoulders. As I sit down I wonder how it's possible for him to look around. I'm musing on this when I realise I was expected to make a reply. 'Oh, yes, I have room enough - happy to take you two guys with me. Where are you two from Christopher?'

'Please - call me Chris. Liam and I are both from Coney Island. We're practically neighbours; known each other for years.'

'I've heard of Coney Island, maybe from the movies, but I don't have any idea where it is.'

Liam places it for me. 'You've heard of Brooklyn? Coney Island is in the south part of Brooklyn. It's not really an Island. It's what they call a peninsula.'

'When are you leaving?' he adds.

'Hopefully tomorrow at 2pm from where I'm staying - Hotel Turk — that's just around the corner. All I need is one more passenger, then I'm viable, and I might have that passenger anyway. There's an American guy called Jon I bought here from Afghanistan. He might come on to London, but he hasn't contacted me yet.'

'Running from the draft, this Jon?' asks Chris with a knowing smile.

'I never asked him, to be honest.'

'Probably,' he continues,' seems like every American you meet on the road nowadays is figuring on how to keep away from home for as long as this war lasts.'

'Seems sensible to me,' I reply. 'What do you two do back home?'

It's Chris who does most of the talking for both of them. 'Liam's a silk screen printer. Not quite Andy Warhol yet, but he has done an advert for Hershey, so he's getting there. As for me I'm a catwalk model,' he laughs at his own joke and we join in. 'No, of course not, 'I do a bit of extra work on films. When they want someone big I'm one of their first choices. I've been in a lot of films but I doubt if any of them have crossed the Atlantic so you probably wouldn't have seen me.' Suddenly, he pulls a stern face and looks quite gangster-like. 'With a bit of makeup, a good camera angle and the right clothes I can look very menacing. Usually I play the heavy bodyguard type, unfortunately without any lines most of the time. Of course, in the film business its lines that make the money,' he sighs.

Liam laughs. 'C'mon Chris. They would have to dub your voice.'

Chris's eyes disappear again as he grins then shakes a huge playful fist at his friend. 'Shut up you'. Then he looks at me and adds humorously, but he's right of course.'

The Yellow Bus

I spend all my time up to my 6.30 deadline sitting and chatting with these guys. I figure if someone wants to find me they will, but I keep an eye out for Jon all the time. His money would make things a little easier.

Come Friday, Chris, Liam, Zigi, and Kati are all sitting with their belongings on the wooden street benches near where the Yellow Bus is parked. With only four of us we don't need to stow the luggage on the roof, so throw it inside.

After sitting for three days, the Yellow Bus is reluctant to get going. *Maybe I'd left a light on and drained the battery?* I try it again. The motor heaves sluggishly but doesn't catch. Not an auspicious start. I slide across from the driver's seat and get out to investigate. I'm contemplating asking my passengers for a push start when a cheerful Australian voice comes from behind me.

'Need a jump start, matey?'

I turn to see a familiar face. I had run into it before, both in Germany and Afghanistan. It's Bruce leaning out his window, parked right behind me in his 'Sundowners' bus'.

'Brucy, good to see you cobber.' I try to mimic his accent. 'You are the right man at the right time, believe me.'

With perfect efficiency Bruce pulls up his Sundowners bus alongside us and quickly connects his jump leads. Yellow Bus starts first time and we both laugh at the billows of smoke it throws out. I thank him profusely. He wishes us Bon Voyage and I sit for a few seconds appreciating the camaraderie travelling brings - before pulling away.

I continue looking out for Jon in case he makes it at the last minute, but he doesn't show. Perhaps he's decided to get a flight back to London after all. We pull away from The Turk Hotel, now with Zigi in the passenger seat, Kati seated behind him and Chris and Liam sitting behind me.

It's a pity Jon didn't make it. He's an easy person to travel with. I've even forgiven him for having a 'magic' credit card, although why I feel I have to forgive him for that I'm not sure. When I think about it I realise I would do the same in his position; travel rough and keep quiet about having access to money. In any place in the world telling people you can get large amounts of cash only puts you in danger. It's not smart to broadcast such a thing. I reluctantly accept my initial confused feelings towards him is just plain envy.

With the distorted music tapes thankfully gone, and many of the others having been reclaimed by their original owners, our music library is down to four tapes no-one else wants. There's Simon and Garfunkel's soundtrack from 'The Graduate', 'The Best of Buffalo Springfield', 'Live Cream' and 'Nashville Skyline' from Dylan. I put on The Graduate tape, as it seems to be the only one that will lift our spirits, even though it's a bit cheesy, and we set off on the long ride home.

As we travel back I realise the battery on the bus is dying. It will start if the engine's hot but if it's left to cool down then it needs either a jump start or a push. Most of the time I park on a hill and let it roll to get up enough speed to start. The passengers are all good natured about it, and Chris's bulk comes in handy on the odd occasion there's no hill around. Although no athlete, he has the natural strength most big people have.

Chris assumes the role of tea maker now, but demands we stop as soon as possible for a jar of coffee.

'American people only drink tea to appear sophisticated,' he says. 'We all know coffee's absolutely essential for ever true American.'

He has to make do with 'instant' owing to our catering restrictions. At one stop Chris demonstrates to us how to roll a cigarette with one hand. He opens a pack of tobacco and sits on the back of the bus, which has both doors open, (the springs depress a good six inches) and we all stand around him and watch him do it. The dexterity of his sausage-like fingers are astonishing to watch.

'I learnt to do this for a part in a movie but when it was released they'd edited me completely out of it,' he chuckles. 'I still got paid though.'

He puts the cigarette between his lips and lights it. 'It's not as impressive as the way Prince Randian used to do it. He was an actor born without arms or legs and still rolled his own cigs. Amazing man. Could speak English, German and French in addition to his native language Hindi. He got married and fathered four children and paid for their education with money made from 'freak shows' and movies.' Chris, the natural story-teller, tells us the story of one of Prince Randian's films in some detail and we are all spellbound.

With his amazing images still fresh in our minds we collect our bits and pieces and climb back into the bus to set off. With the handbrake let off the Yellow Bus rolls, slowly at first, then faster, down the slight incline. At about fifteen miles per hour I let the clutch up, there's a slight hesitation then the engine rattles into life.

There's little conversation generally but after a half hour or so Kati, in her usual direct way, asks Chris,' Are you and Liam dodging the draft?'

Chris looks up from his tea making and shakes his head. 'Too old for that my dear. They sacrifice the young ones first. Liam and I would be useless in a war. I'm afraid we're too intelligent to believe those lies they feed the kids with. 'My country right or wrong' and that kind of thing. Not my style. My country right……..but not wrong. To fight when you know your country is wrong is the lowest form of stupidity… or should that be the highest?'

He passes a freshly made mug of tea to Kati. 'You don't take sugar do you?' Kati shakes her head. Chris continues, 'I guarantee Vietnam will become a holiday resort for American families within twenty years. American boys will fall in love with Vietnamese girls and produce scores of little 'Amerinese' or 'Vietrican' babies and we will all kiss and make up. The only people who'll suffer will be the fools who encouraged their kids to die for what – absolutely nothing.'

Nobody says a word. Chris keeps pouring the tea but the feeling of anger has obviously not left him. 'I imagine American corporations are already buying large chunks of land in Vietnam while it's so cheap; preparing to use inexpensive labour to make white goods for the markets back home.'

It's the first time I've heard Chris speak without humour in his voice and the intensity of his feelings are obvious. I fear Kati will be drawn into a political argument but once again underestimate her complete will in controlling her emotions. She doesn't respond, and I'm thankful; having people argue about politics or religion – well, anything really - is very distracting when you're driving.

It's Liam who speaks, sensitive to Chris's mood. 'Tell 'em about the guy we met from Seattle, Chris.'

Chris passes a mug to Zigi to pass on to me, after having asked about sugar and seen me shake my head.

He thinks for a few moments searching for the memory, then it comes back to him. 'Oh yes. That was repulsive. No I don't want to talk about it – I don't even want to think about it. What an awful guy.'

There is a short silence, our curiosity now stirred. We're all beginning to sense Chris is too much of an entertainer not to tell us the whole story. Sure enough, 'All right, I'll tell you,' he exclaims, as if we'd been urging him desperately. 'Liam and I were in – where were we Liam?'

'Greenwich.'

'That's right. Liam and I were in Greenwich seeing some friends. One night we ran into this drunk fella from Seattle, and he started trying to impress us with some crazy story. He said his name was Ivan…'

'Marvin,' corrected Liam.

'That's right - Marvin. Well, he told us he had a business going with the medical staff of the military who brought body bags back from the war with the dead in them; all totally legal, he claimed. He told us they remove all of the undamaged major organs from the bodies and Marvin then buys them on behalf of his 'clients' to pass on for transplants and experiments.'

'A modern day Burke and Hare,' I comment. The silence that follows demonstrates nobody knows who they are, so I just say, 'Carry on Chris.'

I can see him in the rear view mirror as he screws his face up. 'It's too repulsive to talk about.' But talk about it he does.

'This Marvin character told us he exported organs all over the world for medical research - no questions asked. They give them official clearance at borders so as not to delay them. It seems unbelievable, but they substitute bits of some bodies into others, just to make the bodies look alright, I suppose, well the ones that are meant to be in one piece. It also makes sure they are about the right weight when their coffin's carried; a man must feel quite light without all their major organs in them and…...'

Chris then does something which we later learn is a common experience for his audiences; he interrupts himself.

'Oh, that reminds me about a story of a burial in Haiti. When they carry the coffin in and someone notices fresh blood is dripping from it. They force the undertaker to open it and in it they find….....' He pauses for effect here, and is obviously not going to continue without spectator encouragement.

'What?' Asks Zigi, on our behalf. Chris, obviously delighted at being centre stage, responds like a magician revealing a trick.

'A dead body. In fact it's the proper dead body they were burying that day; but as he was supposed to have died three days before, there shouldn't have been any blood. The family go mad and demand the coffin's opened there and then. The undertaker tries to run but family relatives grab him and hold him until the police arrive. What'd happened, as the undertaker confesses later, was he'd been paid for both the coffin and the funeral by the family and used the money to settle some debts. The body had been stored in a cool place and on the morning of the funeral it was collected and the undertaker and his assistant were shocked when it suddenly sat up. This re-awakened corpse asked where he was. Apparently, he suffered from catalepsy. The undertaker, realising he would have to pay the family back their money, grabbed a knife and killed the guy. '

Chris claps his large hands together in sheer joy at a tale well told. Somehow, without warning, we are immediately transported back to the original story.

'So, think about it. All those moms and dads burying bits and pieces of a number of people and believing it to be their sons. Too horrid to think about.'

Chapter 52. The five gallon air-guitar

Travelling with Liam and Chris is a joy. Chris always takes the lead role but relies on Liam to act as his stooge, which Liam does with good humour. They're obviously very close and care greatly for each other. Liam takes a delight at feeding Chris with prompts for stories, of which there seem an inexhaustible stock. They've known each other since childhood.

The following day Liam tells us how, when he was about thirteen years old, three much older boys tried to mug him. They set upon him down a small street, where few pedestrians were likely to witness anything.

'They'd already given me a few licks,' Liam tells us, 'when Chris suddenly appears out of nowhere. I'd only known him to say hello, so it wasn't like we were best friends or anything. These boys saw him and stopped beating me for a few seconds. He was amazing! I'll never forget how he walked really slowly and menacingly towards them and drew himself to his full size, which even at his young age was formidable. He said in a strong confident voice, 'Leave the boy alone'. I remember - they swore at him and told him to mind his own business, but Chris just pulled those large hands from his jacket pockets and held them in fists by each side of him. They looked like a couple of clubs the way he held them. All the time he was walking slowly towards them. The three boys stared at him for a while and decided to retreat.'

'It was just wonderful; the way Chris just stared them down and then stayed rooted to the spot like a statue until the boys ran away. They were still swearing and jeering but they kept on running down the street until they'd disappeared.' Liam laughed and looked at Chris, who was laughing at the memory with him.

'Do you remember what I said after those kids ran off, Liam?' He chuckled.

'I remember you were shaking like a leaf when you helped me up. You said, 'God help us, I've never been so frightened in all my life.'

We all laughed uproariously.

But Liam wasn't finished yet. 'And then, you said you had no idea what you would have done if they hadn't run away - and would probably have just stood there and wet yourself.' By this time tears of laughter were welling in Chris's eyes.

Over the following days, we travel through Greece and into Yugoslavia without any issues, Chris, with the support of Liam, keeps us entertained with stories and anecdotes from his own experiences in the acting world - plus a plethora of stories from Hollywood, or 'Tinsel Town' as he calls it. He professes to know who's straight, who's gay or bisexual in the acting world: who's going out with who in secret: who's had an abortion: who the father of so and so's child is: who has had plastic surgery etc. etc. The only difficulty in being in Chris's audience is how easily he's distracted from one story to the next. Everything from one story reminds him of another, even funnier one, and you rarely get to hear the end of any of them unless Liam intervenes to keeps him on track with a gentle verbal nudge.

The Yellow Bus

We are listening to one of his Tinsel Town stories, when the Yellow Bus started to steam up. The top water hose has split and starts to release the water from the radiator at a steady stream making the engine overheat. We stop at a shared water tap near a war memorial in the centre of a village with an unpronounceable name, and fill one of the empty jerry cans.

To keep the radiator topped up Chris volunteers to sit in the passenger seat and pour water from the heavy can into the radiator while we drive to the next town to get a repair. It isn't an ideal situation because of the noise, smoke and steam coming from the engine when the cover's removed. It's not helped by Chris deciding now to recall the Isle of Wight festival he and Liam had been to last time they'd been in England, a couple of years back.

'It was better than Woodstock – five hundred thousand people for sure. The Stones were fantastic.' At this point he tries to strum our huge five-gallon jerry can and imitate the sound of Keith Richards playing a riff from Jumping Jack Flash on electric guitar.'

The cap isn't closed and water misses the radiator completely and pours liberally over the electrics of our engine bringing us to a shuddering halt.

'Oops,' Chris exclaims. 'Erm, sorry about that everyone.'

We all push the bus a hundred yards to the next lay-by and I take off the distributor cap and put it in the sun to dry out. We wander up and down the deserted A road looking at the scenery and smoking cigarettes until it's dried out enough for us to get going again. This time it takes hefty push to start it.

After half an hour I pull up at a shop near Skopje and buy a piece of hose. We manage to butcher it into shape to fit. It works a treat and we're able to continue with the engine cover back on. It also frees Chris up to strum his air guitar with more gusto, whilst continuing to tell us all about great rock 'n Roll Festivals he's been to.

The day rolls by. The potholed roads are as I remember them - punishing. As we enter Austria it's apparent to all of us the Yellow Bus isn't going to make it to London after all. One of the front springs has further collapsed which gives the bus a dangerous lopsided look from the front. For me the effect on the steering is dangerous as it always wants to turn right unless I pull against it.

The engine is still running too hot even in the colder weather, although we make sure the radiator is kept full by regular checks. Luckily the weather has now become poor and the cold rain deters the border guards from a closer inspection of the state of the bus. It's not running smoothly and it's difficult to stop it hopping like a rabbit when pulling away from traffic lights. As the speed goes up it improves and gets smoother but the smoke is now visible in my rear view mirror and a number of well-meaning people give us a toot on their horns and point to the back of the bus, as if we need to be told.

The following day we pull into a car park near Graz, and I call a conference.

It's a sad moment to admit defeat and I feel a little tearful when I say, 'I think we have to be realistic. The bus is dying and we need to make a decision as to whether to go on as long as possible, or should we head somewhere, where everybody can continue on their journey.' I feel compelled to add, 'I am sorry about this. I thought we could make it.'

Zigi, who has the map open in front of him, is first to reply. 'I suggest Salzburg, as it has a big main station. It looks like it's about 180 miles. It should be smooth roads all the way. But Alan, do you think Yellow Bus will make it?'

Chris, moves his considerable bulk next to Zigi, and studies the map as well.

'Salzburg isn't too bad for us. I don't pretend to know much about cars and stuff, but I would say this baby of ours is about to burst, and it may be better to abandon ship sooner rather than later. It might be nasty to come to a grinding halt in the middle of one of these big highways.'

'Show of hands for Salzburg then?' I ask. It's unanimous.

The engine which I have left running now stops, as if it's been listening and is showing its resentment. Luckily, as the rain is still coming down strongly, it starts immediately without a push.

Zigi, who has mastered the art of the windscreen wiper, rhythmically tugs at his end of the string as we pull out onto the road again for the last leg of the journey.

The Yellow Bus seems to know we are planning its demise and the intermittency of the engine performance increases. Sometimes, to my embarrassment, it lets out a large bang from the exhaust as if it's clearing its throat, but after that it runs okay for the next few miles.

It's about eight o'clock in the evening when we pull up outside Salzburg railway station. I'm not impressed much by its architecture. I'd imagined a vast gothic construction like St Pancras in London, but perhaps, was really just looking for a symbol to remember the end of the journey with.

I shake the big bear's hand and give him a hug but it's like trying throwing your arms around a Redwood tree. I shake hands with Liam and Zigi and hug them, then I kiss Kati and take one more look into those cat-like eyes of hers. She looks into my eyes and smiles a smile that feels so intimate it takes my breath away.

We all stand about outside the station not wanting to do or say anything much, until eventually Chris says, 'Well, good luck Alan. I guess we better see what time the trains are.' They both pick up their bags and wander off with a final wave.

'Thank you for everything Alan,' says Zigi. 'Maybe we'll be in the papers one day. Don't forget us.'

'I really hope you aren't Zigi. The best of luck to both of you,' I reply sincerely.

They go to walk away before Zigi remembers something and comes back. 'If you can get our flag back home it would be good. It means something to both of us I think, yes?'

I smile. 'You bet.'

Then the two of them walk off merging easily into the crowd, as casually as if they are a couple of young students going home after a day of studying.

I feel so emotional, all I can do is stand and watch the milling crowds for a while. I wipe away the tears and feel a little silly standing there long after they have all disappeared into the busy terminal. It's a chilly evening and after a few minutes decide to travel away from the centre to find a cheap café for a coffee. Jumping into the bus, I try starting the engine but it just gives a click, and then nothing. Damn! It's on a forbidden zone for parking too! By chance, she's parked outside a pricey-looking café I would never have gone in to normally. Cafes near main stations are always expensive; this time I don't care, and go in.

Chapter 53. A reasonable swap

Sitting by the window in this dark café with its traditional heavily carved wooden décor, I study the railway crowds through the glass to see if any of my passengers come out again. A waitress takes my order for a coffee and apple strudel, and parts me from a considerable amount of the cash I have left.

Then I mindlessly watch the evening traffic. I had thought if the bus started I would just keep going for as long as I could. This now changed things. Could I get a jump start from someone? A garage would charge. I didn't speak the language. I sipped my coffee slowly.

In my time hitch hiking, I had learnt the skill of making a coffee last all night. *Hopefully I won't need that skill tonight*, I thought. But it's cold. If I sleep in the bus I'll probably get towed away before morning. I certainly don't have the money spare for a hotel in a big European city like Salzburg.

An hour later, I still hadn't formulated a plan. Then a group of ten or so well-groomed young people come flooding merrily into the place and sit at some other tables by the window. When those tables overflow some of them ask if they could share my table. I nod. They order bottles of beer and chat eagerly. There's a lot of laughter and friendly joke playing, so I guessed they're all good friends.

One young man says something to me, but I shrug my shoulders and say, 'I'm sorry, I don't speak anything but English.'

The Yellow Bus

This guy has a face that looks like the pictures I'd seen of D H Lawrence, handsome and intellectual. 'That's okay, I speak English.' He smiles and puts out his hand. I shake it and ask what the special occasion's for.

'It's Helga's birthday,' he says, pointing over at a laughing brunette at the centre of another table. At hearing her name Helga looks over at us. I raise my cup and shout over the noise, 'Happy Birthday Helga.' She laughs and raises her bottle.

My new companion introduces himself as Martin and tells me he's an engineering student. I tell him my name is Alan.

'So Alan, what do you do?' he asked.

Nodding towards the Yellow Bus I say, 'I drive that - when the bugger will start.'

'I saw it. I saw it when I came in. You mean this is your bus,' he asks excitedly.

He shouts over the din for quiet and then tells everyone I am the owner of the overland bus standing outside.

There's a chorus of noise as a response, some of it in English. Helga stands up and leads a toast; bottles clink and are drunk, then banged onto the table. Suddenly from being a lonely and slightly depressed man, I become a celebrity. Everyone wants to know about our journey, and before I know it beers are appearing in front of me, and I am being transported into a pleasant blurred state.

At some point, Martin leans over to me and says seriously, 'Alan, I want to buy your bus from you,' I laugh. 'Martin, I wouldn't sell you that bus, because there is not a single part that isn't worn out. The only things still working are the light bulbs, and then not all of them.'

'Tell me a price Alan, he insists, as he pushes another beer in my direction.

I think for a moment. 'Okay Martin. You can have the bus in exchange for a suitcase, a jacket and a sleeping bag.'

'What? I didn't hear you,' he moves a bit closer.

'I said, you can have the bus in exchange for a suitcase, a jacket, you know – a coat - and a sleeping bag.'

'A suitcase, a coat and a sleeping bag?' he says it with a smile, as if I'm slightly deranged.
I nod in agreement.

With an effort he stands up and starts to make his way out, and then turns and shouts loudly to me, 'Wait here. I shall be back.'

I get into a few conversations with some of the others around the table. Once again, I'm struck by how many speak perfect English, and reflect on how few English people ever seem to master a foreign language. They're all students at Salzburg University, but from a number of different disciplines. Some of them are studying Performance Art, and I'm watching a really good mime being enacted, when Martin returns. In his hands he carries a worn leather suitcase. He manages to regain the seat next to me and puts the case on the table. He flicks the two catches, which spring back. Inside is a sleeping bag and a green jacket.

'The case is very old but strong, the sleeping bag is my own and only used a few times, for parties, never outside, and the coat – it's the only one I can spare. Try it on.'

To claps of appreciation, I model the student style corduroy jacket. It isn't going to be very warm, but it's definitely an improvement over the thin cotton shirt I have on at the moment. I wish I'd asked for a scarf and gloves as well, but I'm happy with what he has brought.

With great ceremony and applause from everyone I hand the ignition keys over to Martin, whilst warning him the rear doors don't lock and never had; and that he needs to get a jump start before it will go anywhere. Then after refusing requests to stay and join their party, I wish them goodnight and walk out the door.

Stopping only long enough to gather a couple of remaining items from her, I pat the Yellow Bus on the bonnet and with a heavy heart say, 'Thanks girl,' and start walking to find the road heading for Germany. I regret having to leave the German flag behind but figure it'll be a nice surprise for Martin when he see it. It's a clear and drying night and I ask a couple of people for directions. I find myself at a roundabout with a sign 'Deutschland 6km 'on it and decide to walk it.

Chapter 54. Not the hand of friendship

It's at the border of Germany, whilst getting my passport checked, and the inevitable search is being carried out, my eyes stray to a large notice board next to the kiosk. There's a large 'Wanted' poster and underneath the words 'Baadar-Meinhof'. Under that there's a number of black and white photographs. And there they are; Zigi and Kati looking out at me. They appear strangely menacing, not like the people I had been so close to at all. But it's them all right. If I had any doubts about them being genuine, they evaporated at that moment.

I am given a thorough going over as my appearance is rather odd, with my long hair and beard, corduroy student jacket, oil stained jeans and an ancient leather suitcase which looks as if it's been looted at some point during the First World War.

Standing just inside the German border I make myself visible to drivers by the harsh light the border lamps throw out. It feels cold now I'm not walking, and the beer is wearing off. Pulling my new jacket as tightly around me as I can, I stick out a thumb and wait. After a while I start hopping from foot to foot to generate some heat, but still nobody stops. Then, just as I'm starting to curse the entire nation, a large Mann truck slows. It has Turkish number plates and the passenger is leaning out of the high cab, shouting something and waving for me to come on.

Excellent!

I run as fast as I can with the awkward suitcase banging into my knees. The truck stops and the man calls something I can't understand, but offers to shake my hand.

. As soon as he has my hand, he alters his grip and grabs me around the wrist; at the same time he signals to the driver, who lets in the clutch and accelerates. My suitcase goes flying as I try not to lose my balance. Now I'm running and trying to pull away from his vice-like grip. The front wheel's perilously close and I try to stay away from the large protruding bolts threatening to tear into me. I'm having difficulty staying on my feet, but know I daren't fall; at the same time I know I can't run much faster, or for much longer. I hear the passenger laughing and the driver shouting something back to him, but I don't look up as I need all my strength and concentration to prevent myself going sideways under the wheel. There's a large step to help passengers climb into the cab in front of me, but try as I can I can't get to it.

Seconds before I'm about to give myself up for dead, because by then I am convinced these guys really are trying to kill me, the grip releases on my wrist and I am flung away from the truck where I hit the asphalt and roll three or four times, trying all the time to protect my head. The brightly lit truck roars off into the night and I can hear the echo of laughter from it as it disappears.

Checking myself out I find no major injuries, just a few cuts and bruises and a very frayed ego. On returning to where it all started I find the suitcase has burst open and my things are scattered about, but there's nothing in it I feel precious about. The inevitable questions follow that can never bring sensible answers to them, like 'How can people be so dumb? What kind of people are they who get pleasure doing stuff like that?' This is followed by musing on how ridiculous it is to say you love this country, or that country, when every country has total arseholes like them; just as every country has amazingly good people. Turkey just went a notch down in my top ten places.

Chapter 55. Truck race with caravans

I decide to find a place to sleep, if I can. In a way I wish I hadn't drunk so many bottles of beer with the students – it only makes you feel colder to be a little drunk. As I walk away from the lights of the border post, I stick my thumb out without any real belief it will lead to anything. However I'm wrong. A long truck carrying three caravans on the back stops. This time there's no passenger offering me a handshake, but I still approach with caution.

'Wohin gehst du?' asks the driver.

'England,' I reply, guessing he's asking me my destination.

'English? You are English?' I hope being English isn't a bad thing in his eyes and say yes.

'Come in. Ja, I am going to Wiesbaden – you know Wiesbaden?

I climb in the warm cab and shiver.

I think, 'No, I've never heard of it but I don't care because I'm freezing. Is it even in the right direction?'

He shows me where we are on a map and points to Wiesbaden. What a change of circumstance! From a death defying event to an offer of a trip over half the distance to my home.

'Good Ja?,' he smiles.

'Bloody brilliant,' I agree.

He stows my suitcase behind us, then he sees the blood on my hands and face from where I had tried to protect myself. Without asking questions, he pulls out a first aid kit from a shelf over the driver's side, and passes it to me. 'Open it' I do what he tells me. 'Antiseptikum.' He points to the antiseptic pads. 'Understand?'

'Yes, I understand.'

As I open some of the cleaners, and start to wipe at the cuts, he urges me to put some plasters on. While I do this he pulls the huge truck off onto the quiet roadway. After a minute or so, he speaks.

'My name is Walmond,' he says, as he changes into what I count to be the eighth gear of the truck. 'I have been to pick up some caravans in Liezen, where they are made, to deliver to Wiesbaden, where my company has its headquarters. I think this is a good day for you, yes?'

I hold my damaged hands up, 'Good and bad,' I grin.

For the next hour or so we chat easily about our families, work and football, of which I know nothing and Walmond knows everything. Walmond is in his early fifties, has a wife of twenty four years old and four children, which include identical twins – 'Identisch. Absolut identisch.' He says with an enthusiastic laugh. 'Absolut identisch!'

He lives a half an hour's drive from the company. I confess my ignorance of football and he decides to teach me. I learn, without doubt, Germany has the greatest football team in the world; that, although they only managed third place in the last world cup, it was because of injuries. He then patiently explains how they'd been robbed in 1966 when a blind referee gave the win to a poor English team over a superb German one. He is seeing whether I'm going to have a friendly argument, but I'm really too ignorant to do so. He tells me he enjoys the freedom of driving and would hate to work in an office. Business is good as more people are taking caravan holidays, so he's not worried about his future. I offer him a cigarette but he refuses.

'Too many drivers die young from smoking and bad food, he declares, then explains. 'We work hard but do no exercise. I prefer to see my children grow up.'

Unlike many people who give you a lift, conversation with Walmond is easy and unforced. The silences are unstrained and relaxed. Suddenly I jump as a loud blast from a truck horn rents the air. Another truck pulls alongside and the driver is tugging at the rope operating the horn in the same way steam-engine drivers of old used to. He looks like a painting of Casey Jones. I'm pleased to see Walmond is smiling and waving at the other driver, allowing him to pass. It's a near identical truck to the one we're in, with the same cargo.

'That is Rolf, and behind us there is Mervin.'

'All the same company?'

'Yes, all the same company. We deliver nine caravans.'

And so, the slowest race in the world begins.

It turns out the three trucks are made by three different companies. They all have similar top speeds within five miles per hour or so, but one is fractionally better going up inclines, whilst another is fractionally better at coming down. The other will take it on the flat – if it's long enough. We're in the one with a little bit of extra top speed on a long stretch, so I guess Rolf has crept up unseen whilst Walmond is busy talking to me.

Flat out none of them can top sixty miles per hour, but it's hilarious the way they try to overtake each other, grimacing and brandishing their fists at each other, while doing it. On a hill Mervin is able to pull alongside but unless the hill is a long one he falls back again as it levels out. On the straight our truck pulls ahead but it takes about five miles to do so. Then Rolf flashes his lights to show it's safe for us to pull back into the slow lane. All the time they hoot their horns at each other. It passes the time that would otherwise be boring and it keeps them awake.

The only down side is when there's only two lanes and one truck tries to overtake another. Cars behind might have to wait ten to fifteen minutes depending on what the road conditions are like, before the superiority of one or other truck would let it get to the front. Some may think it irresponsible behaviour, but they are very professional drivers, and at no time did any of them do anything unsafe.

Eventually, about three am, they all pull into a truck park for the night. Climbing into his bunk-bed Walmond tells me to put my sleeping bag across the front seats and sleep there. It is a welcome gesture as I am mentally preparing myself to decamp outside. I sleep like a dead thing and am woken by the noise of Walmond's electric razor.

'Sleep well?' he asks.

'Wunderbar ,' I reply in schoolboy German.

We go into a transport café where I finally get to meet our competitors, Rolf and Mervin. Rolf is the older one, in his sixties with a rotund belly and double chins. *He's not following Walmond's health plan,*' I think. Mervin, twenty years younger is much fitter looking. He wears a designer stubble and a new pair of white Nike trainers.

Going by the hand gestures and the modelling on the table, with salt and pepper pots to represent their trucks, they are enjoying the run and laugh a lot. After a good breakfast of pancakes we get going again. Within minutes the race resumes and never ceases, except for a couple of refreshment breaks, until we arrive in the dead of the following night, in Wiesbaden.

Once again, it's in the early hours of the morning when we pull into the large car park outside of Henckleverks, the headquarters of their company. Parking the three long vehicles next to each other the drivers kill their engines and climb out of their cabs. Walmond collects some personal possessions and walks with them to a black Mercedes car, whilst I pack my few bits and pieces in the suitcase and put my jacket on. The three drivers talk amongst themselves for a few minutes, then Walmond comes back over to me.

'Alan, It is my wife's birthday tomorrow, otherwise I would invite you home.'

'No, no, please it isn't necessary. You have taken me a long way towards my destination…'

He holds his hand up to stop my protestations. 'So Rolf is going to put you up tonight. He lives a lot closer than I do. He will be able to put you on the right road for England tomorrow.'

It turns out Rolf is a single man who has a flat within a few minutes' walk. It's a nice place but obviously lacking any female influence. There are posters of racing cars and their drivers on the walls. Rolf has to wash a couple of glasses to pour the inevitable beer. It's been a long day and his face looks tired and drained.

'Usually we do this trip in two days but it is Walmond's wife's birthday so we kept going,' he explains. Please, Alan, help yourself to beer or any food in the fridge. I don't want to be rude, but I'm very tired.'

He shows me where I can roll out my sleeping bag in the front room. We wish each other goodnight and he goes to his bedroom.

I finish the beer he's poured me and turn out the light. We have come over four hundred miles in one go and I'm feeling on top of the world; and so far, not a single night out in the freezing weather. An early start suits me fine and I awake refreshed, and excited to keep going.

Chapter 56. Jan the communist spy

But the next morning is just the opposite of the day before. I have a number of lifts but all short ones by local people. An old man drives an Audi up to me and drives off when he hears my English accent.

Bit by bit, I make my way slowly across Germany by a number of small hops. That night I sleep in the open, in a field near Hennef, and am lucky the rain keeps off. It's cold and dewy when I wake and my bag is wet, but otherwise I'm okay. The sleeping bag proves its worth and is much better than the cheap one I'd originally travelled with. I check the label; it's 'tog 30', the same as Mike's. *No wonder he was warm enough to strip off at night*, I thought

The rain doesn't stay away for long, for within half an hour of thumbing the drops start to fall. There's a bus shelter just a short way off, so I run for it and get in just before the heavens open and the rain pelts down. It allows me to carry on thumbing and keeps most of my body sheltered at the same time. After an hour or so, a small commercial van stops and the driver asks where I'm going.

'England,' I say.

"Koln?' asks the man.

'That suits me fine.'

This man speaks no English and I speak no German, but we still enjoy each other's company. I offer him my last cigarette, he declines and pulls out a fat cigar and offers it to me. The usual pantomime follows with me declining and him insisting; it looks like quite an expensive gift, which was confirmed when we light them. It's a good quality smoke. He reaches into his glove compartment and shows me a box with 'Romeo y Juliet' on it. I was right, they are expensive.

Somehow the 30 odd miles passes by in a flash. He drops me off at Koln Station and lets me know his destination is down the side streets somewhere. By now it starts to rain again. *If it gets too heavy I can always shelter in the station,* I think.

Standing in the drizzling rain outside of Koln Station where I've been dropped, I stick my thumb out. No more than five or six cars have passed when an elderly Skoda pulls up. After previously hitching in Germany and deciding it was one of the worst places in the world I am amazed; I've had nothing but good luck and met some really nice people. But it isn't a German who picks me up but a Czechoslovakian. He is about thirty-five, well dressed, and he speaks perfect English. He must have guessed I was English or American.

'Where are you going,' he asks.

'London - eventually,' I answer.

'Yes, I am going towards London too. Get in.'

Offering prayers of thanks to the god's under my breath, I climb in, stowing my case on the back seat.

'I don't like to go too fast,' he warns, as we chug down the road at about forty miles per hour.

'As long as we are going in the right direction,' I laugh, unable to believe my good fortune.

We introduce ourselves. He tells me his name is Jan and he comes from Prague. Then he asks me where I have been, and how come I have arrived in Koln. I briefly explained about the Yellow Bus and how I had swapped it for the suitcase. He laughs loudly and offers me a cigarette, I decline. After the cigar I feel I need to give my lungs a break.

The cheap old Skoda feels quite luxurious in comparison to the Yellow Bus; at least it's reasonable quiet and the suspension works. We get to the motorway and I expect him to accelerate, as there's no speed limits on these roads. No, he keeps it at forty miles per hour and it feels like we are standing still every time we're overtaken by one huge lorry after another. After a while I realise just how long we're going to be together if we travel at this speed.

'So Jan, what brings you to these parts and heading for London,' I ask cheerily. He looks at me out of the corner of his eye and says nothing for a while, as if deliberating on something.

'I will tell you something Alan, but you must promise not to tell anyone – ever. Do you agree?' What he says sounds faintly ridiculous, but I can tell by the sound of his voice he isn't kidding. My curiosity is now aroused and I want to hear what he has to say, so I reply, 'Sure, I promise.'

Jan draws on his cigarette a couple of times and I am wondering whether he's going to change his mind, or worse just laugh and say he'd been joking. Instead, in a confidential tone, he says, 'I am a scientist in my country. My specialist area's laser research. Czechoslovakia is at the forefront of this technology at the moment. It's very exciting. The reason I'm travelling to London is to attend a scientific conference to discuss various breakthroughs in laser technology.'

There's silence for a few minutes as Jan concentrates on overtaking a couple of vintage vehicles travelling even slower than us. Then he looks at me and laughs.

'You are wondering why a successful scientist is driving an old Skoda rather than a big BMW or Mercedes Benz I expect.'

He's spot on. It's exactly what I'm thinking. 'It does seems a bit odd I guess,' I say.

'You see – Czechoslovakia isn't in such a good state at the moment. Salaries there aren't comparable to those in the west.' He went to stub out his cigarette, but his ashtray was full to overflowing. He throws the butt into the foot well on his side.

'So what's it like living in a communist country, Jan?' I ask.

'It's shit,' he says, with some bitterness. 'Look Alan I am telling you the truth because there's no one I can talk to without fear of reprisals. It's been years since I have been able to tell anyone how I feel. There's no one I can trust.

The sincerity in his voice was unmistakable; this was no act.

'How do you know you can trust me then?' I ask.

He smiles. 'Simple, you are hitch hiking. They would never try to catch me out with something so... so random. They could have no idea whether I would pick you up or not. No, Alan, you have not been planted, that much I'm sure of.

The reasoning is sound, but I'm troubled by the thought anyone should live in a state of full alert like this.

'Have you been to England before, Jan?'

'Yes, once. I have a sister living in Croydon. Do you know Croydon?'

'Just down the road from where I live in Thornton Heath.'

'I thought you were going to London, Alan?'

I laugh. 'I always say I come from London when I travel. Who's heard of Thornton Heath?'

'That's good, excellent. I do the same. I can drive you to your house. Would that be good?'

'That would be brilliant Jan, thanks. But you were telling me about your sister.'

'"Yes, you're right I was. I last saw her two years ago when I stayed with her and Gregory, her husband. It was only for a few days last time.'

'And how long are you staying this time?'

'One week, but of course they allow one day travelling each way.'

'Sounds to me like they can't afford for you to be away for any length of time. Are you that important?'

He shakes his head. Then his voice takes on a more serious tone.

'Every road I take's been mapped out for me by the authorities. Every mark I spend has been calculated in advance; nothing's been left to chance. My timetable's exact and I am expected to follow it precisely. I may be followed the whole journey or perhaps just a part of it – I just don't know.'

It feels altogether odd to hear this coming from a man who we, in the west, would have the greatest respect for. 'Forgive me Jan, but that sounds a little paranoid. Are you a political activist or something? It sounds like you have upset the authorities somehow.'

Another cigarette is lit and Jan draws the smoke in heavily. He's not just an occasional smoker. *This man certainly needs his nicotine.*

'In Czechoslovakia today everyone is 'political' as you call it; you have to be, to survive. Perhaps you'd be surprised if I told you I'm an active member of the communist party – even though I hate the communist party.'

'That's weird. How does that work?'

'You have to belong to the communist party if you want your children to go to school and you want a job. Of course, if you want your children to go to a 'good' school or you want a 'good' job - maybe get promotion, then you need to be more than just a member of the party, you need to be 'active' in the party. You have to become their ears and eyes; report any suspicions you have that may be against their interests…,' his voice trailed away into silence.

'What about non-communists.'

'Nobody will talk to them, give them work or help them in any way. They are frozen out of society until they change their ways. Believe me unless you want to commit suicide you make an effort to let everyone you know how good you think the party is, and how decadent and controlled the people in the west are, compared to us.' His voice had taken on a tone of anger now. 'That's why it's dangerous for them to let people like me out of the country, of course.'

'Because you will go back and let people know it's just propaganda, and it's much better in the west than they're being told?'

'Of course. I become a dangerous element to them just by travelling. But this conference is too important to us to ignore. They have no choice.'

We sit for a while in silence. I am trying to put myself in Jan's shoes. What would I do? Here I am, unemployed, broke, no qualifications or discernible talent, but feeling I wouldn't want to change places with this young successful scientist for all the tea in china. It's a strange feeling for someone so well-versed in envy.

'I can understand with colleagues you may need to be careful, but in private, Jan you can talk openly with your own friends and family. You can give each other support surely?'

'Colleagues? – no. Friends? – no. Family? – it depends. To be reported for anti-communist behaviour is a serious affair. You could lose everything. You must remember Alan, they control everything, absolutely everything. Maybe with your own mother or father or someone very close to you, you could share your feelings; someone you grew up with so closely you trust them with your life – otherwise, you keep your opinions to yourself.'

Jan concentrated on his driving for a while. I am trying to understand how people could allow their lives to get into such a mess that all normal freedoms are curtailed. Also, my uninformed and budding socialist tendencies are offended by this.

Back home I loathe the unfair distribution of wealth, the automatic right to succeed in any and every walk of life if you have rich parents. There's no way I can dress my feelings up as an academically informed argument for fairness, or pretend I felt this way for the overall good of my country – it was personal.

It hurts me to acknowledge, I'm just another angry young man who's been born to poor parents; who can't find a way to be appreciated by his own society. But as uneducated as I am, I believe in a force that will eventually tip the balance towards some kind of meritocracy. In my mind, this force is socialism. Now I am hearing a different truth, and I believe it to be just that; of what it is like to live in a country where the state has assumed the power to make things fair and decent for its citizens - and does just the opposite.

'Why don't you apply for political asylum in England Jan? Surely the British would offer you work in your field. There can't be too many laser research scientists in the world.'

He chuckles before he speaks – it is full of irony. 'Oh Alan, I wish it was so simple. Before I left I was interviewed by men from the state security service. I am not married, but they made it very plain what would happen to my parents, should I choose not to return. You suggest I may be paranoid, but I can guarantee I will be under surveillance during this trip and I will be visited at some point to make sure I stay – how shall I say - focussed.'

'How did your sister get out then?' I ask.

'She married an Englishman when he came to Prague on holiday. They had no option but to let her go.'

I suggest we stop for coffee as he'd been driving for many hours and must be tired. He shakes his head. 'I have to make the eight o'clock ferry. It's on my schedule. There will be trouble if I miss it.'

'Christ Jan, this sounds like a real crap way to live. I feel really sorry for you.'

'You want to know the icing on the cake, as you call it?'

'What?'

'I'm a spy.'

'You're kidding me?'

'It's true. Last month I was on the train coming home from work when two plain clothes secret police got on and asked everyone for their identity papers. When they came to me they told me to get off with them at the next station. For a while I was quite panicked, thinking it was something to do with my work. Had I said something to my colleagues that could be seen as critical of the party? I went through all the conversations I'd had with my friends that day, but couldn't think of anything. Perhaps I had forgotten to lock some important document away in the safe? I just didn't know. '

'When we got to Rudna I was driven to a police station and taken to the interview room. It was one of the most stressful experiences of my life. The feeling of helplessness was total. Nobody knew where I was. The policemen refused to say a word to me in the car, and my mind was racing trying to imagine what was going to happen. In the interview room were two more men who were obviously senior to the ones who brought me there. The first two just left without a word to me – the other two didn't introduce themselves or tell me what department they were from.'

'What did they want?'

'Well, they made it obvious they knew everything about me, my family, where I worked, lived – everything - and about my planned journey abroad. It is a strange feeling, my friend, to be interviewed by these unknown people who have no manners, who don't feel the need to explain themselves to me, but who can make me disappear if they want. When they had played with me mentally and reduced me to a state of near panic they asked about my commitment to my country, and, of course, the party. I assured them I was a loyal citizen, and then they got down to business. They said I must write reports for them about everyone I meet in London in the scientific community. I'm supposed to find out their sexual preferences: Do they prefer girls or boys: Whether they had an addiction to drugs or alcohol: Perhaps they have financial problems – all this I am supposed to report on.'

I am certainly taking notice now. 'What did you say?'

'I said I am a scientist not a spy, anyway how could I find out such information about my colleagues. We would be talking science, not about who they spend their nights with, or whether they liked cocaine, besides it is only for a few days. I told them it was ridiculous. But they said they could teach me to get information from people in a number of innocent sounding ways. All I needed to do was attend training, at the nearest police station to my house each evening for a week. They would arrange everything.'

'Did you?' I ask, sitting up.

'I had to. It's not something you can refuse - if you want a career.' He is silent for a minute or so, then adds, 'I have no idea what I'm going to report, but I will have to make something up for them.'

We come to the ferry booking office and buy our tickets. Jan is disturbed. 'They seem to have used an old brochure when they worked out my costs. The fare has gone up since the beginning of this month.'

On the ferry, we sit drinking coffee next to the rain slashed windows and listen to the deep throb of the big diesel engines pushing us across the channel, I ask Jan, 'Seriously Jan, what are you going to do?'

He looks quizzically at me. 'What do you mean Alan – to do?'

'Well, you can't just go along with this spying stuff surely?'

He seems less concerned than I am. He smiles, 'Don't worry about me. It may sound serious to you but I have lived with this madness for a long time. They are not very bright and easily fooled, if you are clever at it. I know how to keep them happy without anyone getting hurt.'

He reflects on something for a moment before continuing. 'You know Alan, sometimes I think the people who become our leaders are by their very nature unsuitable to be leaders. The process we insist on them following is almost guaranteed to filter out the most able, and make them fail. Most of the decent people I meet don't want to climb to the top in any way, except perhaps in their own professions. They don't want to direct and bully and threaten people, and act as if they know what is best for everyone else. Unfortunately these are necessary qualities to become a politician, particularly in Czechoslovakia at the moment.'

'Isn't that true of all countries?' I suggest cynically.

We sit and stare at the blackness out the window. I am feeling overwhelmingly sad about returning home so soon. Although no time had been set, in my enthusiasm I'd expected to be away from home for years, rather than a couple of months. The faith I had in 'something good happening' which I had no realistic reason to believe in, had not materialised.

I felt I had given the gods a chance to show good will towards me, and they'd let me down. I know I would feel better if I had managed to bring the Yellow Bus back home. Now, I had nothing but an old leather suitcase, a sleeping bag and a green corduroy jacket to show for it. I muse on the fact I have no job and nowhere to live when I return, and the weight of these thoughts come down on me heavily, as if the whole escapade has been a failure.

Jan reads my thoughts, and asks me what my current problems are.

'No problems really Jan, just some decisions to make now.'

In our drive together I had outlined some of the adventures of the past weeks, so he was aware of the Yellow Bus and our travels.

'How many young people did you meet from my country?' he asks seriously.

'What?'

'How many young Czechs are there on the road?'

It doesn't take a lot of reckoning. 'None,' I reply.

He smiles. 'Exactly. There are no young Czechs on the road because they are not allowed by the authorities. Don't you realise how lucky you are Alan? You have a freedom we can only dream of. Of course you have anger for the way things are. There's no Utopia on this planet yet, but you have the main ingredient already – you have the freedom to make things happen.'

The positive and uplifting mood we generate between ourselves continues as we drive off the ferry into a windy, rain-swept and shabby looking Dover. As we head along the A20 in his old Skoda we treat ourselves to singing a couple of Beatles songs, and are surprised how well we harmonise.

I write my address down on a piece of his notepad and say, 'Anytime you need somewhere to stay, my parents have a spare room, and they will always know where I am.'

'Thank you Alan, you are very kind, but perhaps you are still thinking I will not return home after all?'

'Well, it's a possibility,' I say.

He shakes his head. 'No. I may not like my country the way it's governed, but I love Czechoslovakia. I would never leave it to live in exile. It will change – everything does. People will get fed up living like prisoners in their own houses. Freedom will emerge – maybe not this year or the next, but it will eventually – it is part of humanity, we need freedom like food and water.'

We spend some time in silence just watching the countryside go by, and chain smoke his cigarettes. I can't help juxtapose the violent struggle of Zigi and Kati with the patient faith of Jan; both are desperate – No, in truth I have to include myself – all of us are desperate for a change in our societies, and angry at the injustices we perceive in our own countries, but all in our very different ways.

Zigi and Kati's direct action is awe inspiring, but still doesn't resonate in my heart as being right. Jan is determined to see it through by patient perseverance and a belief in the common need of people to live in a more just society. Zigi and Kati believe in creating an implosion, and as quickly as possible.

What do I believe?

My life had been so concerned with survival there hasn't been much time for politics. I have no solid beliefs. I can't alter anything other than my job, clothes, and which drugs I take. My father is a hard-working impoverished working class man who voted Conservative. I told him he was a turkey voting for Christmas – not very original, but heartfelt nevertheless. But the limited choice of voting for one bunch of people over another seems pathetic and pointless when they're so alike.

Then, perhaps Sandappa's right to forget the world of causes altogether, and concentrate on personal freedom. For a moment I think of her and wish her well wherever she is, and in whatever she's doing. But in all of this human concern, I am lost. Sometimes, when talking to people who believe in some cause or other, I feel like a simpleton even when I agree with their principles. What can I say when asked, what are you doing for the poor? What are you doing against animal cruelty? What are you doing to help the homeless? – orphans? – stop the war? – the list is endless; and always I have to acknowledge, I do nothing.

Perhaps I will find the selflessness to do something one day, I think. Right now I have to get a job and find a place to live; maybe a squat again. Damn, I don't want to think about that until I have to. I kill the thought. Perhaps I haven't ever met a person whom I can look up to enough to want to follow? Was there a 'Baba Mia' whose feet I wanted to sit at? No, it isn't for me, and I know it. Deep down I distrust all human groups with a common aim; you can't be inclusive of your group without being equally exclusive of others. Is that just my excuse for being a hedonist?

'What are you thinking Alan?' asks Jan.

'Oh, just beating myself up again,'

'Yes, we all do that sometimes. I also think badly about myself sometimes, why I didn't do this or that. Am I a coward, am I brave? Why isn't it clear which is which? Sometimes you choose to do the hardest thing, believing it to be a brave thing, then afterwards everyone tells you what a coward you were. It is not so easy this living - is it?'

After a couple more miles I ask him, 'Jan, do you think it is possible to really know yourself – in a way that you can't play these tricks – so you can really know all your own motives?'

He laughs. 'I like to dabble with inventions in my spare time, Alan. One day I will make a machine to do just that.'

After a slow drive from the ferry we arrive at Thornton Heath and I show Jan how he can continue on to Croydon. He refuses to come inside, saying the authorities will expect him to make contact with them as soon as he arrives. He's a little behind schedule as it is.

We shake hands. I thank him for the lift and we wish each other luck. As he drives away I think about how travelling is all about saying goodbye to people. How you meet some of the most interesting and wonderful people for just a short while, and then comes the hug, the handshake, the wishes of good luck and sometimes even the promise you will meet up again someday.

It would be nice to do so.

Chapter 57. My dog pees on me!

As I ring the doorbell I guiltily realise I haven't bought anything back for my mother from all the exotic places I'd seen. Mum opens the door and a bright beaming smile lights up her face.

'Welcome home, son. Are you hungry?'

We both turn at the sound of whimpering. At the top of the stairs sits Toby, our black and white crossbreed dog. Although only medium sized, Toby is pure muscle and he is now sitting on the top of the stairs, shifting frantically from side to side, and whining like a pack leader.

Suddenly all that muscle springs into action and he bounds down the whole flight, only touching the stairs once. He leaps up so strongly I'm knocked over and fall full length in the hall. Mum's laughing. Toby sits on my chest and pins me down with his weight, and the fact he is licking my face so hard I can hardly breathe. Suddenly I feel a warm wet something on my chest. It's the dog peeing on me in his excitement. A welcome I hadn't expected.

The following week is all about telling and retelling the story of the Yellow Bus to friends and family. In quieter times alone, I wrestle with the conflicting thoughts and philosophies I'd heard from the people I'd met on the journey.

Gradually a sense of positivity enters my thinking. When I remember the Buddha's story where he drew an open circle and said that opposites are like the ends of the circle, but the middle-path is the furthest from either of them.

It becomes clear to me, there's a middle path of politics, room for both socialism and capitalism – it just depends where we use them. Should the government be dictating how much a bar of chocolate costs? Of course not. Should education, transport, health, and the utilities be open for profit? Absolutely not. Other than that a person's duty is to their own happiness – how else can happiness be spread? It seems nothing now but it was my little epiphany at the time.

It's two months later when I receive a letter, redirected from home. It's from Odette telling me she's on her way back to England and wants to come and see me. [iii]

There's always been an unexplainable certainty about this in my thoughts, but I smile every time I re-read it.

I'm feeling the need to make plans again. I've returned to my job with Harmony Foods, and am now squatting in a house with four other people in Bermondsey, South-East London.

The weather is appalling. Every day I cycle to work, and try desperately to get dry and warm in the big warehouse that stores the grain, pulses and beans we market. I look at the large sacks of Hunza apricots from Afghanistan. I remember the country they've come from, and want desperately to be back there.

Every spare penny is being put aside, and I have the next trip all planned; next time it will be a forty-seater coach. And I will learn a lot more about mechanics before I leave. And this time we will get to India.

Maybe I'm only a hedonist at heart, but I will just have to learn to live with it.

THE END

Endnotes:

[i] *Sad Sack was an American comic strip and lovable comic book character created by Sgt. George Baker during World War II.*

[ii] *I didn't know at the time what really happened to the amazing Kunst brothers. For more information see this link:-* https://en.wikipedia.org/wiki/Dave_Kunst

[iii] *To find out what became of me and Odette you will have to wait for my sequel – but -'spoiler alert' - it was a good outcome.*

Printed in Great Britain
by Amazon